Living and Working in
China

WITHDRAWN
FROM
STOCK

Also by Andrew Williamson

The Chinese Business Puzzle

How to work more effectively with Chinese cultures
This book is aimed at Westerners who wish to do business
with China, whether in China or at home, face-to-face or at
a distance, during a long-term posting or on a flying visit.

howtobooks

Please send for a free copy of the latest catalogue:

How To Books
3 Newtec Place, Magdalen Road,
Oxford OX4 1RE, United Kingdom
email: info@howtobooks.co.uk
http://www.howtobooks.co.uk

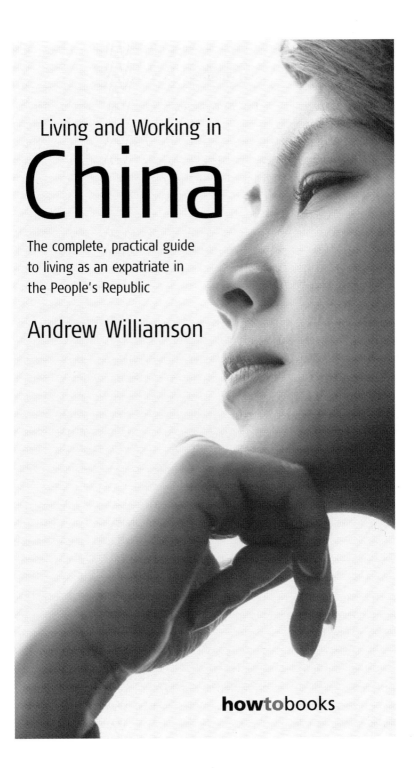

Living and Working in

China

The complete, practical guide
to living as an expatriate in
the People's Republic

Andrew Williamson

howto**books**

915.1 / 2601939

First published by
How To Books Ltd,
3 Newtec Place, Magdalen Road
Oxford OX4 1RE, United Kingdom.
Tel: (01865) 793806. Fax: (01865) 248780.
info@howtobooks.co.uk
www.howtobooks.co.uk

All rights reserved. No part of this work may be reproduced
or stored in an information retrieval system (other than for
purposes of review) without the express permission of the
publisher in writing.

© 2005 Andrew Williamson

First edition 2005

British Library Cataloguing in Publication Data
A catalogue record for this book is available from the British
Library

Cover design by Baseline Arts Ltd, Oxford
Produced for How To Books by Deer Park Productions,
Tavistock, Devon
Typeset by PDQ Typesetting, Newcastle-under-Lyme, Staffs.
Printed and bound by Cromwell Press, Trowbridge, Wiltshire

NOTE: The material contained in this book is set out in good
faith for general guidance and no liability can be accepted
for loss or expense incurred as a result of relying in particular
circumstances on statements made in the book. The laws and
regulations are complex and liable to change, and readers should
check the current position with the relevant authorities before
making personal arrangements.

Contents

About the Author

Andrew Williamson (born 1945) is a scholar of Repton and graduate of Bristol, where he studied modern languages.

At the same time, he developed a lifelong interest in classical choral music, which he was fortunate to combine with his degree – in particular reading music at the Sorbonne and directing a student choir at Heidelberg University (courtesy of a German government scholarship).

Whilst at Bristol he met his wife, Eileen, also a musically-gifted modern language student, whom he married in July 1969, and with whom he has continued to 'make music' ever since.

Keen to travel, Andrew joined a major United Kingdom (UK) international financial services company and subsequently spent 12 of his 30-year career overseas in three continents – Europe (Spain and Italy), South America (Colombia) and Asia (China) whilst Eileen taught English, primarily with the British Council.

Whilst abroad, they always became fully involved in the local and expatriate communities. For example, Andrew was elected in:

- **Spain**: president of the property owners' association on several occasions by his all-Spanish neighbours
- **China**: to the Committee of the British Chamber of Commerce in China by the British business community.

Two of their sons were born and initially educated abroad, speaking Spanish before English; whilst Number Three first saw light of day in the UK, and had to contend with spending school holidays in China.

Andrew held some very senior appointments with his employer abroad (e.g. General Manager for Colombia) and at home (e.g. Distance Learning Manager) before being appointed Director and Chief Representative for China in the late 1990s with the brief to direct the company's China Market Entry Team.

In China, Andrew was involved amongst other things with:

◆ raising the **company's profile and influence** in China-based Chinese and British government, diplomatic and business circles;
◆ establishing a 'circle of friends' from which to select a **joint venture** partner;
◆ **market intelligence**.

In recognition of his services, the People's Bank of China appointed Andrew a guest (i.e. unpaid!) professor of its Shanghai Finance College (now upgraded to Shanghai Finance University under the government of the Shanghai Municipal Government).

As a result, Andrew has first-hand, in-depth and relevant practical expertise in and experience of:

◆ **In general**: the cross-cultural challenges that face inexperienced and seasoned foreign business(wo)men working in established and emerging markets; and sadly witnessed many ventures which failed due to insufficient attention being paid by employers to their employees' cross-cultural needs.

◆ **In particular**: the issues facing foreigners who wish to work with the Chinese, including building a business presence in China virtually from scratch.

Consequently, now retired and living in Suffolk, he and Eileen act as freelance China consultants, primarily to Farnham Castle, briefing foreign business people and their spouses on working with the Chinese and living in China; and spend their spare time exploring the English waterways on their aptly named cruiser *Guanxi*, visiting their Spanish home-from-home, and entertaining their grandchildren.

Andrew completed his first book about China, *The Chinese Business Puzzle*, on how to work more effectively with Chinese cultures, in 2003, which was also commissioned by How To Books and endorsed by Farnham Castle International Briefing and Conference Centre.

Further information: www.minim.biz

Andrew M. Williamson
BA, FCII, Chartered FCIPD, DipCMus
Chartered Insurance Practitioner
Guest Professor, Shanghai Finance University
Managing Partner, Minim Consulting

Foreword

It is a truism that with a shrinking world we are now totally
blasé at visiting places which, a generation ago, would have
seemed impossibly remote and exotic. A recent radio programme I was listening to concerned a group of business
people from Stockport visiting Tieling, a small city in Liaon-
ing Province in the north east of China. They were negotiating
leases on industrial land, discussing joint ventures and planning major business developments. I was fascinated: it was
impossible not to be carried along on their wave of enthusiasm, but at the same time not to feel apprehensive. I was
reminded of recent comments by the managing director of a
local company manufacturing industrial waste treatment
equipment, a product that should be of enormous interest
to the Chinese market. He was meeting his umpteenth visiting
delegation of Chinese business people. He said all these
groups of Chinese visitors had shown great interest in his
products, leading him to anticipate new orders from
China. Yet, after they had left, he had heard nothing
more from them. 'How do I turn interest into orders?'
was his plea.

What is offered in this book is a timely reminder that we
should not allow our enthusiasm and Chinese hospitality
to lull us into a false sense that China is no different
from our home environment. China, for both locals and
foreign residents, is a much kinder place to live in than
twenty-five years ago, particularly in material comforts
and convenience. Then the restaurants were state-owned,

they closed at seven or eight in the evening, the daily beer allowance had probably run out, tables were for eight people and if you were a party of just three or four you would be slotted in with a group of random strangers. Even worse, I remember going to a famous Peking Duck restaurant in the centre of Beijing and being told by my host, as our meal was drawing to a close, to get up at her signal and move rapidly away from the table. I was slightly puzzled, but the golden rule in this situation is always to follow your local host's advice. We got up and retreated, then I saw people I had not even noticed before descending like vultures on our leftovers, grabbing plates and tureens, with food and soup flying in all directions. I was glad I had heeded the advice.

China now is superficially just like being at home, except that the food is better, the service is quicker, the hotels and restaurants are smarter and only the traffic is worse. It is easy in this situation to forget that great differences remain, many of them buried in details of language and social etiquette that completely bypass most visitors. I hope this book will help you become part of the aware minority. I do particularly commend Andrew Williamson's emphasis on risk and insurance. The risk of accidents and medical emergencies is not greatly higher than at home, apart from the carnage on the roads, but, as I know from personal experience of cases, the consequences of having inadequate medical insurance cover can be disastrous. Similarly, punishment can be draconian, with capital punishment regularly used for drug and corruption-related offences. The civil legal system, in crucial business areas such as contract law, offers far lower levels of protection than Western business people are used to. This is one reason why *guanxi*, relationships or connections, is so vital.

Sun-zi, the military strategist of the 6th century BCE, famously said: 'Know your enemy and win a thousand battles.' An up-to-date version might be: 'Know your customer and win a thousand orders.' Knowledge is important, but understanding is even more so. I hope reading this book will help you achieve both.

Don Starr
Head of the Department of East Asian Studies
University of Durham
Durham
November 2004

Introduction

Judge not, that you be not judged.
Gospel according to Matthew, Revised Standard Version, 7.1

So, you have been posted to China! Congratulations! Or should it be commiserations?

Well, that depends on your point of view.

If you are a:

- **Xenophobe**: who struggles with the language, hates eating 'foreign muck', cannot stand the heat, is frustrated by *mañana* whilst on holiday in Spain, and cannot wait to return to familiar surroundings at home and routines at work then China is definitely *not* for you.
- **Xenophile**: who relishes a new challenge every day, and is prepared to learn from a people whose language, culture and education may put yours to shame then China might suit you...or, rather, you might just be acceptable to the Chinese.

They say pre-warned is pre-armed. However, as regards China, in our experience:

- **Previous expatriate service**, even in a developing country, may be an advantage, but does not necessarily guarantee success.
- An **orientation visit** – such as my employer insisted we

undertook before allowing me to accept the posting – can only scratch the surface.

Thus, although my wife and I had read languages at university and been career expatriates – spending ten years abroad working (for the British Council and a UK multinational respectively) and raising a young family – no amount of prior instruction could have adequately prepared us for what lay in store, despite our own and others' best efforts.

One reason was that, like so many foreigners, our concept of China in the mid-1990s was still based on the films of Fu Manchu or *The Inn of the Sixth Happiness*. Indeed, even in the 21st century, half the population of the United States of America still considers China an unfriendly country (according to a Harris poll conducted in September 2002).

We shared this misconception and were, therefore, pleasantly shocked to discover:

♦ In 1997: on first arriving in **Beijing** a city in some respects more advanced than elsewhere we had lived in the world with, inter alia: imposing architecture; attractive shops with high-quality goods; smart clothes; excellent food; luxury cars; and modern technology, with computers and mobile phones galore!
♦ In 2003: on returning to **Shanghai** a city that could rival if not surpass any European capital, whose inhabitants eat in chic restaurants, wear designer clothes, drive smart cars, and live in spacious apartments with fine furniture and the latest household appliances, and much more besides...and that is only the Chinese!

Above all, we found that the Chinese have time for each other. The streets of Beijing, for example, are full of people strolling, talking, sitting, taking exercise, eating, watching, standing, singing, dancing, and in many other ways just making the most of every minute – not rushing headlong from A to B to save seconds, as is so typical in many Western capitals.

That is not to say that all is sweetness and light, despite the best efforts of the foreign-language Chinese press, far from it. Neither is it all doom and gloom, as the Western media would often have us believe. Rather the truth lies somewhere between, and can only be truly appreciated by an extended stay in China, mingling with the Chinese.

This last point is important. China is not found in the venues of sanitised package holidays and orientation visits, such as foreign housing complexes, bars and club-houses, international hotels, restaurants and shops, city tours amongst neat 'hutongs', and expatriate-dominated enterprises.

I was asked recently what key advice I would give to anyone about to live and work in China. Here is a summary of my answer:

1   Each old China-hand will counsel you differently, based on what worked for them. Seek not just a second opinion; but a third from a Chinese person; and a fourth from someone who really knows, understands and is respected by both sides.
2   Judging the Chinese by your standards shows an arrogant disregard for, and ignorance of, their way of life and is fraught with dangers. The more you understand and

respect – without condemning or accepting – Chinese culture and values, the happier and more successful you are likely to be.

3 Above all do not underestimate the Chinese...you can learn much from them.

ACKNOWLEDGEMENTS

To quote a joke doing the rounds in China a few years ago:

What is the difference between a China 'expert' and a China 'consultant'?

An expert is anyone who has been in China for 30 minutes; a consultant is someone who knows more about China than you do.

I claim to be neither. However, during my time in China I met many who do but was privileged to befriend a handful who really are, both foreign and Chinese, and who took the time and trouble to share their expertise with me. To them I acknowledge my debt of gratitude and dedicate this book.

ORIGIN

The motivation behind this book is twofold.

1 To pass on my passion for and experiences of China and the Chinese to others, in the hope that they will catch the vision and learn from my mistakes.

2 To thank my wife, Eileen, without whose altruistic support and encouragement such experiences, let alone this book, would have been impossible.

It all started in December 1996, when I casually asked Eileen, just as I was slipping out of the cottage into the garden (as husbands do, when they are not sure how violent the reaction is going to be!): 'There's a vacancy in China...how do you fancy going?' and she replied: 'Yes!' Our family was astounded. All that any of us knew about China was from the film *The Inn of the Sixth Happiness* and a biography of Gladys Aylward (the book of the film) that I had read some 40 years earlier. The rest, as they say, is history.

CREDENTIALS

Although we returned to the UK less than two years later, our training as linguists and previous expatriate experience greatly accelerated our learning curve whilst in China. Also, the nature of our work (mine obtaining an operating licence; Eileen's working with the British Council) rapidly and constantly exposed us to the key issues of living and working amongst senior Chinese officials and foreign executives. Subsequently, we have maintained our momentum through continuing study and occasional return visits in support of our work on behalf of Farnham Castle International Briefing and Conference Centre in the UK, which has in turn given birth to this book.

AUTHENTICITY AND CONFIDENTIALITY

An erstwhile boss and friend of mine once said that mistakes are learning opportunities; for which reason this book tells it as it is, warts and all, not only suggesting and illustrating best practice but also quoting my own 'learning opportunities'.

To protect the third parties involved, and respect the confidentiality of my employer (of which I am now a pensioner), I have anonymised some examples quoted where and as appropriate. Nevertheless, all such illustrations are wholly genuine and suggestions are based on hard fact.

TARGET AUDIENCE

There are probably more books about living and working in China than you or I have had hot dinners. The majority of such books, however, seem to be written for foreign tourists, students, junior executives and similar short-term visitors or low-ranking (in Chinese terms) workers and it would be a foolish waste of time to try to compete with them.

This book, therefore, concentrates on the issues facing the more senior members of the foreign expatriate community on longer-term postings, whose lifestyle at home and work in China may be so very different – lavish and demanding, respectively – from anything that they have previously experienced as to be initially quite bewildering and overwhelming for them and their families.

STYLE

As a direct consequence of the many and varied 'how to' questions at our briefings at Farnham Castle, mentioned above, I have organised much of the material into standalone guidelines for specific subjects, supported by real examples. In this way, I hope that you can quickly find specific answers to specific questions, grouped by topic, without having to plough through masses of prose.

TERMINOLOGY

By the terms 'Chinese' and 'China', I specifically mean the people, Provinces and Municipalities of the People's Republic of China in general, and the major centres of industry and commerce in particular.

While the Special Administrative Regions (Hong Kong and Macau), Autonomous National Minority Areas (Guangxi, Inner Mongolia, Ningxia, Tibet and Xinjiang) and Province of Taiwan (aka the Republic of China) undoubtedly have close similarities, China is such a large, diverse and quickly evolving country that it would be imprudent of me to make such bold assumptions.

Because of its size, however, there is a danger in adopting an identical approach to all Chinese in every part of China or elsewhere in the world when, in fact, they are as diverse as the many nationalities that make up Europe, and their regional loyalties rival each other just as fiercely as the supporters of the White and Red Roses in England!

I have, therefore, tried to reflect the eternal truths of China and its culture, but apologise in advance for overlooking any significant regional or ethnic variations.

DISCLAIMER
The pace of change in China, in all walks of life, moves so fast that what was unheard of yesterday and is news today may be out of date tomorrow.

Consequently, this book is obsolete even as I write it, for which reason it should be used as an illustrative rather than exhaustive good-practice guide to be supplemented by your own more recent experience and research. You should always seek up-to-date advice if in doubt.

I have tried to be as objective as possible, describing what happens and explaining why, but without knowingly justifying or condemning Chinese practice.

POST SCRIPT

Enjoy living in China and working with the Chinese ... they are well worth the effort!

Farnham Castle International Briefing and Conference Centre

A lack of cultural understanding and local practices can be a major obstacle to the effectiveness of conducting business in another country. The ability to relate quickly and effectively with colleagues and clients in a new country is very important to long-term success.

Farnham Castle International Briefing and Conference Centre is widely acknowledged as the world's leading provider of intercultural management training and briefing and has an unmatched reputation for helping individuals, partners and their families to prepare to live and work effectively anywhere in the world.

Through its unrivalled faculty of trainers and experts, Farnham Castle offers a totally flexible and comprehensive range of programmes providing the first-hand knowledge and skills required to be successful in international business including:

- ◆ workshops on developing cross cultural awareness
- ◆ working effectively with specific cultures or nationalities
- ◆ cross cultural communication, presentation and negotiation skills training
- ◆ country and business briefings for any country in the world

◆ intensive tuition in any language.

Full details available on website at: www.farnhamcastle.com

$$\left(1\right)$$

Overview of
Living & Working in China

LIVING AND WORKING ENVIRONMENT – CHAPTER 2

Chapter 2 summarises the first three chapters of my book *The Chinese Business Puzzle* (see p. 361), which you should read in their entirety for a fuller understanding. It briefly describes the relevant:

1 **Business environment**
2 **Domestic environment**
3 **Underpinning behaviours**

that foreigners working and living in China may expect to encounter.

Section 1 – Business environment

The first section of Chapter 2 briefly describes the relevant background to the business environment in which foreigners may expect and be expected to work in China, under four headings:

1 The logical starting point is the **philosophical environment** of **Confucianism** which, albeit out of favour at present, has so permeated Chinese life for the last 2,500 years that its effect is subconsciously all-present, including in business.

2   Next is the **political environment** that has marginalised
    Confucianism to dominate China since 1949: **Com-
    munism** – which has evolved into '**socialism with
    Chinese characteristics**'.

3   Integral to its political environment is China's
    economic environment where 'socialism with Chinese
    characteristics' translates into a '**market economy with
    Chinese characteristics**'.

4   Last but not least is the **legal environment** that
    legislates how business should operate within the
    preceding three environments.

Section 2 – Domestic environment

The second section of Chapter 2 briefly describes the
relevant background to the social environment in which
foreigners may expect and be expected to live in China,
under three headings:

1   The relevant aspects of its **geography** and **history** that
    have moulded China's **cultural heritage**.

2   The **domestic environment** in which today's Chinese
    have been raised.

3   The relationship that, consequently, the Chinese enjoy
    with **foreigners** (to ignore which is one sure-fire way
    for foreigners to fail in China).

Section 3 – Underpinning behaviours

The third section of Chapter 2 briefly introduces the
relevant behaviours that underpin the business dealings of
the Chinese as a consequence of their business and social

environments, including:

- **personal relationships** (*Guanxi*);
- **collectivism, collective decision making** and **consensus**;
- **face** (*Mianzi*) and **harmony**;
- **modesty** and **humility** (*Keqi*);
- **hierarchism** and **authority** (*Laoban*-ism).

Although many modern Chinese will forgive your lack of expertise, you may well encounter those traditionalists who still lay great store in adherence to the ritual behaviour expected of a Confucian 'Superior Man', for whom outward form may be more important than inward motive. Hence the reason for devoting so much space in *The Chinese Business Puzzle* to the correct observance of Chinese business etiquette.

RISK ENVIRONMENT – CHAPTERS 3 TO 5

Chapters 3 to 5 examine in detail and at some length the main:

Ch. 3   Threats to the **safety** of **persons** and **property**
Ch. 4   **diseases, infections** and other **illnesses**
Ch. 5   **health** and **hygiene** risks

to which China-based expatriates may be personally and peculiarly exposed, since – in my experience as a consultant at Farnham Castle – these are the foremost concerns worrying most foreigners, and especially the spouses.

- **Assume** a rudimentary knowledge of, and therefore only refer en passant to, basic health and safety practices and procedures at home and when abroad, such as on holiday.
- **Exclude** any reference to **business risks**, as being outside the scope of this book and already underlying *The Chinese Business Puzzle*.

Approach

I have taken a simplified **risk management approach** – that is briefly:

1   **identifying** the risks;
2   **evaluating** the frequency and severity of their impact;
3   suggesting appropriate **control** measures.

Sources of expert advice

There is a plethora of detailed expert advice on risks facing travellers abroad in general, and Westerners in China in particular, from reputable sources far more qualified than I am.

For the sake of simplicity, therefore, I hope that I may be forgiven for understandably:

- **preferring** the specialist UK and US (as well as international) sources listed in the Bibliography;
- **synthesising** the key points;
- **sign-posting** further information.

Caveat

Although I have made every effort to consult, verify and

cross-check only reliable sources, as well as back them up from personal experience, neither they nor I can:

- guarantee the success of;
- accept liability for injury, illness, loss or damage resulting directly or indirectly from

any advice or statement contained in these chapters, since:

- such advice and statements reflect the general situation at the time of writing, which may have subsequently changed;
- your individual circumstances may not necessarily be the same as our family's.

Thus given their general and timed nature, these chapters are *not* intended to replace any particular up-to-date specialist advice that you might and should otherwise seek.

Exposure to risk in china

Identification

1 Before travelling to China, as to any country, you should find out about any potential risks to which you and your family may be personally exposed as unwitting and innocent victims.

2 It is unlikely, however, that your local Chinese Consulate will be too forthcoming in this respect, even in the era of China's 'Open Door Policy' (outlined in *The Chinese Business Puzzle*).

3   For the latest authoritative information, therefore, you:

   a) Should not only visit the appropriate web-page of your home government's **ministry of foreign affairs** and **health** or equivalent, but also subscribe to its ongoing e-mail alert service.

   b) Could join an **international travel advisory service** such as the e-mail alerts issued by organisations listed in the Bibliography:

      ◆ **ExpatExchange.com**
      ◆ **International SOS**

4   Whilst in China: keep abreast of changing circumstances by:

   a) Registering and maintaining contact with your local **Consulate**.

   b) Following the foreign-language and international **press**, **television** and **radio**.

Evaluation

5   Just because I have included a specific risk does not necessarily mean that either you will or we did face it. Rather, on the premise that 'forewarned is forearmed', I have preferred to err on the side of caution – perhaps even going overboard at times – to ensure that you are prepared for most eventualities, however remote.

Control

6   From the experience of our family and many friends, both foreign and Chinese, I believe that – subject to the foregoing caveat and evaluation – China is quite safe and healthy as long as you take sensible, appropriate precautions, as you would in any country.

7   With my insurance background, you would expect me strongly to recommend you **insuring** yourself, family, property and liabilities as comprehensively as possible whilst in China.

a) Except for short business trips to China – for which you may be able to obtain travel insurance – you will need to effect local policies in local currency to cover local risks, in accordance with Chinese law and increasingly international practice.

b) Unfortunately, **insurance intermediaries** – as we understand them in the West – hardly exist in China, if at all. Thus, you may have difficulty in shopping around for reputable alternatives to the state-owned People's Insurance Company of China (PICC).

c) I suggest, therefore, that you contact:
   –   your **normal insurer** for details of their China office;
   –   a **specialist in expatriate insurance**, such as: **Clements International**
   –   your national **insurers' trade body**, such as (in the UK) the **Association of British Insurers** (ABI).

8   If all else fails, you should negotiate with your employer suitable arrangements for **emergency repatriation** from China in the unlikely event of a sudden deterioration in the political situation and/or threat of **civil unrest**, especially targeted at foreigners.

> **EXAMPLE**
>
> In the mid 1970s, when we were living and working in Spain during the last days of the Franco regime, there was so much speculation amongst some of the expatriate community at the prospect of a possible *coup d'état* that I felt constrained to seek assurances from my employer that, should the situation ever warrant it – which it never did – they would send the company jet to evacuate all their expatriate families.

9 Similarly, you should negotiate with your employer suitable arrangements for **emergency evacuation** from China in the unlikely event of **serious illness** or **accident** requiring specialist attention.

> **EXAMPLE**
>
> In the late 1990s, Hong Kong was a favourite destination. Indeed, when my wife and I required dental treatment in Beijing involving the replacement of crowns, these had to be made by dental technicians in Hong Kong.

AT HOME – CHAPTERS 6 TO 8

Chapters 6 to 8 examine in detail and at some length the main considerations facing China-based expatriates with respect to:

Ch. 6   finding **accommodation**;
Ch. 7   hiring and firing **domestic staff**;
Ch. 8   keeping **dogs**.

In my experience as a consultant at Farnham Castle these are amongst the foremost concerns worrying most foreigners, and especially the spouses.

Accommodation – Chapter 6
Chapter 6 deals solely with accommodation for expatriate business(wo)men – since for diplomats, foreign experts, and language teachers and students (the other main categories of foreign residents) accommodation is normally provided in special complexes and/or by their Chinese host organisation.

Caveat
I have made every effort to consult, verify and cross-check only reliable and up-to-date sources at the time of writing, as well as back them up from personal experience.

However, please bear in mind that:

◆ the property market in China – as elsewhere in the world – is volatile and, hence, subject to changes in law, price and availability;
◆ your individual circumstances may not necessarily be the same as our family's.

You should, therefore, seek up-to-date specialist advice from a reputable international property consultant, such as one of those listed in the Bibliography.

Domestic Staff – Chapter 7
Chapter 7 offers advice on how to interact with the two main categories of Chinese domestic staff with whom expatriate business(wo)men commonly deal – often provided at their employer's expense – and of whom they may probably have no previous experience:

1   **maids**
2   **drivers**.

Drivers
Most senior expatriates are provided with a company car, and many (like ourselves) with a driver too, for reasons of personal safety and 'hassle-free' convenience, as follows.

1   China does not recognise **international driving licences**, but requires foreigners to:
    a) Surrender their **national driving licence** which can cause a problem during home leave to which the only solution, according to the motoring organisation that I consulted, is to retain an authenticated photocopy.
    b) Take a **driving test**.
    c) Undergo a **physical examination**, including a Human Immunodeficiency Virus (HIV) test with the attendant risks described in Chapter 4.

2   If you cannot read Chinese characters, you will not make much sense of the **road signs**!

3   Geographical **restrictions** also apply to expatriate drivers, whose cars are easily identifiable by their distinctive number plates.

4   The **traffic conditions** are, according to one guide book, 'anarchic' as detailed in Chapter 3.

5   If you have an **accident**, expect to be held absolutely and strictly liable, since the accident would not have occurred had you – as a foreigner – not been driving! This is not dissimilar to the situation in some Middle

Eastern countries; or Colombia, where whoever stops to assist a road-traffic victim is automatically deemed the perpetrator acting out of a sense of guilt! No wonder that apocryphal stories abound of foreigners driving straight to the airport and leaving the country after accidentally running over Chinese pedestrians.

Caveat
The advice that we give is:

♦ **experiential** – that is: based on real experience;
♦ **generic** – that is: not specific to any one particular maid, driver or household.

For example, I have also included references to our experience of maids in other countries (Spain and Colombia) where appropriate.

Hence please understand that it:

♦ neither necessarily guarantees success;
♦ nor is automatically suitable for each and every maid, driver or household.

Keeping dogs – Chapter 8

I never cease to be amazed by the number of expatriates for whom a major concern, when posted to China, is taking the family pets with them.

EXAMPLES

I know wives who have:
1 Refused to accompany their husband rather than be parted from the dogs.

2 Been more concerned about leaving behind the cat than an elderly, ailing mother.

To one and all – as an only child brought up with dogs – my advice is simple and straightforward: **moving to and settling in China is challenging enough without unnecessarily adding to the trauma by worrying about family pets!**

From personal experience, I can assure you that it is better to:

- find a good home – temporary or permanent – for them in your country of origin;
- send for them once you have settled into China;
- acquire pets locally.

The same applies, in reverse, on leaving China especially when moving to a country requiring extended quarantine (such as the UK).

In all cases the animals' interests should prevail over those of their owners. What suits the latter may not always benefit the former.

EXAMPLES

1 On the one hand – unhappily:
We took our valuable Siamese cat from Spain to Italy, on the verbal assurance of the landlady that pets were allowed, only to find that she expressly forbade them in the written contract. All credit to my employer, who volunteered to indemnify us, should the landlady find out. She did not, but only thanks to a large sea-trunk in which we were able to hide the cat and its accoutrements during her visits.
On moving from Italy to Colombia, my employer insisted on our taking

the cat, rather than replacing it, as we requested. Naturally, we agreed and arranged for the cat to be boarded at an Italian cattery whilst we were in transit to South America via the UK. During that time, unfortunately, the cat became terminally ill and had to be destroyed. All credit again to my employer for footing the bill.

2 On the other hand happily:

We subsequently purchased pets in both Colombia and China, for all of which we eventually found good homes locally on returning to the UK, rather than consign them to the rigours of a lengthy quarantine. The pointer became a contented mother and excellent working gun-dog in the Andes; whilst we still receive photographs each year of the basset, living blissfully with our Chinese driver's family in the countryside outside Beijing.

Thus, Chapter 8 provides guidelines for:

♦ **acquiring**
♦ and **keeping**

a dog in China – but not importing or repatriating – in accordance with government regulations.

Caveat

Everyone's experience of acquiring and keeping dogs in China is different – particularly depending on where they live and, thus, how strict or lax the local authorities are in applying the pertinent regulations.

Thus the guidance we give is based on our circumstances in the late 1990s and may not necessarily wholly apply to yours today.

OUT AND ABOUT – CHAPTERS 9 TO 11

Chapters 9 to 11 explain, in broad terms, what China-based expatriates may expect to experience outside their home as regards:

Ch. 9 **climate** and **clothing** – including **dress codes**;
Ch. 10 **communications** – both business and personal;
Ch. 11 **internal transport**.

Since such experiences are similar to those of anyone visiting China, I have tended to concentrate on the aspects peculiar to the resident expatriate business community rather than attempt to compete with the many excellent general tourist publications (listed in the Bibliography).

Climate and clothing

Chapter 9 concentrates on the **climate** of, and corresponding appropriate **clothing** for, the three principal Chinese business centres of **Beijing**, **Shanghai** and **Guangzhou** where, typically, the largest expatriate communities are to be found.

Because of their geographically strategic locations (the three principal climatic zones of **North-East**, **Central** and **South China**, respectively), conditions in other nearby parts of the country, however, may be guesstimated by analogy. For example Tianjin is close to Beijing, Suzhou to Shanghai and Shenzhen to Guangzhou.

Caveat

With apologies to my colleagues at the UK Meteorological Office (whom I briefed on China in late 2002 at

Farnham Castle): when I was young, my mother used to say: 'Little boys who lie, grow up to be weather-forecasters!' By which she meant that it is very difficult accurately to predict in detail the **weather** from one day to the next, let alone weeks, months or years ahead.

Climate, on the other hand, as the 'general weather conditions prevailing in an area over a long period' (*Concise Oxford Dictionary*, 10th edition, Oxford University Press, 1999), may be easier to anticipate, based on historic data, if only by virtue of obfuscating what constitutes 'a long period'. Nevertheless, the data sources which I have consulted do not always agree, for which reason I have sometimes had to compromise when quoting temperatures.

Thus you should:

◆ treat what follows as a general indication of what you may typically find in China; but...
◆ be prepared for a totally different experience!

Note: more detailed figures for Beijing, Shanghai and Guangzhou appear in Appendix 7.

Communications

For expatriates and families, friends and colleagues whom they leave behind, keeping in touch with each other is often a concern, especially if posted to the more remote parts of China.

However, far from lagging behind the West – as you might be forgiven for thinking – China is in some respects at the cutting edge of global communications technology. If this surprises you, just consider: how else could a central system of autocratic government removed from the common people – whether imperial or communist – have retained control over such a large country (in terms of area and population) for so many hundreds of years, if not by highly-developed means of communications (which the cynics might be tempted to call 'propaganda')?

Chapter 10, therefore, outlines the different methods of **business** and **personal communication** available to expatriates in China.

Health warning
Whichever communication channel you choose, remember that 'big brother' may be monitoring you.

Transport
Travelling in China can be a challenge, despite the many recent improvements. Queuing at booking offices can take ages and procedures often seem illogical. As with everything else in China, stay calm and be patient!

To make things easier for you, therefore, Chapter 11 offers detailed and specific advice on **internal travel** by **air**, **rail**, **road** and **water**.

Meanwhile, in general terms, I suggest that, when and wherever possible, you should:

- Book tickets through your office (or otherwise your hotel or the **China International Travel Service** (CITS) – whose service, although much improved, can be slow).
- Be prepared to pay in cash since, as everywhere else in China, not all travel outlets take credit cards.
- Book well in advance and then confirm.
- Arrive early at your departure point.

EXAMPLES

We relied on my Chinese Personal Assistant (PA) to handle all our family travel arrangements, especially air and hotel bookings, including hotel cars from/to the destination airport.

Be aware that sometimes you may:

- not be able to purchase a **two-way** air or train **ticket** within China;
- have to buy the return portion of the journey on arrival at your destination.

WORK PRACTICES – CHAPTER 12

Chapter 12 summarises Chapters 4 to 7 of *The Chinese Business Puzzle* (see p. 361), which you should read in their entirety for a fuller understanding; and briefly describes the relevant protocols for:

1 **exchanging gifts and favours**;
2 **negotiating techniques**;
3 **business meetings**;
4 **business entertaining**;

with which the Chinese will expect foreigners working and living in China to be familiar.

Human resource management (HRM)

Rightly or wrongly, I have chosen not to include here any guidance on HRM in China, since it is quite possible and legitimate for some foreigners to live *in* China without working very much or at all *with* the Chinese.

Nevertheless, suffice it to say that implementing Western HR practice lock, stock and barrel could be as disastrous as the wholesale acceptance of the Chinese status quo if not more so, should your workforce resist the former (insofar as, and in whatever form, the Chinese are wont to 'resist').

Thus, rather than throwing out the baby with the bath water, I – as an ex-HR professional:

◆ Contest the view of those commentators who maintain that China is hostile to Western HRM practice: otherwise why do so many Chinese prize an overseas MBA degree?
◆ Recommend adapting the best of the former to take account of the underpinning protocols and behaviours of the latter to produce **Western HRM with Chinese characteristics**.

For further details, please refer to *The Chinese Business Puzzle*, Chapter 10.

Section 1 Exchanging gifts and favours

A key concept of Confucianism (*Analects,* Chapter 17) is **generosity**, of which two of the most obvious and tangible forms are: **giving presents** and **doing favours** or rather exchanging them, following Confucius' Golden Rule of **reciprocity** and in the spirit of the Chinese proverb that 'courtesy demands reciprocity'.

Moreover, it is the **act of giving** – not the gift – that counts, according to the Chinese saying that: 'the gift is nothing much, but it is the thought that counts' (*li qing; ren yi zhong*).

Thus, an integral part of the Chinese business scene is **exchanging gifts** as a means of building *guanxi* – for which reason giving gifts is not a one-off, but should be repeated from time to time.

The first Section of Chapter 12, therefore, summarises the protocol for **exchanging gifts** and **favours** between the Chinese and foreigners.

Section 2 Negotiating techniques

The second section of Chapter 12 briefly:

1 **Lists** the protocol and suggests tactics for **negotiations** between the Chinese and foreigners, the correct observance of which should improve the chances of the latter securing a successful outcome.

2 **Assumes** a basic knowledge and understanding of **negotiating techniques** in general, onto which such specific protocol and tactics may be grafted.

3 **Concentrates**, therefore, purely on the aspects peculiar to China.

Nevertheless when negotiating with the Chinese, remember that – given the importance of *guanxi*, as described in Chapter 2 – they set greater store on personal trust than paper-based contractual terms and may, therefore, be more interested in building a working relationship with you than crossing every 'T' and dotting every 'I' of an agreement.

Section 3 Business meetings
The third section of Chapter 12 details the protocol for **business meetings** between the Chinese and foreigners, the correct observance of which should improve the chances of your securing a useful meeting and successful outcome.

Section 4 Business entertaining
As stated above a key concept of Confucianism is **generosity**, of which one of the most obvious and tangible forms is **entertaining**.

Thus an integral part of the Chinese business scene is **entertaining**, which normally takes the form of a **banquet** as a means of:

- exercising **generosity** and demonstrating **prosperity** (by offering a large range and number of dishes, to the extent of purposely over-ordering);
- building *guanxi*;

for which reason constantly hosting and attending **banquets** is a regular feature of doing business with the Chinese.

The fourth section of Chapter 12, therefore, summarises the protocol for business entertaining in general, and **banquets** in particular, between the Chinese and foreigners – the correct observance of which should help you build *guanxi*.

EXPAT LIFE – CHAPTER 13

Chapter 13 summarises, in broad terms, two issues that are often painted in far rosier terms than their reality sometimes proves, namely:

1 **non-work activities**;
2 **terms and conditions of service**.

and includes a **post script** with final thoughts on how to survive China.

If you do not fully consider the implications and/or prepare for the consequences of these issues *before* you go to China, it may well be too late to do anything about them after you arrive.

With a few exceptions, all sections concentrate on aspects peculiar to China, and merely point to sources of information on those issues common to all expatriate postings, on the assumption, hopefully correct, that the majority of senior expatriates posted to China, such as those of our acquaintance, will already have served elsewhere outside their home country, or know somebody who has, and thus be familiar with such common issues.

Section 1 Non-work activities

Rather than compete, and poorly at that, with the plethora of up-to-the-minute tourist guides, detailing every conceivable excursion, entertainment, sport, pastime, restaurant, cultural activity, etc that you could possibly think of, and more besides, the first section of Chapter 13 briefly challenges you to think about:

- how much **spare time** you may actually be able to enjoy outside the hours that you will be expected to work;
- how your **trailing spouse** is going to cope when you are not at home as often as you had expected.

The issues surrounding **dependent children** are not peculiar to China and, hence, outside the scope of this book (although **schooling options** are summarised in the next section).

Section 2 Terms and conditions of employment

Rather than provide a model expatriate employment contract, with every 'I' dotted and 'T' crossed, the second section of Chapter 13 briefly prompts you to identify some of the issues that you should agree with your employer before leaving for China.

Section 3 Post script

As the Chinese say: 'enjoy!'

The Living and Working Environment

BUSINESS ENVIRONMENT

Philosophical environment – Confucianism

Confucianism is a form of humanism, based on the teachings of **Confucius** (551–479 BC). Once China's official state ideology, it fell from grace after the collapse of the Chinese Empire (1911) and subsequent founding of the officially atheist People's Republic of China (PRC) (1949), and no longer dominates the country's political life and institutions. Nevertheless, **Confucianism** still underpins the Chinese ethics and the rules governing their accepted standards of behaviour. Hence, a basic understanding should help your relationships with them – as follows:

According to Confucius, social cohesion is achieved by correctly observing **ritual behaviours** – rather than any legal code – which serve to:

- promote **mutual understanding** by sharing in communal acts;
- exercise **self-control** by directing emotions in the right direction.

EXAMPLES

1 When dealing with other people, 'the **superior man** in everything considers **righteousness** to be essential. He performs it according to the rules of **propriety**. He brings it forth in **humility**. He completes it with **sincerity**' (*Analects*, Chapter 15).

2 When asked to summarise his teaching in one word, Confucius replied '**reciprocity**', saying: 'What you do not want done to yourself, do not do to others' (idem). This is Confucius' **Golden Rule**, which – albeit negative – seeks to achieve the positive behaviour of '**Do as you would be done by**' (*The Water Babies*, Charles Kingsley, 1863).

3 Another key concept of Confucianism is **filial piety** (the respect of children for their parents): 'In serving his parents, a son may remonstrate with them, but gently; when he sees that they do not incline to follow his advice, he shows an increased degree of **reverence**, but does not abandon his purpose; and should they punish him, he does not allow himself to murmur' (*Analects*, Chapter 4). Albeit one-sided, this command seeks to engender **mutual respect** between not only parents and children but also – by analogy – all partners, whether equal or unequal, in any relationship.

Political environment – socialism with Chinese characteristics

The PRC is a multi-party, multi-national state under leadership of the **Communist Party of China** (CPC) and defined in the current **constitution** (1982) as a 'socialist state under the people's democratic dictatorship led by the working class and based on the alliance of workers and peasants.'

This is the '**socialism with Chinese characteristics**' into which **Communism** has evolved in China – one of only a handful of countries where it has survived as the ideology of a nation state, probably due to being continually adapted to suit the country's needs, rather than copying the Soviet ideological model as most other communist regimes did, as follows.

1 **Mao Tse-Tung**, the founder of the PRC, preached a peasant type of Marxist-Leninism, with a principally rural and military outlook, reflecting his own background, as enshrined in his *Little Red Book*. Unlike his contemporaries, he held that, once economic revolution had been achieved, the state should remain the dictatorship of the proletariat rather than become the state of the entire people. Unfortunately, his policies led to the ill-fated:

   (a) *Great Leap Forward* (1958): reorganising agriculture into collectives and ultimately causing widespread famine;

   (b) *Cultural Revolution* (1966): purging Chinese Communism – with the support of the Army – of the bourgeois influences of the upper middle class (such as art and academia), many of whose members were conscripted into agricultural labour.

2 On his death (1976), the ensuing chaos led to Mao's policies being officially criticised, leaders sanctioned, and many innocent victims reinstated – including **Deng Xiaoping**, who succeeded him to promote '**socialism with Chinese characteristics**', advocating **economic reform** in place of revolution. Thus he dismantled the collectives and allowed farmers to sell spare produce on the open market (known as the '**Responsibility System**').

3 **Deng** succeeded where **Mao** failed because he recognised that ability was more important than ideology

(saying: 'It doesn't matter if the cat is black or white; what matters is how well it catches mice'), whereas Mao held the opposite view (saying: 'Better Red than expert').

4 On his death (1997), the CPC declared **Deng Xiaoping Theory** its guiding ideology.

Big brother
One of the less pleasant aspects of a dictatorship is the '**big brother**' syndrome – as portrayed in George Orwell's *Nineteen-Eighty-Four* – which need not concern those foreigners who 'mind their Ps and Qs' and 'keep their nose clean'. Any who behave otherwise, however, may expect to attract the unwanted attention of the **public security agencies**, as they well might elsewhere in the world. Thus, to be on the safe side: 'enter village, follow customs' – the Chinese equivalent of the Latin proverb 'when in Rome, do as the Romans do'.

Economic environment – market economy with Chinese characteristics

More recently, China has been transformed from a planned system into a '**market economy with Chinese characteristics**' (a euphemism for 'capitalism'?) including gradually opening to the outside world as follows.

1 Under **Jiang Zemin** (who succeeded Deng in 1997) and the then new Premier, **Zhu Rongji**, China embarked on ambitious plans to restructure loss-making **State-Owned Enterprises** (SOEs) in order to improve productivity and efficiency, and thereby maintain competitiveness in a **socialist market economy**. To cure an ailing

command economy with modern commercial principles is no ordinary task, but then Zhu was no ordinary Prime Minister, being an economist (the first in the country's history to hold that office), a leading proponent of a **market economy**, and acclaimed as the most able manger of the country's economy.

2 At the same time, Zhu affirmed that China would maintain its **open-door policy** (see below) to foreign business, improve the **investment environment** and eradicate **corruption**, now re-classified as an '**economic crime**' (see below).

3 The accession of **Hu Jintao** and **Wen Jiabao** to the leadership, as President and Premier respectively, in 2003, has seen further major reforms to the economy and financial systems including the admittance, for the first time, of senior **Privately Owned Enterprise** (POE) managers as representatives to the 16th CPC Congress, thereby giving political recognition to the status and functions of the non-State and private sector. At the time of writing, the most immediate foci for such reforms are **over-investment**, **inflation** and **unemployment** (see below) according to the *China-Britain Trade Review* of May 2004 (listed in the Bibliography).

4 The pace of **political change**, however, is another matter. China has learnt from Russia the danger of simultaneously reforming economic and political systems. Nevertheless, the inextricable relationship between the two means that the latter cannot mark time for very long while the former continues to move forward.

Corruption

That **Zhu Rongji**, when Premier, was serious about eradicating **corruption** is best illustrated by his once allegedly ordering coffins for corrupt officials and one for himself in case he was killed in his battle against them. On another occasion – at the 2002 National People's Congress (NPC) – he censured those officials who were using public money to stage lavish festivals, visit fine restaurants and travel abroad privately.

Iron rice bowl

Just as Confucius extended his concept of **filial piety** to advocate a paternalistic-style government that provides food, security and education for the people, so Mao's government, in its early years, promised workers an '**iron rice bowl**' of lifetime employment, housing, healthcare, pensions and education provided by employers.

Naturally, some strings were attached, including:

- A **job allocation system**, whereby employment was allocated, not chosen, nor always consistent with employees' abilities or location.
- **Unmarrieds** having to live with parents.
- Restrictions on the **movement of labour**.
- **Transgressors** such as parents of **illegitimate children** or more than one child, and professing **Christians** being dismissed by their employers and hence denied access to such provisions.

Today, however, in line with China's economic reforms (described above), such **cradle-to-grave provision** by the state is being gradually phased out in favour of a greater **personal self-sufficiency**.

Which begs the question: in the future, who will provide and/or pay for **unemployment** (see below), housing, hospitals, pensions and schools? The strain on these will be exacerbated by people moving from the countryside to the cities as **residency restrictions** are gradually lifted. The answer is outside the scope of this book

Unemployment

To put **unemployment** into context, in approximate figures:

- at the end of **2002**:
  - 4% of the registered urban workforce was unemployed and growing;
  - the number of **unemployment insurance** policyholders was 35% higher than in 1989;
- in **2004** (at the time of writing):
  - unemployment is expected to rise, despite the anticipated creation of 9 million new jobs (*ibid.*).

One child policy

Since the late 1970s, to help solve the problem of feeding about 20% of the world's population living on approximately 5% of the earth's cultivatable land surface, **married couples** have been restricted to having only **one child**, with severe penalties for **additional** or **illegitimate children** – a policy reiterated in 2002 by the 16th CPC National Congress.

Demography

As a result of the **one child policy**, however, the country now faces the unwanted, undesirable, unforeseen but not unforeseeable:

- repercussion of a generation of **spoilt only sons** or '**little emperors**' – allegedly incapable of tying their own shoelaces;
- prospect of 20% of citizens being **aged over 65** by 2040.

Worse still against the background of the:

- preceding '**baby-boom**' (encouraged by Mao);
- gradual withdrawal of the **iron rice-bowl**;
- current emergence of China's '**dinky** (double-income, no kids yet) **generation**'

the country faces the additional prospect of the growing **third-age generation** – with scant means of support – having to rely on a dwindling pool of progeny, the so-called '**pivot generation**' who in turn need to support themselves and any **dependent children** in the face of **increasing unemployment** (mentioned above).

And if that were not bad enough, significant numbers of married couples are now refraining from having children, who 'are no longer viewed as a link to maintain the family' and 'starting to value their **career development** and **life quality** more, instead of the so-called **social responsibility**' (*Shanghai Daily,* 15 Feb 2003) whereas, until recently, the Confucian concept of **filial piety** would have made it unthinkable for grown-up children to negate their duty towards helpless parents.

Perhaps that is why new legislation was introduced in 2003, allowing parents who are both **only-children** to have two offspring. Viewed logically: in purely mathematical terms the population might otherwise suffer significant reversal, if each generation were to reproduce no more than half itself!

Open door policy
China's commitment to its '**open door policy**' is evidenced by its:

- joining the **World Trade Organisation** (WTO);
- hosting the **2008 Olympics** in Beijing and **World Expo 2010** – the world's leading trade exhibition – in Shanghai.

The **open door** swings both ways: thus the Chinese are now the fastest growing group of international travellers, following the government's easing of restrictions on obtaining a passport – previously the main obstacle to their leaving China – including a growing number of **Chinese working abroad** on short-term assignments as a means of bettering themselves before returning home to enjoy an improved quality of life long-term in China. In this respect, the Chinese are no different from Westerners working in the Far or Middle East!

Long-term commitment
Despite the foregoing, we should not expect China suddenly to fling wide the gates and welcome all-and-sundry like some long-awaited messiah. Were that to happen, there is the real danger – that China fears – of out-moded domestic ventures being destabilised by the superiority of modern foreign adventurers.

Rather, as the lengthy WTO negotiations proved, the Chinese way is to hasten slowly. Thus, foreigners intent on doing business must be **patient** four-fold (the four 'Ps' of marketing in China!); whilst those who grow tired of waiting are sadly mistaken if they think they can pull out of China one day and return the next. Similarly, 'hit-and-run' entrepreneurs wanting to make a fast buck. What the Chinese are looking for is **commitment to China**, which they will test by deliberately playing waiting games.

In other words, in a country where **patience** is a virtue: the longer you are prepared to wait, the sooner you are likely to arrive.

Legal environment

Traditionally in China (in line with Confucian anti-legalism, mentioned above): '**the law is made for man, not man for the law**' – a practice which, whilst theoretically favouring the legislated, rather than the legislators, has some disadvantages.

EXAMPLE

Until new legislation is published, it is hard to know its content and import. Meanwhile, when you ask, more often than not the likely reply will be a Confucian and face-saving: 'We are still thinking about it' (rather than: 'We do not know'). It is possible, therefore, that no two answers to the same question will be the same, leading to inconsistent practices.

As a member of the WTO, China now needs to develop a **Commercial Code** in line with international trade practice. It is an encouraging sign, therefore, that a draft **Civil Code** was submitted to the Standing Committee of the NPC in 2002.

SOCIAL ENVIRONMENT

Cultural heritage

Geography of China
In Western eyes – whose map-makers have traditionally described the world around the Greenwich 0° meridian, with the Americas to the left or 'West' and Asia to the right or 'East' – China is geographically 'off centre', relegated to the far-right edge or 'Far East' of the world-map.

In the Chinese mind, however (as pictured in Figure 1), China lies at the centre of a world that revolves around it – a view emphasised by its Chinese name *Zhōngguó* meaning **The Middle Kingdom** (the first character of which, illustrated in Figure 2, is a pictogram of the world with a vertical axis); and that has been a stumbling block to Sino-West relations in the past (as explained below), and may still be for foreigners who choose to work against, rather than with, it.

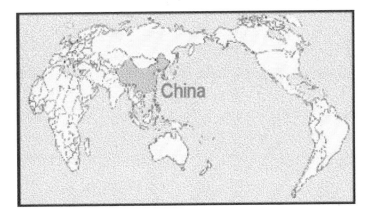

Fig. 1. World map from China's perspective. *Source: ChinaTour.com*

Fig. 2. Pictogram of the first character of *Zhōngguó*:
The Middle Kingdom.

History of China

China is one the world's oldest civilisations, with a **recorded history** of nearly 4,000 years that boasts the **invention**, over a millennium ago, of **paper**, **printing** with movable type, recreational **gunpowder** and the **compass.**

In **literature** on a time-line between **Confucius'** writings (c. 500 BC) and today, the earliest post-Latin texts of the so-called 'civilised' Western world (such as *Beowulf*) appear only at the mid-point.

If this surprises us today, no wonder **Marco Polo** was called the 'Man of a Million Lies' when, over 700 years ago, he claimed that the Chinese were using **paper money**, **paddle-boats** and **coal**.

However, China's fortunes were forcibly changed for the worse some 200 years ago, when **Western traders** invaded China in search of **porcelain**, **silk** and **tea** in exchange for contraband cheap Indian opium for the masses of poor Chinese who could not afford the locally grown opium.

Relations with the West

China's attempts to outlaw the illegal importation of cheap **opium** were fiercely opposed by the Western trading nations in the course of the two so-called **Opium Wars**

(1839–1842 and 1856–1860) characterised by each side's ignorance of the other, as follows.

1 **China's attitude to the West**

The Chinese emperor could not conceive of a community of independent, equal nations. In his eyes, the world comprised China and the rest of the world – a view that branded those who encouraged greater flexibility in its dealings with the West as '**Westerners with Chinese faces**'; and still persists today, to a certain extent.

2 **The West's attitude to China**

The behaviour of the key players (Britain, France, Germany, Russia and the USA) was contradictory, as they tried to:

♦ On the one hand:
   – **undermine** what they deemed restrictive trading practices;
   – **carve up** the country for their own purposes,
♦ On the other hand:
   – **support** the emperor;
   – **keep** China **together**.

In the process, the West humiliated China by:

(a) **reducing** it to a semi-colonial and semi-feudal country;

(b) **forcing** it for approximately the next 100 years to replace Confucianism with Western practices;

(c) **relegating** it to just another backward country under the heel of imperial powers (especially Britain, France and the USA).

However, the West's continual demands for ever-increasing trade concessions gave rise to **anti-foreign popular uprisings** – most notably the Taiping (1851–1864) and Boxer (1898–1900) Rebellions – and were eventually thwarted by the outbreaks of the Chinese Revolution (1911) and First World War (1914).

The Unequal Treaties

During and at the end of the **Opium Wars**, the Western powers forced China to sign the so-called **Unequal Treaties** that, *inter alia*:

♦ On the one hand: **subjugated** China and the Chinese, by:
  - **dictating** China's relations with the West, at home and abroad, for the next 100 years;
  - **prohibiting** it from isolating itself from the rest of the world;
  - **down-grading** the Chinese to second-class citizens in their own country (for example: subjecting them to local courts presided over jointly by Chinese and foreign judges).

♦ On the other hand: **elevated** the West and Westerners by:
  - **exempting** citizens of the Treaty Powers resident in China from Chinese law as answerable only to the laws of their own country, as exercised by their own judges or consulates (a practice known as '**extra-territoriality**').

The Chinese regarded such treaties as unpleasant but necessary concessions dictated by unruly barbarians –

who today are sadly unaware of, or choose conveniently to forget, their inglorious colonial past, much to their shame and China's chagrin: 'plus ça change, plus c'est la même chose!' (*Les Guêpes*, Jean-Baptiste Karr, 1849).

Is it any wonder then that, having been treated so badly, the Chinese may still be cagey about doing business with foreigners?

Domestic environment

Sexual mores
In line with Confucius' teaching that the **Superior Man** should guard against **lust** in his youth, the Chinese official attitude to **sex** is still quite puritanical, disapproving of **pre-** and **extra-marital relations**.

EXAMPLE
In the event of a **birth outside wedlock**, the **parents** may be expelled from the CPC and excluded from the 'iron rice bowl'; and the **child** denied a birth-certificate and condemned to a lifetime as an illegal – rather than illegitimate – 'non-person'.

Similarly, yet paradoxically, some Chinese may still:

- On the one hand: **refrain from** and disapprove of **public displays** of **heterosexual physical contact** beyond a handshake – even between foreigners.
- On the other hand: **publicly indulge** in **same-sex physical contact** without there necessarily being any **homosexual** overtones (which is repulsive to most Chinese).

In practice, however, there is increasingly more **sexual freedom** than meets the eye, if not a **sexual revolution**, with an increase in **pre-** and **extra-marital sex** and **sexually transmitted infections** (STIs), all of which were unthinkable only a few years ago.

Foreigners, on the other hand, are seen as extremely permissive and should, therefore, not take **sexual relationships** with Chinese citizens lightly. And men should even be prepared for rough justice if caught *in flagrante delicto* with Chinese girls, who themselves may be punished in consequence.

As a general rule, steer clear of situations where you might be alone with a member of the opposite sex.

Sexual equality
Today, China is a model of **sexual equality – at work**, at least – with many well-educated wives enjoying as successful careers as their husbands, and not always in the same city or even country. '**Trailing spouses**' are not a Chinese phenomenon; whilst any **child** of the marriage may be farmed out to grandparents in a third location. The **virtuous wife** finds favour under the law, which allows her to **divorce** her husband for co-habiting with another and keep the whole of his estate including the marital home, which he must leave (as the Chinese put it) 'only with his pants'.

However, as elsewhere in the world, this was not always so in the past, when Chinese women were subservient to men in a **patriarchal** and **sexist society – at home**, especially – of which vestiges nevertheless still linger.

EXAMPLES

(1) **Women** who **drink alcohol** and **smoke** in public are 'not nice'; and drivers still open the car door for the man before his wife.
(2) Although considered to share the rank of their husband, Chinese wives seldom show up at social occasions.

Privacy

Many Chinese have no concept of **privacy**, especially if brought up in a family where several generations have shared cramped living-quarters.

EXAMPLE

In 2002, some Western friends checked into a five-star Shanghai hotel, accompanied by their Chinese host. On reaching their room, the wife announced she was going to take a bath – to which the Chinese host, sitting down in a comfortable chair, replied 'Go ahead' without making any attempt to leave!

Another explanation is the alleged **big brother** regime (mentioned above) which may excuse paranoid foreigners for being suspicious of those service personnel who burst unannounced into their hotel room!

Whatever the reason you will find that the Chinese may tend to:

- invade your **privacy** – especially domestic staff (see Chapter 7);
- stand a bit too close to you for comfort (as they are more comfortable with shorter **personal distances** than many Westerners).

EXAMPLES

1 To reach my office from reception, I had to walk past that of my senior Chinese colleague, who would invariably 'jump out' into the corridor and block my way in order to be the first to tell me what had been going on in my absence, without first giving me a chance to make myself comfortable.

2 She also had great difficulty understanding why my office door was not always open to her, even when shut to others and with the instruction 'please do not disturb'.

Family and friends

The importance of loyalty to **family** and **friends** is enshrined in the Confucian concept of **filial piety**.

Erosion of traditional values

Despite millennia of **tradition**, a new set of **social value**s is now being embraced by the so-called '**dinky generation**' or '**Chuppies**' – Chinese 'young urban professionals, with a handsome income, working like dogs in multinationals and lingering in discos or bars until midnight; they marry late, mostly in early thirties or even older; they prefer DINK (**double income and no kids**) families; they drink coffee, watch Hollywood movies and listen to Western R-and-B or hip-hop music, which may be condemned by their parents though. But they don't really care; the older generation is a little out of time (sic). Most of all, **fashion** is above everything else, because that's the soul of being modern, being a **yuppie**, at least in appearance' (*Beijing Review*, 23 Jan 2003).

Amongst **China's youth**, 'Chinese **tradition** is disappearing... Some are westernized; some prefer Japanese or Korean lifestyles and some even wear clothes with national flags of other countries... Many Chinese children like McDonald's or KFC (Kentucky Fried Chicken) while cannot even use chopsticks well (sic)' (*op. cit.*, 16 Jan 2003).

Education system
The Chinese still tend to **learn** by rote and **be examined** by multiple-choice tests, methods considered in the West to **impart** and demonstrate **knowledge** and **stifle** powers of reasoning and **understanding**, respectively. Which may explain why, as you will soon discover, they possess **phenomenal memories**, show **little individual initiative**, and prefer **collective decision making**.

Relationship with foreigners

As a result of their contrasting cultural and domestic backgrounds, not to mention history, today's relationship between China and the West has been described by one Chinese commentator as: 'Americans are from Mars, Chinese are from Venus. We are ready to be your friends while keeping our characteristics. How about you?' (*op. cit.*, 23 Jan 2003).

Attitude to foreigners
Because of China's **centrism** and **isolationism** (mentioned above), foreigners may still be:

- **judged** by Chinese norms;
- **disparaged** as inferior '**foreign devils**' or '**barbarians**' just because they are not Chinese, to be stared or shouted at;
- **stereotyped** – such as bowler-hatted men stumbling around in the London fog.

This attitude is displayed especially by uneducated Chinese and/or in rural areas.

EXAMPLE

Many young educated urban Chinese still believe the UK 'to be populated by a stiff and reserved people; a nation stuck in the past.' Some see the British 'as men in bowler hats walking at a clip with noses in the air; doffing servants living below stairs in large country houses; regal pomp and circumstance by every turn' (*City Weekend*, 13 to 26 Feb 2003).

Nevertheless, most educated Chinese are hospitable to foreigners, but still may be wary about developing friendships with them that would bring mutual obligations, according to the extended Confucian concept of **filial piety**. Thus, should a Chinese person befriend you, beware lest their sole aim is just a ticket or passport to the West.

In particular – if you are a businessman on your own:

♦ pity the gullibility, rather than be jealous, of your middle-aged colleague sporting a trophy Chinese girl on his arm: all she may want is access to the West;

♦ take your spouse to China – we have seen too many marriages fail.

Attitude to foreign women

The Chinese view of the West is **schizophrenic**, perceiving it as **technologically highly advanced**, but **morally corrupt**. Thus, although they are not attracted to **Western women**, Chinese men believe them to be promiscuous and thus fair game.

However, the Chinese show more respect in business circles where:

- **foreign businesswomen** are accorded the respect due to their positions;
- **wives of foreign businessmen** are welcomed at social occasions (and accorded the same rank as their husbands);
- **foreign women** are expected to wear sober clothing (see Chapter 9);
- **female foreign guests** may drink and smoke in public, even when their Chinese counterparts may not – a concession indicative of the fact that the Chinese expect foreigners to behave strangely!

Overseas Chinese (**huáqiáo**)

Do not assume that those foreign businesses who include **overseas Chinese (*huáqiáo*)** in their negotiating teams and/ or appoint them as their local Chief Executive Officers (CEOs) instead of their own country(wo)men, will enjoy more favourable treatment. If this surprises you, just bear in mind the parallel of the UK and USA: two countries divided by a common language!

UNDERPINNING BEHAVIOURS

Personal relationships (*Guanxi*)

Guanxi is the 'special **personal relationship** in which **long-term mutual benefit** is more important than **short-term individual gain** and contains the key elements of **indirect relationship** between two people through proper introduction by a **third party**, and **direct relationship** between two people who **trust** each other and the contact person...It is the **mother of all relationships**' 'Chinese Cultural Values and their Implications in Business Transactions', Wei-ping

Wu and Li Yong in: *Doing Business with China*, Kogan Page, UK, 2000, pp. 192 and 193).

Simply put: *guanxi* is akin to the **old boy network** in the UK, but with the added feature of **reciprocity** (as per Confucius' **Golden Rule**), **lasts for life**, and contrasts with the Western superficial, short-term, and results-oriented practice of **networking**. It is what oils the wheels of life, and glues together social and business intercourse.

The **punishment** for breaking the rules of *guanxi* is ostracism from the network – which is incentive enough for the Chinese to obey them.

Building and maintaining Guanxi
The Chinese lay such emphasis on *guanxi* as a measure of **personal ability** and **influence**, that they disdain anyone who has none as only **half-Chinese**. Thus the more a foreigner or **outsider** builds *guanxi* in China, the more they will be accepted by the Chinese as being one of them or an **insider**.

Guanxi takes time to **build**, particularly between parties with nothing in common. You can accelerate it by using the services of an **intermediary** who is respected by the Chinese and has established *guanxi* within the circles you wish to enter – but only as a short-term kick-start since, by its **reciprocal nature**, *guanxi* cannot be permanently bought. Longer term, the traditional way for foreigners to build guanxi is by **exchanging gifts** and **favours** with the Chinese, and **entertaining** them (as explained in Chapter 12).

To **maintain** it, you need to stoke your *guanxi*, since it is not an inexhaustible supply – as some foreigners mistakenly believe – but, like a bank account, needs deposits to cover withdrawals and maintain a balance of payments. Otherwise, the Chinese may withdraw their goodwill or, worse still, pre-empt you by requesting a favour you cannot grant.

Guanxi in action

Since *guanxi* is the **personal networking** that opens doors via **exchanging favours** rather than greasing palms – **bribery** is an 'economic crime', as intimated above – succeeding in China depends as least as much on **whom you know** as what you know. Thus results-oriented foreigners who ignore this, and concentrate on contractual rather than personal relationships in business – as the Chinese do – are likely to be disappointed.

This difference in behaviour is explained by the fact that in China:

◆ The approach to **problem solving** is: 'whom do we *know* who can help us?' rather than, as in the West: 'what can we *do*?'

◆ '**Business may flow out of friendship** whereas, in the West, friendship may flow out of business' (*Doing Business in China*, Tim Ambler and Morgen Witzel, Routledge, London, 2000, p. 198).

Moreover to be successful, *guanxi* must be as much '**business to business**' as '**person to person**', since the Chinese tend not to distinguish between the two, but use personal *guanxi* to secure business advantage. This is especially true with foreigners. After all, the prime value to them of building *guanxi* with you, a 'foreign devil', is to secure whatever contribution your business can make to China's progress. Again, foreigners who ignore this, and boast of and rely solely on their personal *guanxi*, are likely to be disappointed.

Using Guanxi

The simplest way of using *guanxi* is via **a friend of a friend**. For example: if you wish to meet Mr X, and his and your right-hand Chinese employees have *guanxi*, ask the latter for an introduction via that *guanxi*, who will gain 'face' if they were not senior enough to have made the connection without you. (This method is similar to **Newton's Cradle**, using contiguous connections to move up the chain of influence.) Afterwards, do not forget who facilitated, or rather 'lent' you, that connection – since to take over another's *guanxi* without further involving the introducer could cause resentment and close more doors than it opens. If *guanxi* is hard to **build**, it is even more difficult to **recover**.

Warning

One word of warning: do not exaggerate the scope of your *guanxi*, nor imply that it will necessarily yield results. Otherwise, you may not be able to grant a particular favour, and thereby cause offence.

Collectivism, collective decision making and consensus

Given the influence of *guanxi*, Maoist **collectivism**, lack of **privacy** and the Confucian values of **harmony, modesty** and **respect for authority**, is it any wonder that the Chinese put:

- **group allegiance** *before* individual loyalty;
- benign **group harmony** and **dynamics** *before* (potentially) divisive individual behaviour, ambition and assertiveness;
- the preservation of **insiders'** *guanxi before* the conflicting interests of outsiders?

As a result, also given their **uninventive education system**, the Chinese prefer **collective decision making** and **consensus**; and will debate issues until everyone agrees to a **group decision**, regardless of their personal views.

Hence '**agreeing to disagree**' is not an option in China.

Intellectual property rights (IPR)
A peculiar consequence of collectivism has been China's hitherto Confucian view of **copyright** as anti-social, and **plagiarism** as acceptable, contending that sharing knowledge benefits society and restricting it impoverishes. After all: who is to say that my idea is original, just because I first made it public? Today, however, faced with **mass-copying techniques**, the Chinese have been obliged to introduce appropriate regulations similar to elsewhere in the world.

Face ('*mianzi*') and harmony
'**Face**' (*mianzi*) is '**the regard** in which one is held by others or the **light** in which one appears' (*Dealing with the Chinese*, Scott D. Seligman, Management Books 2000, UK, 1997, p. 50); 'an intangible commodity that is vital to a person's **reputation**, **dignity** and **prestige**' (*Chinese Business Etiquette*, Scott D. Seligman, Warner Books, USA, 1999, p. 198).

Simply put: 'face' is your '**status**'; and to lose it, and thus incur **shame**, is the worst thing that can befall you.

Face in action

What distinguishes *mianzi*, however, from other cultures is that it can be not only **lost**, **saved** or **gained**, but also **given** as follows.

1　If you criticise a Chinese person in public they will '**lose face**'; and you lose their goodwill, suffer retaliation, lose the respect of bystanders and anyone that they tell, and consequently **lose face** yourself. In such an event the best way to '**restore face**' – theirs and yours – is to ask a Chinese intermediary for help.

2　Thus, to '**save face**': you should use **positive criticism**; and deliver it in a mutually face-saving way – privately, discreetly and tactfully.

3　Unlike losing or saving face – which normally involve a third-party – you can '**gain face**' on your own: typically by acquiring **status symbols**.

4　You can also '**give face**' to someone: for example, by praising their work in front of others. Since the Chinese lay special store on face given them by foreigners, you may consequently be regarded with particular favour.

Whose face is it anyway?

In the Confucian spirit of **reciprocity**, you should **protect** the face of others as well as your own. When it comes to foreigners, however, some Chinese may be less considerate and try to save their own at your expense, even if you are boss.

In such an event, I suggest that you tactfully remind them that your face is also your employer's face, to lose which will reflect badly on them too. Since the actions of individuals reflect not only on themselves, but also on their immediate associates, being linked to others' **failure** could undermine one's own sway – and no Chinese wants to be tainted by failure, albeit vicarious.

Saying no and preserving harmony

'**No**' means 'no' to the Chinese, for whom to recant is a sign of weakness and thus **loss of face** – and will shut the door in your face. It is the antithesis of *guanxi* which, once destroyed, is hard to re-establish.

In dealing with the Chinese, therefore, you should *never* say, nor put them in a position where they are compelled to say, a bald '**no**' – such as in response to a request for an **impossible favour**. Rather, leave yourself a way out and forward, using such Chinese tactics as:

- Saying 'let me think about it and get back to you' or 'have you thought of such-and-such an alternative?'
- Sucking in air through clenched teeth, to give the other person time to think again.
- Telling an **abject** or **white lie**.

Far from being devious, you would be respecting the Chinese tactics of:

- **Circumlocution** in preference to the Western 'fault' – in their eyes – of blunt speaking.
- **Lying** as a dishonourable means to justify the honourable end of **avoiding conflict** and **preserving**

the **harmony** of *guanxi*, which transcends each party's version of the truth, whatever that may be.

In other words: the greater good of the other outweighs **self-interest**.

Being economical with the truth
The Chinese use similar tactics as a 'cover up' – such as for a **mistake**, **ignorance**, or something they do not want to own up to; and, in my experience, sadly some would rather lie than lose face, even when the means and end are equally 'dishonourable' by their own standards.

Conflict management
The best way of **handling conflict** is to state objectively your **annoyance** and reasons, and allow the other person a face-saving way out.

EXAMPLE

One acceptable method that saves both parties' faces is to use a mutually respected **intermediary**. This is especially useful when foreign employers need to give bad news to Chinese employees, to avoid the added indignation of losing face to a foreign devil.

Modesty and humility (*Keqi*)
'*Keqi*' is the **humble** and **modest behaviour** expected of the Confucian **Superior Man** (as in the expression for 'you're welcome': '*buyao keqi*' meaning 'you shouldn't be so kind and polite to me'); and encouraged by Mao, who said: 'We should be **modest** and **prudent**, guard against **arrogance** and **rashness**, and serve the Chinese people with heart and soul' (23 Apr 1945).

Indeed, to be **arrogant** and boast about you and yours is considered so impolite that the Chinese have made a virtue out of **public displays** of **ritual modesty**; and foreigners should follow suit.

EXAMPLES

1 **When complimenting** your Chinese hosts on a sumptuous and magnificent home-cooked meal, do not be surprised if they reply: 'I am glad you like our simple food: we are very poor and unadventurous cooks'.

2 **When complimented** on your spoken Chinese, you should reply along the lines of: 'Thank you, but my grammar and pronunciation are very bad' rather than boast about having a master's degree in the language from an ivy-league university.

One purpose is **ritually** to **cede superiority** to others by **praising them** and **deprecating oneself**, in accordance with the practice of **hierarchism** (explained below).

Although **ritualistic**, such displays are not necessarily **false modesty** nor **hollow flattery** as some sceptics might think: the mere fact that the Chinese bother to observe their code of gentlemanly behaviour when dealing with unequal 'foreign devils' is in itself a sufficient demonstration of genuine respect.

Nevertheless, the Chinese may use **false modesty** or **hollow flattery** to put you in your place or get their way. Do not be fooled, but check your ego: they may really mean the opposite and are just 'trying it on' in line with the Western saying that 'flattery will get you anywhere'.

EXAMPLE
When you, in halting Chinese, compliment their genuinely excellent command of your language, do not be fooled when they reply: 'But not as good as your spoken Chinese' or 'your Chinese calligraphy makes mine look like a child's scrawl'.

Hierarchism and authority ('*Laoban*-ism')

In line with the extended Confucian concept of **filial piety**, the Chinese are taught not to 'kick against the pricks' of social order; but to respect and defer to **age**, **authority**, **rank** and **seniority**.

Dead men's shoes

In the past, respect for age and seniority has meant being **promoted** to fill '**dead men's shoes**' according to **age rather than ability**.

In the future, however, this practice should change, according to the last of Jiang's *Eight Dos and Don'ts*: 'Appoint people on their merits; do not resort to malpractice in personnel placement' (*www.chinadaily. com.cn*, Nov 2002)

Meanwhile, in business, **rank** and **reward** should correlate to **age**.

EXAMPLES
1 Bosses are expected to be older than their staff; leaders of a delegation than its members; and senior colleagues than younger ones.
2 Older colleagues expect to earn more than younger ones, even if the former are performing identically or worse in the same or a smaller job.

Thus, **foreign 'high flyers'** who are too young for their seniority and thus insufficiently experienced by Chinese standards may not be taken seriously, and even be misconstrued as an insult on the part of the home office for not appointing someone of sufficient **gravitas**.

One exception to this rule seems to be young well-paid short-term foreign graduates, probably because they are transient, not blocking their Chinese colleagues' promotion.

'Laoban-ism'

Laoban-ism is the term coined by me – as far as I am aware – to describe the **blind obedience to the boss** or laoban, and the subjugation of truth to hierarchy, both of which are rife.

EXAMPLES

1 *Laoban* is always right (even if only by virtue of being older and when obviously wrong): that is why they are the boss – otherwise they would not be.
1 Because **infallible**, *Laoban* should never be openly challenged – which would be a loss of 'face', as explained above.
3 *Laoban* makes and is expected to make every decision – the Chinese workers' means of **'upward delegation'**.

For the foreign boss who does not understand their ways, the result may be disastrous as Chinese staff stand by and watch *laoban* make all the mistakes in the book and lose face, whilst ensuring they do not lose their own.

Changing your mind

For the average person, **changing your mind** is a loss of

face; but for *laoban* it could be mistaken for a lack of ability or show of weakness – when, in fact, the opposite may be true.

Business hierarchy

In business, hierarchical distinctions (i.e. **rank** and **status**) are important to the Chinese and at the root of China's **bureaucratic structures**.

In theory, therefore, to maintain face – as explained above – you should ideally interact with people of similar rank and, therefore, age. Otherwise, you may detract from the 'face' of a more senior or much older person; or lose face when dealing with a more junior or much younger one.

Thus, at work, junior staff will often ask senior staff to sound out the boss on their behalf, rather than making a direct approach.

EXAMPLE

Since drivers spend more time with their bosses than many of the staff do, it is common practice for employees to ask the driver to bend the boss' ear in the car or to eavesdrop on in-car conversations.

In reality, however, this is wholly impractical and I recommend that you should behave, when dealing with people of:

- **Higher rank**: **deferentially** and **diffidently**, even using **flattery** and **self-deprecation** (as intimated above).
- **Lower rank**: neither as if you consider yourself more important than the other person; nor too informally.

Exercising authority

As a corollary of being conditioned to respect their 'elders and betters', those Chinese who fall into this category expect **natural respect** in the exercise of their authority.

Consequently, they may feel threatened by those Western modern management practices that turn traditional business hierarchies upside down to cast the boss in the role of facilitator with responsibilities rather than leader with privileges.

Similarly, some Chinese staff may be confused by and/or lose respect for foreign bosses who try to be 'one of the boys'.

Deferring to authority

Self-deprecation and **deferring to authority** must be interpreted in the afore-mentioned contexts. Do not be surprised, therefore, if:

- Younger or less senior colleagues present you with a problem and expect you to solve it for them; but also be aware that they are not normally averse to suggesting a solution, when you ask them.
- Even senior Chinese employees fail to recognise, and hence take advantage of, genuine opportunities that you offer to them to behave otherwise.

Paternalism

As a result of the **paternalistic nature** of the employee-*laoban* relationship – consequent upon the Confucian concept of **filial piety** – the latter may freely advise, or be consulted by, the former about personal as well as work matters.

Contrary to the Western management tradition of keeping personal problems out of the workplace: in China, good bosses are those who look after their employees' general welfare for the **collective good** of the whole staff. A happy worker is a productive one.

Conformity and disagreement

From the foregoing, it will come as no surprise to learn that the basic rule (*Beyond the Chinese Face: Insights from Psychology*, Michael Harris Bond, Oxford University Press, Hong Kong, 1991, p. 83) is: '**Honour the hierarchy first, your vision of the truth second**'. Since the Tiananmen Square incident (of 1989), however, there is less reserve amongst younger Chinese to challenge authority.

Social hierarchy

When discussing jobs and careers – 'safe' subjects, as mentioned below – do not be surprised by an apparently inverted **social hierarchy** (in Western terms) left over from Maoism.

EXAMPLE

Whilst practising conversational Chinese with my first driver, I struggled to explain that my father had been a doctor, only to be trounced by the driver who replied, with obvious pride and superiority, that his father was a peasant!

Topics of conversation

What constitutes a **taboo** may depend on the relationship that you and your Chinese counterparts enjoy. If in doubt, as at all other times when dealing with the Chinese, take your lead from them.

Meanwhile, I offer the following guidelines.

Chinese politics

1 Do not criticise **Chinese government leaders** or **policies** (past or present), which may offend some Chinese – even if they criticise them to you. Indeed, it is probably better not to discuss **Chinese politics** at all, until you have been in China long enough to know for certain what you can say to those whom you can really trust (not to report you to a local CPC official) should you deviate from this advice.

2 In addition, avoid those areas of Chinese politics that the West openly challenges, such as: **human rights**, **Tibet**, **Taiwan**, and the treatment of so-called **dissenters**. Otherwise, you may well find that you are *persona non gratis* in Chinese business circles.

Sensitive subjects

3 You need to be careful, circumspect and sensitive to Chinese views when discussing: **crime**, **drugs**, **foreign politics**, **freedom**, **one child policy**, **sex**, **spiritual matters** or **superstitions**.

Safe subjects

4 As elsewhere in the world, subjects safe to discuss with the Chinese include (in alphabetical order): **books** (non-political), **clothes**, **cooking**, **customs** and **traditions**, **entertainment** (TV, films, music), **family**, **festivals** and **holidays**, **folk-arts**, **home-town**, **grandchildren**, **hobbies** (especially stamp collecting), **jobs** and **careers**, **landscapes**, **music**, **sport**, **tourist attractions**, **weather** but not **pets**, which urban Chinese tend not to have.

5 On the other hand, however, the Chinese have no qualms about asking **personal questions** to which, if embarrassed, your best response is a non-committal humorous answer. Never react in any way that suggests that they have committed a cultural gaffe, since this would cause them a loss of face.

Forms of address

Addressing Chinese with sufficient **respect** (which you can never over do) is a complicated matter, on which you should seek guidance from a Chinese colleague before meeting someone new, as follows.

1 Chinese are rarely addressed by their **first names**, except by family, close friends and, today, close colleagues.

2 Address a Chinese person by their **surname** (which comes first as in: *Hu* Jintao) preceded by their title or rank.

3 Alternatively, you may just address someone by their **rank**, dropping any 'vice' or 'deputy' **prefix** to give them face.

4 At subsequent meetings, you may precede a man's surname with the word **xiao** (young) if under 40 or much younger than you – or **lao'** (old) if over 40 or several years older than you.

5 The Chinese may reciprocate by addressing you by your surname followed by *xian-sheng* (Mister) or *nüshi* (Madam).

6 Say *ni hao?* (how are you?) or, more politely, *nin hao?* (where *nin* is equivalent to the French vous).

7 Limit physical greetings to brief single **handshakes**.

Behaviour

To avoid your committing a *faux pas*, I offer the following guidance.

Non-verbal behaviour

1 Use appropriate **body language** by: maintaining proper **posture**; signalling or manipulating something by using your **hand(s)** only; and signalling someone by waving, never **pointing**.

2 Whilst the Chinese dislike too much **eye contact** and avert their gaze, they are not averse to **staring** at strangers.

3 The Chinese hide their **discomfort** at others' misfortunes by **laughing**.

4 If the Chinese **nod** or **grunt** while you are talking, it indicates that they are listening, and not necessarily that they agree.

5 Avoid **physical contact** with the Chinese beyond **shaking hands**; or, with someone of the same sex, lightly guiding them (such as through a door).

6 The Chinese consider **silence** a virtue, which they use as a sign of **courtesy**, meaning 'please carry on speaking' and a **ploy** to ferret out information, by making you say anything just to break the silence.

7 The Chinese tend not to **smile**, having been conditioned to control their feelings in public, as explained below. Should they do so, however, do not assume that it is a sign of friendliness: it could be a decoy for **embarrassment** or **anger**.

General behaviour

8 In accordance with the Confucian value of **harmony**, the Chinese are conditioned to control their **emotions** and **feelings** in public; and you should follow suit by, above all, never losing your **temper**. It is acceptable, however, to say how you feel in an objective and firm but fair and friendly manner.

9 The Chinese may show you **respect** by using **formal behaviour**, which should not be mistaken for a lack of warmth or friendliness. As you get to know them better, however, they will loosen up.

3

Safekeeping

The main threats to the **safekeeping** of your **person** and **property** include (in alphabetical order by risk classification):

- Arrest and imprisonment.
- Crime:
  - assaults on foreigners;
  - drug trafficking;
  - financial scams;
  - kidnap;
  - sex offences;
  - street crime.
- Fundamental risks:
  - natural disasters;
  - terrorism.
- Immi/emigration control:
  - dual nationality;
  - entry/exit regulations;
  - passport loss/confiscation.
- Restricted activities:
  - religious activities;
  - other restricted activities;
  - restricted exports;
  - restricted imports.

- ◆ Safety and security:
  - – fire protection;
  - – gas appliances;
  - – intruder protection;
  - – public transport;
  - – road safety.
- ◆ Other risks:
  - – bereavement and death;
  - – business disputes.

OVERALL EVALUATION

At the time of writing, the UK Foreign and Commonwealth Office (FCO) and US Department of State (DOS), according to their websites (listed in the Bibliography), respectively agree and anticipate that your stay in China should be:

- ◆ **trouble-free** with a **low risk of terrorism**;
- ◆ **safe** with a **low but increasing crime rate**.

ARREST AND IMPRISONMENT

Identification

1 Under **Chinese law** – to which you are subject in China – you may not enjoy the same protection and rights as in your home country.

2 **Foreign citizenship** neither affords immunity nor is a 'get out of jail free' card as some have mistakenly or arrogantly thought to their cost in the past, even in the event of your innocently, or being wrongly accused of, contravening that law.

Evaluation

3   For example (according to the DOS website), Westerners detained:

   (a) For **questioning**: may not be allowed to contact their local Consulate until after being questioned.

   (b) Pending **trial**: have often waited for more than a year to come to trial.

   (c) Are rarely granted **bail**.

4   Foreigners who are convicted of breaking the law may expect:

   (a) More severe **punishment** than in their home country including: fines, detention, arrest, expulsion and imprisonment.

   (b) Harsher **prison** sentences and conditions than in their home country – see Appendix 3 for details.

5   China has traditionally taken a hard line on crime and punishment; and still practises **capital punishment** for a wide variety of offences, from which **foreigners are *not* exempt**.

EXAMPLES

1   First the bad news: it is probably no exaggeration to say that, in any one year, more people are executed in China than in the rest of the world put together.

2   Now the good news: this may explain why, reputedly, there is no lack of donor organs in China for **transplant surgery**.

6   The Chinese police may also contact your home police if you are arrested for **drugs** or **violent** or **sexual offences**.

Control

7 Provided that you **behave** appropriately in general and **respect** local laws and customs in particular as described here, you should not have any cause to worry.

8 Nevertheless, should you be (wrongfully) **detained** or **arrested**:
   (a) **Remain calm** and **co-operate**.
   (b) **Refrain from abuse** and **violence**.
   (c) Insist on your legal right that the arresting authorities **notify your local Consulate**.
   (d) Request your employer, friends and family to do the same.

9 For further expert advice on what:
   (a) you should do for yourself
   (b) your **local Consulate** can and cannot do
   please refer to the appropriate web-page of your home government's ministry of foreign affairs.

10 Meanwhile, please note that **local Consuls** (see Appendix 2 for details):
   (a) Are not (usually) legally trained and so cannot give **legal advice**.
   (b) Can, however, help you find a **local lawyer**, who is better placed to advise you.
   (c) Cannot get you out of **prison**, since in China you are subject only to Chinese law.

11 For these reasons amongst others I strongly advise you to **register with your local Consulate** as soon as possible after your arrival in China.

CRIME

Assaults on and crimes against foreigners

Identification

1 There were allegations in 2001/2002 of the occasional foreigner in **Tianjin** being threatened with **syringes** claimed to contain the **HIV virus** – a practice not peculiar to China – but nothing since.

Evaluation

2 Otherwise, we are aware of only very few assaults specifically targeted at expatriates **outside their home** and certainly neither our friends nor we experienced any in the late 1990s.

EXAMPLE

On the eve of the return of Hong Kong to Chinese rule (30th June 1997), I spent a long time mingling with the celebrating crowds in Tiananmen Square, where I was often asked by Chinese revellers to pose for photographs with them. Indeed, I was possibly the last white face around that afternoon, and only left when asked to do so by the police for my own safety. Later, in the early hours of the following morning, I walked freely through the thronged streets near my hotel, without anyone taking any notice of me, very obviously an Englishman.

3 Indeed, sad to say, the only country where I have been physically assaulted is my own, when on home leave after many years abroad and hence 'foreign-looking'.

4 We are aware, however, of **foreigners' homes** being specifically targeted.

EXAMPLE

Crimes suffered by our expatriate friends **inside their home** have usually been attributable to their maids or similar 'insiders' acting in collusion with the perpetrators – such as purposely:

◆ **leaving unlocked** doors and/or windows;

◆ **lending keys;**

◆ **conveying** such **sensitive information** as:
  – dates and/or times when the owners were away and/or the premises vacant;
  – security arrangements and/or codes.

5 Similarly – as mentioned in Chapters 2 and 7 – since the Chinese view the West as technologically advanced but morally corrupt, it is not unknown for:

(a) **Maids**: to 'come on' to **Western men** while the wife is away.

(b) **Drivers**: to 'try it on' with **Western wives** while the boss is away (not out of any sense of attraction, which generally they do not feel; but in the mistaken belief that these are promiscuous and thus fair game).

EXAMPLES

When I was away from home overnight on business:

1 In Colombia (in 1974) my wife had to lock the **armed guard** out of our personal quarters at night, and sleep with a gas-pistol under her pillow, in order to ward off his advances

2 In China (in 1997) one dark winter's night, my wife became aware of our then **driver** temporarily slowing the car down in the unlit road leading to our housing complex, and using the rear-view mirror to 'eye her up' as she sat alone in the back seat, just as they were approaching our home. To her credit, although understandably scared, she averted his gaze, prayed hard, entered the house as quickly as possible on arrival, and locked the doors.

6 According to the DOS: 'there were 11 reported violent attacks on **American citizens** between 2000 and 2002' in China.

Control

7 The Chinese **legal system** seems to act as a deterrent since, apparently, the local:

   (a) **Police** tend to treat and investigate **crimes against foreigners** more seriously.

   (b) **Courts** impose heavier penalties on the perpetrators.

8 Nevertheless, since **pre-crime prevention** is better than post-crime punishment you should negotiate with your employer the provision of a **mobile phone** (vulgarly known as a '**rape phone**') for any member of your family potentially exposed to **lone attack**.

> **EXAMPLE**
>
> After the incident in China described above, my employer insisted that my wife always carry a **mobile phone** at their expense.

9 If you are **alone** never enter a (near-empty) lift if there is a suspicious looking person inside.

10 Protect your home (as recommended below).

Drug trafficking

Identification

1 Even the innocent possession of **prescription medications** vital to your wellbeing in quantities larger than the Chinese authorities deem necessary for personal use – which is quite feasible if you intend to work and/

or live in China for any length of time – might lead to your being arrested on suspicion of **drug trafficking**.

Evaluation

2   The **penalties** for **drug-related offences** are most severe, ranging:

(a) From at worst, the **death penalty** – including for foreigners.

(b) To at best, at least ten years in **prison**.

This is not surprising, given the indignation heaped on China in the 19th century by the West during the Opium Wars (as mentioned in Chapter 2; and outlined in *The Chinese Business Puzzle*, pp. 33–36, 211–213).

EXAMPLE

You may well have read in the press of the **public executions** of **convicted drug traffickers** who are taken straight from the court room to a public place – such as a football stadium – to be summarily dispatched by a shot to the head.

3   Indeed, it is not unknown for **foreigners** to be **executed**.

Control

4   **Specific precautions**:

(a) Carry a **prescription** and **explanatory letter** from your **doctor**, in English and Chinese, justifying any **prescribed medications** for personal use.

(b) Leave **prescribed medications** in their **original labelled containers** (so that they coincide with the corresponding prescriptions).

(c) Consult your **local Chinese Consulate** *before you arrive in China.*

5 **Standard common-sense precautions:**
   (a) *Do* **always:**
   - **pack** and **securely fasten** your own **luggage**.
   (b) *Do not* **ever:**
   - **leave** your **luggage unguarded**;
   - **carry** or **look after** packages or **luggage** for **anyone else**.

Financial scams

Identification

1 You may be asked by locals to exchange **foreign currency** at a preferential rate.
2 There is a large volume of **counterfeit currency** in China with which, for example, **taxi drivers** in particular may try to palm you off when changing large notes.
3 If working in China you are subject to **Chinese tax laws**, the **penalties** for breaking which range from **fines** to **imprisonment**.

Evaluation

4 It is illegal to exchange **foreign currency** except at banks, hotels and official *bureaux de change*.

5 'Due to the large volume of **counterfeit currency** in China, **unofficial exchanges** usually result in travellers losing their money and possibly left to face charges of breaking **foreign exchange laws**' (DOS).

6 At the time of writing, several Americans are in Chinese prisons for being implicated in **fraud schemes**, including falsified bank and business documents, and **tax evasion** schemes (*ibid.*).

Control

7 Only change **foreign currency** at official outlets.

EXAMPLE

Shortly after arriving in China (in 1997), I was approached by a Chinese colleague who was travelling to the UK for legitimate study purposes and wanted to take with her more foreign currency than was officially permitted (at the time: US$ 3,000). Otherwise, given the (then) non-convertibility of Chinese currency abroad, she would have been unable to cover her expenses for a whole year.

Innocently, I agreed to exchange some US$ 7,500; and was rightly chastised by my international Head Office for jeopardising their and my reputation. Mistakenly, I had thought that only my colleague might be running a risk by 'smuggling' out of China foreign currency that I had legally brought in.

8 Carry **small change** for paying **taxis**; and ensure you get a **receipt** from the driver.

9 File and settle any outstanding **tax declaration** before leaving China.

10 Keep abreast in the local news and media of any **known scams**.

Kidnap

Identification

1 I am unaware (at the time of writing) of foreigners being purposely **kidnapped**, **abducted** or **ambushed** in China – unlike Colombia, where my employer had to hire an armed bodyguard for the family.

Evaluation

2   Nevertheless, 'women outside hotels in tourist districts frequently use the prospect of companionship or sex to **lure foreign men** to isolated locations where accomplices are waiting for the purpose of **robbery**' (*ibid.*).

EXAMPLES

From personal experience (which I resisted!) I can bear testimony to groups of young **Chinese women** in major Chinese cities:

1   **propositioning foreign men** outside five-star international hotels and restaurants;

2   **molesting foreign men** in their five-star international hotel rooms at unsocial hours.

Control

3   ***Do not ever:***
    (a) **accept lifts** from, or **offer lifts** to, **strangers**;
    (b) open your **hotel room door** to **strangers**;
    (c) **discuss travel plans** loudly or with **strangers**;
    (d) **venture alone** into dark and/or remote areas;
    (e) adhere to a **predictable routine**;
    (f) use **unlicensed travel guides**.

4   From personal experience in South America where such advice was routinely issued, ***do always***:
    (a) Be **unpredictable** – for example vary your **route** and **timetable** if making regular journeys (a good excuse for arriving late at the office and leaving early for home! or should it be the other way round?)
    (b) Check your **car** is empty before entering and, once inside, keep the **doors** and **windows locked**.

Sex offences

Identification

1 In line with earlier comments regarding crimes and assaults against foreigners, as a general rule **foreign women** in China are normally:
    (a) Not at any serious risk of **sexual harassment**.
    (b) Only infrequent victims of **sexual assault**.

2 Indeed, most **rapes** are reputedly of Chinese women.

3 One explanation may be, as intimated above, that Chinese men are not normally attracted to **Western women** (but still believe them to be promiscuous and thus fair game).

4 On the other hand, **mixed-race relationships** are not as acceptable as in the West. Hence, you should not take relationships with Chinese citizens lightly; and even be prepared for **rough justice**.

Evaluation

5 Foreigners who invite Chinese citizens to their hotel rooms may be **detained** or **fined** for having **improper sexual relations**.

EXAMPLE

In the late 1990s apocryphal stories abounded of foreign men caught *in flagrante delicto* with Chinese girls, resulting in the latters' punishment.

Control

6 As a general rule, to avoid being misunderstood and/or compromised, steer clear of situations where you might be alone with a member of the opposite sex.

7 As mentioned above, **foreign women** should negotiate with their (husband's) employer the provision of a **mobile phone**.

8 To avoid harassment, as elsewhere in the world, a **lone woman** should:
   (a) Not publicly announce that she is alone.
   (b) Wear a **wedding ring**.
   (c) If she thinks that she is **being followed**:
      – step into a shop or other **safe place**;
      – wait for the suspected person to pass by;
      – not be embarrassed to **ask someone for help**, including to check if all is safe for her.
   (d) Act **confidently** and be **assertive**.
   (e) **If lost**, ask directions only from families or women with children.
   (f) In hotels:
      – ask **security staff** to accompany her at night;
      – **lock** the room door and windows.
   (g) Not draw attention to herself, but wear appropriate **clothing**, modest **makeup**, and simple **jewellery**.

Street crime

Identification

1 Although, as mentioned above, China is a safe country with few **threats to foreigners**, **street crime** does exist – both urban and rural.

2 For example:
   (a) **Armed robberies** have occurred in western China.
   (b) **Robberies** and **assaults** have been reported (*ibid.*) along remote mountain highways near China's border with Nepal.

(c) **Beggars** and **pickpockets** are a fact of life in many parts of the developing and so-called 'civilised' world; and China is no exception.

Evaluation

3 From my experience and observation, Chinese **justice** is so swift, and **punishment** sure and severe, as to be an effective deterrent.

Control

4 *Do not* ever:

(a) **Travel alone** into **remote, isolated, sparsely populated** or **poorly policed areas** – even near the Great Wall – in case you inadvertently stumble upon **armed bandits** and/or **drug smugglers**.

(b) **Resist** attempted **robbery**, which could lead to your being attacked (often with a knife); although **muggings** are reportedly rare. 'Give up your valuables. Your money and passport can be replaced, but you cannot' (*ibid.*).

(c) **Shout**, lose your **temper**, or get involved in an **argument** – which, as un-Chinese behaviours (as mentioned in Chapter 2), may do you more harm than good.

5 *Do* always:

(a) Leave an **itinerary** with someone (detailing the dates, times and places of your journey).

(b) Be **vigilant**:

– at **street markets** (such as Beijing's Silk Market), **festivals, popular expatriate bar areas** and **major tourist sites** all of which also attract **thieves** and **pickpockets** 'often with the complicity of low-paid security guards' (*ibid.*);

- on **public transport**, where **petty theft** is common;
- in **un/poorly-lit areas, narrow alleys** and **short-cuts** – which you should preferably avoid.

(c) Avoid **public demonstrations** and other **civil disturbances** (as mentioned above).

(d) Generally keep a **low profile**.

6 Take normal **anti-pickpocket precautions**, including:

(a) Secure **valuables** (such as money, credit cards and passport) in inside zipped or buttoned pouches or pockets – otherwise front, but never hip, pockets.

(b) Do not carry more **cash** than necessary for your immediate needs – albeit difficult in a primarily cash-economy – or **credit cards** surplus to requirements.

(c) Button up your jacket or coat.

(d) Close all hand and shoulder **bags**; lock your **briefcase**; and carry them firmly at all times:
- by a **strap** across your chest;
- tucked under your **arm** and **to your front** (so that it cannot be snatched from behind);
- away from the **curb** (to avoid **drive-by opportunists**).

(e) Treat **portable equipment** (such as **cameras, mobile phones** and **laptop computers**) in like fashion; and never leave them unguarded or out of your sight.

(f) Do not wear conspicuous clothing, or expensive **watches** or **jewellery**.

(g) If you are **lost**, keep moving, and only ask directions of someone in authority.

EXAMPLES

1 In **France** failure to follow our own guidelines resulted in my wife having a camera taken from her **open handbag**.
2 In **Colombia** to combat pickpockets, we also had to:
   (a) wrap our arms around in front of us;
   (b) wear **watches** on the 'wrong' wrist;
   (c) keep **car windows** and **doors** closed and locked at all times.

7 Have no compunction in shooing away **beggars**, when they should not trouble you again.

8 **Always carry a mobile phone and guard it as if your life depends on it – which it may do.**

FUNDAMENTAL RISKS

Natural disasters

Identification

1 As is well know from press reports and for which I can vouch from my own experience:
   (a) China is an **active seismic zone**; and, therefore, susceptible to periodic **earthquakes**.
   (b) Parts of central, southern and western China – particularly near the Yangtze River – are susceptible to **flooding**.
   (c) The coastal areas of Hainan, Guangdong, Fujian and Zhejiang provinces are subject to **typhoons** during the summer rainy season; and apparently 'often cause the closure of airports in some parts of the country' (*ibid.*).

Evaluation

2 During 2003, **four earthquakes** occurred in China (one each in Gansu and Yunnan Provinces, and the Inner Mongolian and Xinjiang Autonomous Regions), measuring an average of just over 6.0 on the Richter scale.

Control

3 It is common sense to **check your route** and **local weather condition** before visiting affected areas – although this is not always fool-proof.

EXAMPLE

In June 1998, I flew to Hong Kong on a glorious summer's day, only to be engulfed the following morning in the worst rain-storm for very many years, that was of such a magnitude and so unexpected that people were washed away by and drowned in over-flowing culverts.

---

4 Should a **natural disaster** occur while you are in China let family and friends know that you are safe and well even if you are nowhere near the affected area. They may not know exactly where you are and, hence, worry unnecessarily if they still think that you are in potential danger. Your **local Consulate** may be able to help contact them (although its priority will be those who have suffered).

5 In the unlikely event of an **earthquake**, based on our experience of living in a high-risk area (Bogotá, Colombia):
  (a) You may not even notice, mistakenly thinking that you are drunk, and that is why pictures on the wall appear to be crooked, or the lamp-shades swinging.

(b) **Get outside**, to avoid being shut in by doors jammed in their distorted frames.

Terrorism

Identification
1 At the time of writing, there is 'no evidence of a threat to western or other interests from **global terrorism** in China' (according to the FCO website).

Evaluation
2 China is considered to be **generally safe** (DOS).

3 The small number of crime or protest related **local bombings** have tended to be:
   (a) **Isolated** incidents.
   (b) In **Beijing** (e.g. two Universities in February 2003) and areas inhabited primarily by **ethnic minorities**.
   (c) **Not** directed **against foreigners**.
   (d) Mainly the result of **commercial disputes between Chinese**.

Control
4 Nevertheless, according to FCO, you should:
   (a) **Keep abreast** of 'the risk of indiscriminate, **terrorist attacks** in all countries of the world, against civilian targets in public places, including **tourist sites**' – such as by the various means described in Chapter 1.

EXAMPLE

In the mid 1970s in Spain where the Catalan press (*La Vanguardia*) once carried a cartoon characterising the local news as a bunch of flowers, and international news as a skull-and-cross bones: when Franco was dying, we had to listen to the World Service of the British Broadcasting Service (BBC) to find the truth about his failing health and the quelling of the consequent uprisings in Spain's North African territories.

(b) **Check** with your ministry of foreign affairs, local diplomatic mission, or other reputable travel advisory service.

(c) '**Look out for** anything suspicious (for example an unattended bag at an airport, or a group of people acting suspiciously around an obviously "Western" institution or gathering).'

(d) '**Report** anything that you think is suspicious to the local police – many terrorist attacks have been foiled by the **vigilance** of ordinary people'.

4   If – like most senior expatriates – you have a driver, (s)he is likely to find out before you if the car is **booby-trapped**. Enough said!

IMMIGRATION AND EMIGRATION CONTROL

Dual nationality

Identification

1   China does not recognise:

(a) **Dual nationality** (i.e. citizenship of China and another country).

(b) **Foreign citizenship** of children born:

– *in China of mixed marriages*, where one parent is a Chinese national;

– *outside China to Chinese parents* who are neither lawful permanent residents nor citizens of that country.

2 In other words, you may be considered a **Chinese citizen** if:
  (a) You were born in China.
  (b) At least one of your parents is or was a Chinese citizen even if you are a **(naturalised) citizen** of **another country**.

Evaluation

3 All such persons are regarded and **treated in China as solely Chinese citizens** and may, therefore, not be entitled to:
  (a) Enter China on their **foreign passport** (which might even be seized).
  (b) Formal assistance from the **local Consul** of the other country (especially after entering China on their Chinese passport).

Control

4 If these issues potentially affect you and/or your family members, you should:
  (a) **Before travelling to China** check with your **local Chinese Consulate**; and, whenever possible, subject to their advice, act as follows:
  (b) **When arriving and leaving China** present only your **foreign passport** and Chinese visa.
  (c) **Whilst in China** demand you be treated as a **foreign subject** (which may not necessarily help, but should do you no harm).

Entry and exit regulations

Identification and evaluation

1 **Before travelling to China** you must obtain a **valid entry**

visa. Otherwise, the Chinese authorities may **fine** and **deport** you at your expense.

2 **If you intend to work in China** ensure that you obtain the **appropriate visa**. Otherwise, the Public Security Bureau (PSB) may consider your subsequently applying for **change of visa** to be a violation of the law and impose similar **sanctions**.

3 **Before your visa expires** you must **renew it** or **leave China** and in good time. Otherwise, you may be **fined** and/or **detained** and/or your departure delayed by the Chinese authorities.

4 Adults entering and/or leaving China with children may be asked to prove their relationship, in an effort by the Chinese authorities to contribute to the prevention of **international child abduction**.

Control
5 **Do not** rely on or trust:
   (a) **Host organisations** claiming to provide a visa on your arrival.
   (b) **Employers** who ask you to start work on a tourist visa, promising that they will later obtain a work visa.

6 When **accompanying children**, always carry:
   (a) Documentation showing your relationship to them.
   (b) Written **permission** from their parent(s) or legal guardian(s), if not your own.

Passport loss or confiscation

Control

1 For whatever reason (such as the result of a **crime**; or in the event of **confiscation** by the Chinese authorities, mentioned above):

(a) **Report** the **loss** or **confiscation** of your **passport** to your local Consulate (who, depending on the circumstances, may require you to notify, and obtain a declaration from, the police).

(b) **Never lend** your **passport** to a Chinese person – as this could lead to your or their **arrest**, if the police think the loan was for illegal purposes.

(c) **Make two photocopies** of your **passport**:
  – keep one secure (in the safe) at home or alternatively **e-mail** a **scanned copy** to yourself;
  – carry the other separate from your passport.

RESTRICTED ACTIVITIES

Religious activities

Identification

1 The Chinese authorities impose stringent restrictions on certain **religious activities** such as **public worship**, **proselytising**, **preaching** and distributing **religious materials**.

EXAMPLES

1 On the one hand, **Chinese citizens** are not allowed to attend **foreigners' places of worship**. Thus:

(a) The entrance to one of the international English-speaking Protestant churches in Beijing in the late 1990s was manned by stewards checking passports to ensure that only non-Chinese entered.

(b) I had to explain to a Chinese colleague that the reason why she could not celebrate Easter at our church was because her authorities, not ours, forbade her.

(2) On the other hand, **foreigners** are:

    (a) Not only allowed to attend **Chinese places of worship** – as the then US President did, for example, when visiting Beijing in 1998.

    (b) But also prone to being **proselytised by tourist guides** when visiting Chinese shrines – as we experienced, for example, when visiting Shanghai's Jade Buddha Temple in 2003.

Evaluation

3 The Chinese **customs authorities** may and do seize:

    (a) **Publications** such as books, documents, letters, literature.

    (b) **Recordings** such as films, records, tapes, compact disks.

to determine whether they violate Chinese prohibitions on **religious activities**; and only return them, even if lawful, after several months, if ever.

4 Persons entering China with more **religious materials** than are deemed necessary for personal use, may be **detained** and/or **fined**.

5 Individuals believed to be engaged in **religious prose-lytism** may be **detained** and/or **fined** and/or **expelled**.

6 The punishment for distributing **unauthorised Christian material** may range from **expulsion** to **imprisonment** of three to five years.

Control

7 Nevertheless there are many other appropriate and legal opportunities for foreigners to share their beliefs with the Chinese.

EXAMPLES

Quite safely, openly and legally, we:

1 Used our office premises for **church committee meetings** that my bilingual Chinese PA was happy to organise, including circulating agendas and minutes by fax and/or e-mail.

2 Answered questions from Chinese friends and colleagues in private (sometimes in exchange for equally sensitive information, such as about the Tiananmen Square incident).

3 Took **English Bibles** for the personal use of a Chinese Christian, when visiting Shanghai in 2003.

Other restricted activities

Identification and evaluation

1 **Public demonstrations** that do not have prior approval from the authorities are likely to be forcefully **suppressed** by the same; and foreign participants summarily **imprisoned** and/or **deported.**

EXAMPLE

Foreigners who overtly challenge the authorities – such as participating in **pro-Falung Gong** meetings and/or '**Free Tibet**' demonstrations – have only themselves to blame and no legal grounds for complaint when dragged from their hotel rooms by the Chinese security services.

2 Even **recording** (such as videotaping or photographing) such activities may be regarded by the authorities as provocative.

3 **Recording other sensitive activities** (such as military establishments) may also incur the displeasure of the Chinese authorities; remember the case of the British plane-spotters in Greece in 2002.

4 There are a number of **'closed' areas** in China that you may not visit without special permission.

5 **Selling** personal possessions or household goods or other **items that you have imported into China** might infringe Chinese **customs regulations**.

Control

6 **Do not participate** in such activities.

7 When in doubt as to the legality of an activity – consult:
   (a) *Before travelling to China*: the **Chinese Consulate**.
   (b) *Whilst you are in China*: your **local Consulate** and/ or the **PSB**.

Restricted exports

Identification and evaluation

1 The Chinese **Antiquities Bureau** strictly regulates the legal, and penalises the illegal, export from China of **antiques** (that is: valuable cultural relics and rare books relating Chinese history, culture and art).

Control

2 Details of how to apply for and obtain an antiques **export licence** are given in Chapter 6.

3 Deal only with **reputable dealers**.

4 You should acquire **receipts** for all your purchases, attesting to their **provenance** – including for any **reproductions**, which the authorities may otherwise mistakenly treat as genuine (although, in my experience, if they spot one, their normal Chinese inscrutability momentarily gives way to professional derision).

Restricted imports

Identification and evaluation

1 Once you have obtained a residence permit, you should normally be able to import a container of **household goods** quite easily, subject to a satisfactory customs declaration. However:
   (a) **Without a residence permit** (as in our case) you will probably have to contend with bringing items from home in dribs and drabs on several flights as part of your standard luggage allowance and/or excess baggage.
   (b) Should you not properly declare **high-worth items** (such as very expensive cameras, computing equipment and jewellery) you may eventually be charged **export duty** when leaving China (when Chinese customs will require a full inventory).

2 Should you wish to take your **pet**(s) to China:
   (a) **Normal pets** (such as **cats** and **dogs**) usually present no problems, provided that they:
   – have an authenticated and notarised up-to-date **international vaccination certificate** and a **veterinary certificate of health**;
   – conform to **size restrictions** (explained in Chapter 8).

Otherwise they will be refused entry and **deported** by the Chinese customs.

(b) **Exotic pets**, however, must be pre-approved by customs.

3 The importation of **political, pornographic, religious** (see above) and similar **material** considered 'detrimental to China's politics, economy, culture and ethics' (DOS) is strictly prohibited, including carrying letters and/or packages from **Tibetan nationals** to be posted in other countries.

4 If you are thinking of **importing your car** it must meet with Chinese standards (!) or will be refused entry.

5 **Drugs**: see above.

Control

6 The Chinese customs encourage the use of the **Admission Temporaire/Temporary Admission** (ATA) **Carnet** for the temporary and duty-free import of **professional equipment, commercial samples** and goods for **exhibitions** and **trade fairs**.

7 When in doubt: consult your local **Chinese Consulate** beforehand.

SAFETY AND SECURITY

Fire protection

Identification

1 From personal observation, **fire protection standards** in many Chinese buildings do not always meet current Western standards.

2 However, according to the China-Britain Trade Review of October 2003: 'some 50 local companies, most of which have entered the [**fire detection systems**] market in the last five years, now produce products that are certified and meet the local standards', predominantly in the regions of Beijing, Guangdong and Shanghai – which augers well for the future.

Control

3 Check **fire precautions** where you are living and working (such as: fire fighting and extinguishing equipment; and doors, escapes, exits and evacuation procedures).

EXAMPLE

To my shame – despite an insurance and human resource management (HRM) background – I now realise that we never instituted, let alone rehearsed, any **fire drill** in our offices in China.

4 Install (at home and, if possible, at work):
  (a) **fire extinguishers**;
  (b) **fire blankets**;
  (c) **smoke detectors**.
  You could bring the last two from your home country.

Gas appliances

Identification

1 Sadly, in some parts of China, foreigners have reportedly (DOS) died from:
  (a) The use of **odourless natural gas**, whose **leaks** and concentrations are consequently undetectable.

(b) **Poorly-ventilated gas heaters**, causing a build-up of excess **carbon monoxide.**

Evaluation

2 Fortunately, we did not experience directly or vicariously such problems with modern housing aimed at the expatriate market.

Control

3 Where appropriate, install **gas** and **carbon monoxide detectors** at home (which you may need to obtain elsewhere, as they are not widely available in China).

4 Ensure that all **gas appliances** are properly **vented**.

Intruder protection

Identification and evaluation

1 Foreign housing complexes (in our experience at least) are normally very safe places, with all or some of the following:
   (a) **Perimeter fence** or **wall**.
   (b) **Security guards** at the entrance gate and patrolling the grounds.
   (c) **Close-circuit television** (CCTV) **security cameras** at strategic points.
   (d) All-night **street-lighting**.

2 Individual properties may be fitted with a range of **intruder protection equipment** (such as intercom entryphones, burglar alarms, security locks and lights, strong entry-doors with spy-holes, boundary walls or railings, and electric gates).

3   Occupants, drivers and maids are usually required to carry **identity** (ID) cards issued by the housing management; and visitors somehow to identify themselves.

Control

4   Nevertheless, **burglaries** and **attacks** do occur occasionally (as mentioned above in relation to **crimes against foreigners**); for which reason – as we did – you should:

(a) Lock **valuables** in a cupboard (if not install a safe).

(b) Carry a **personal alarm** or **mobile phone**.

(c) Reclaim **keys** and **ID cards** when dispensing with the services of **maids** and **drivers**.

(d) Be aware that the landlord and estate management probably have spare **door keys** for tradesmen to carry out maintenance and repairs, not always with your prior knowledge – for which reason you may want to consider temporarily changing the **door locks** (for the duration of your occupation).

(e) **Never flaunt** your possessions: they may not be worth much to you, but could represent a small fortune to some Chinese.

5   Since most landlords allow pets – subject to local laws, described in Chapter 8 – and many Chinese are unaccustomed to and so afraid of them, **dogs** are an excellent deterrent (for whom gardens may be fairly easily secured).

Road safety

Identification

1 **Driving etiquette** (such as **rights-of-way, lane discipline** and other courtesies) is only in its infancy, if indeed it has passed the gestation stage. Generally, the rule of the road seems to be: 'every person for themself'.

2 **Poor roads** and **low driving standards** cause many, often serious if not fatal, **accidents**.

3 Some **personal drivers** will drive as fast and riskily as you allow them.

EXAMPLES

1 One of our drivers was prone to doing **u-turns** in the main avenue running East from Tiananmen Square.

2 Another was determined to get me to my destination as quickly as possible even if it meant breaking the **speed limit**, or driving on the **wrong side of the road** or in the **wrong direction** to avoid traffic jams

3 Neither ever caused an accident!

4 **Foreign drivers**:
   (a) May not be able to read **road-signs** and/or **names** in Chinese.
   (b) From the UK and some (ex-)Commonwealth countries do not always find it easy to adapt to driving on the **right-hand side** of the road.
   (c) (Whose cars are so identified by their number plates) may be victims of the '**chicken game**' – that is: **Chinese pedestrians** who deliberately provoke accidents in order to sue for compensation.

EXAMPLE

One friend of ours – who had turned down his employer's offer of a driver in favour of driving himself – was caught this way; and received scant sympathy from not only the police but also his employer.

5 **Road traffic accidents** are a major cause of death, judging by the number of **corpses** of dead **pedestrians** and **cyclists** purposely left in the road by the police as a warning to others.

EXAMPLE

We first lived outside Beijing at the end of a freeway dubbed 'death alley' by the expatriate community, on account of the virtually **daily fatal accidents**, the evidence of which was not always scraped off the road until some time later. Despite our previous experience of traffic accident victims being displayed at the side of the road in Colombia (South America), the regular sight of **mangled bodies** was too much to stomach, and we moved into the city.

6 Some **taxi** and **bus-drivers** show scant respect for the safety of their passengers.

EXAMPLE

We stopped using the Dragon Villas' shuttle-bus after it raced along 'death alley', hurling passengers down the aisle despite screams of protest. On arrival at our destination, I rang the bus operator to request they supply another driver for the return journey (which they did).

7 One unusual hazard for Westerners, though perhaps not peculiar to China, is the practice of **drying maize on the public highways** in the countryside and suburbs. At

the appropriate season, it is not uncommon suddenly to be confronted with a 'yellow maize road', often of several hundred metres, which you or your driver should avoid at all cost in order not to incur the wrath of the local farming community.

8 **Cycling** and **bicycles** are a nightmare, since:
   (a) Vehicles do not respect **cycle lanes**.
   (b) Bicycles are not required to carry **lights** at night – since to do so would allegedly blind car drivers!
   (c) **Cyclists** often go against the flow of the traffic, especially in **cycle lanes**.

EXAMPLES

1 On the outskirts of Beijing, some cycle and car lanes are of almost equal width, giving rise to the quip that 'it's safer to walk in the cycle lanes because there are less cars'.
2 When I fitted lights that I had bought in the UK to my bicycle, my Sino-Australian neighbours accused me of being anti-social!

Evaluation

9 The DOS evaluates **road transport** as follows:

Measurement		Evaluation
Safety of public transportation		Good
Urban road conditions/maintenance		Good
Rural road conditions/maintenance		Fair
Availability of roadside assistance	in/near large cities	Fair
	rural areas	Unavailable

10 Most **road traffic accidents** tend to involve **pedestrians** or **cyclists** who:

(a) Are involved in **collisions**, especially with vehicles in the **wrong lanes**.

(b) Encounter **unexpected road hazards** (such as **potholes** or **unmarked open manholes**).

Control

11 Only take **authorised taxis** – clearly identified with official markings – and, if you are concerned, make note of **the registration number** and **driver identify number** (which many hotels now do automatically for you).

12 Adhere to **standard car safety measures** (in addition to **anti-kidnap precautions**, mentioned above), such as:

(a) Fit **child safety seats** (which you may have to bring from home, as they are not widely available in China).

(b) Wear **seat belts**.

(c) Do not leave **valuables** in the car.

(d) Avoid using the car at **night**.

(e) Only use designated, wardened **car parks**.

(f) Drive **defensively** – that is: 'keeping an eye out for potentially criminal pedestrians, cyclists and scooter riders' (DOS).

13 Ideally – like most senior expatriates:

(a) **Do not drive – use a driver** instead.

(b) Ensure the driver stays with the car.

14 When cycling, wear a **cycle helmet** meeting international safety standards (which you may have to bring from home, as we did).

15 Always be careful while **walking** near traffic.

Public transport

Identification

1 **Air transport.**

   Although there have been some spectacular **air accidents** in China, from personal experience of having flown extensively in Europe, South America and China, I can confirm that my family felt very safe when flying with **Air China** although not always with some other domestic Chinese airlines (see below).

2 **Water transport.**

   (a) Although several incidents have been reported in the media of overcrowded **ferries** sinking, leading to loss of life, from personal experience I can confirm that the Guangzhou, Hong Kong and Shanghai ferry boats were safe when we took them (in 1997, 1998 and 2003, respectively).

   (b) According to the DOS: watch out for **pirates** in the **South China Sea**.

   (c) Meanwhile: if the Three Gorges Dam project has not put a stop to **Yangtze cruises**, why not take one?

3 **Rail transport.**

   (a) Regretfully – or happily? – I am unable to find any authoritative official statistics on **rail safety** in China (or offer any opinion from personal or vicarious experience), except to warn against **thieves**, especially on **overnight trains**.

   (b) However judging from the popularity of books and websites on **rail travel** in China, it cannot be that unsafe!

Evaluation

4 **Air transport**.

(a) According to **AirSafe.com** (listed in the Bibliography): between 1970 and the time of writing, there have been 17 **fatal air accidents** of PRC airlines involving some 1,125 persons, both passengers and crew (see Appendix 3 for details).

(b) According to the **US Federal Aviation Administration** (FAA), (listed in the Bibliography): the PRC civil aviation complies with the safety standards of the **International Civil Aviation Organization** (ICAO).

Control

5 **Rail**.

(a) **Do not**:

– allow yourself to become blocked between two (or more) people in the **train corridor** or on the **station platform**;

– accept food and drink from **strangers**: it might be contaminated (accidentally or on purpose).

(b) On **overnight trains** (in order of effectiveness), **do**:

– lock your compartment **door**;

– sleep **in shifts**;

– stay **awake**;

– secure your **luggage**;

– sleep on top of your **valuables**.

EXAMPLE

If this seems over the top, let me assure you that once (1971) I had to deal with a claim for a suitcase, allegedly containing everything the insured owned in the world, stolen from the Paris-Barcelona overnight train.

OTHER RISKS

Bereavement and death

Identification and evaluation

1 This is the **number one worry** for most expatriates, because it may be a sudden and unforeseen event over which they have no control – and not so much their own **death abroad**, as of loved ones at home, and especially **elderly parents**.

2 Happily, there are not usually any restrictions on foreign residents temporarily leaving China in a hurry, unlike some other countries.

> **EXAMPLES**
>
> 1 In **Colombia** (in 1974):
>   (a) One friend had to file his tax-return over a weekend before flying home for his father's funeral.
>   (b) My very down-to-earth pathologist father urged me not to feel compelled to return for his funeral in the UK – a promise that, thankfully, was not put to the test.
> 2 In **France** (in 1991): my wife immediately flew back for her father's funeral, which then had to be postponed until one sister returned from holiday abroad where was she was incommunicado.

Control

3 Should you **die in China**, your family should contact the **local Consulate** immediately.

4 Meanwhile:
  (a) **Before you go to China**:
    ♦ Agree with your family back home what you:
      – will do if someone **dies back home**

- want done if you or a family member **dies in China**
♦ Leave your affairs in order at home.
♦ Make two **wills**, each referring to the other:
  - one according to the law of your home country
  - the other under the **Chinese legal system**
  to avoid disputes over the disposal of any assets in China.
♦ appoint an **attorney**; and – if leaving them behind, such as at boarding school – a **guardian** for dependent children.

EXAMPLE

We appointed our personal solicitor and chartered-accountant son as joint:

♦ **attorneys** with enduring powers;
♦ **guardians** to our 16-year old son.

(b) While you are in China, maintain **regular contact** with your family back home.

Business disputes

Identification and evaluation

1 The Chinese authorities have been known to detain foreigners involved in **business disputes** by:
  ♦ **confiscating** their **passports**;
  ♦ placing them under **house arrest**;
  until such disputes are satisfactorily resolved.

2 Asking your local Consulate for a **replacement passport** is no solution, since you will still need a valid Chinese

visa to leave the country, which the authorities will understandably not grant you.

Control

3 **Before doing business with Chinese enterprises**, you should:

(a) Check their integrity by means of **due diligence**.

(b) Establish whether they have had, and if so investigate, any **previous disputes**.

4

Epidemiology

In China, you may be exposed to **illnesses** (the all-embracing term I have chosen to include **diseases** and **infections**) not normally found in the West as a result of:

- ◆ **poor** standards of **hygiene** and **sanitation**, and especially in **rural areas,** in many:
  - **eating places**;
  - **toilets**, both public and private;
  - **hospitals**.
- ◆ environmental **pollution** – especially (as explained below) of:
  - **food** production;
  - **water** treatment;
  - **air** quality.

Such illnesses include (in alphabetical order by risk classification):

- ◆ **Air-borne**
  - air pollution
  - nose-blowing and sneezing
  - passive smoking
  - spitting and coughing
  - tuberculosis
- ◆ **Communicable**
  - influenza

- poliomyelitis
- SARS
- **Food and water-borne**
  - brucellosis
  - cholera
  - diarrhoea
  - dysentery
  - fluke
  - giardiasis
  - hepatitis A and E
  - schistosomiasis (aka bilharziasis)
  - typhoid
  - worms
- **Insect-borne**
  - dengue fever
  - filariasis
  - Japanese encephalitis
  - leishmaniasis
  - malaria
  - plague
  - typhus
  - yellow fever
- Transmittable
  - chlamydia
  - gonorrhoea
  - hepatitis B, C and D
  - herpes genitalis
  - HIV/AIDS
  - syphilis
- **Other**
  - altitude sickness
  - Chinese restaurant syndrome

– cold
– haemorrhagic fever with renal syndrome
– heat and dehydration
– meningitis
– rabies.

OVERALL EVALUATION

'**Under-reporting** is...rampant among China's 100 million-strong **migrant population**' – about one-twelfth of the country's total population – 'which relies on health care from **unlicensed fly-by-night clinics** that rarely report epidemiological figures to local centers for disease control' *(Unhappy Returns*, Hannah Beech, *Time Asia*, 8 Dec 2003, Vol. 162, No 22).

Hence, it is not always possible accurately to evaluate the full extent of some illnesses in China (as specifically indicated below, where appropriate).

OVERALL CONTROL

Based on the premise that prevention is better than cure, you should – in addition to any medical regimen to which you are already subject – take serious note of the above-mentioned illnesses and:

1 **Protect yourself** appropriately (as recommended below).

2 **Eat well**: you will need a healthier diet than you do at home.

3 **Keep fit**: your body will need more strength than usual to stay healthy and overcome illness.

EXAMPLE

As mentioned in Chapter 6, many expatriate housing complexes offer some form of sports or exercise centre.

4 Consider taking **vitamin supplements** (but only on medical advice, given doubts about their efficacy in the UK press during 2003).

5 Keep all your **inoculations** up to date (see below).

6 Take your **malaria medication** regularly (if in an infected area).

7 **Register with your local Consulate** so that it can contact you in the event of an epidemic.

EXAMPLE

In 1971 all expatriates in Barcelona (Spain) were dramatically urged by the British Consulate-General to attend the Clínica de Extranjeros for an urgent **anti-cholera vaccination** following the death of several foreign holiday-makers.

INOCULATIONS

1 Opinion varies between the sources consulted as to those illnesses against which expatriates intending to live in China should be inoculated, depending on a number of factors such as their age, location, lifestyle, propensities, etc, as well as the risk evaluation of such illnesses.

2 You should, therefore, seek authoritative, up-to-date information from your personal and/or company physician and/or the specialist sources listed in the Bibliography.

3 Meanwhile, from personal experience, such **inoculations** are likely to include those as:
   (a) *Required by law*: **yellow fever** and **severe acute respiratory syndrome (SARS)**.
   (b) *Recommended:* **malaria** and **SARS**.
   (c) *Standard:* **hepatitis A** and **B, polio, tuberculosis** and **typhoid**.
   (d) *Boosters:* **diphtheria, measles** and **tetanus**.
   (e) *Appropriate:* **Japanese encephalitis** and **rabies**.

AIR-BORNE ILLNESSES

Air pollution

Identification
1 The **air quality** in China is generally **very poor**, caused by the:
   (a) Rapid **industrial development**.
   (b) Burning of local **coal**, very high in **sulphur** content.
   (c) High **traffic density** in major cities.
   (d) Resulting **acid rain**.

EXAMPLE

In Beijing I was once caught in a short April **'dirty rain'** shower that left my pin-stripe suit looking like a combat jacket!

---

2 Air pollution may cause **catarrhal colds**, and **eye** and **ear infections**; and exacerbate **asthma**.

3 Additionally, the dry dusty atmosphere of North China may cause **sinusitis, laryngitis** (aka a **sore throat**), **cracked lips** and **dry skin**.

Evaluation

4 'China has nine of the world's ten most **polluted cities**' ('Chasing the China Dream', Paul Morrison in *Strategic Risk Magazine*, UK, Dec 2003), such as Beijing, Shenyang and Wuhan where **pollution levels** 'can reach three to four times the maximum level advised by the World Health Organisation (WHO)' (*China Business Handbook 2003*, p. 45).

5 Although various members of our family living in or visiting Beijing are variously susceptible to **sinusitis**, **laryngitis** and **allergic rhinitis** (aka **hay fever**), I cannot recall their being adversely affected.

6 On the other hand, my **skin** suffered very badly in Beijing.

Control

7 **Asthma sufferers** (of whom we have had to brief some) should:
   (a) Take ample supplies of their normal **medication**.
   (b) Avoid **industrial zones** (insofar as work obligations allow).
   (c) Pay frequent visits to the **countryside** to get some **fresh air**.

8 Carry **throat lozenges**, **lip salve** and **moisturising cream**.

9 From personal observation, I can vouch that pedestrians, cyclists and street-sweepers in Beijing have worn **face-masks** since long before SARS.

10 With the prospect of hosting the Olympics in 2008, the Beijing authorities have reportedly embarked on an **air purification plan** that apparently is already having a beneficial effect.

EXAMPLE

In Beijing in summer, I quickly came to understand why there were so many advertisements on the English-language television for healing **cracked soles of the feet**.

Nose-blowing and sneezing, spitting and coughing

Identification

1 With apologies to Admiral Lord Nelson: 'China expect_orate_s'.

2 Anyone who has seen the famous photograph of the meeting between Margaret Thatcher and Deng Xiaoping (when British and Chinese leaders, respectively) prominently figuring a spittoon will know that **spitting** is endemic in China – to the extent that some commentators have dubbed it China's national sport!

EXAMPLE

My predecessor alleged that even his most senior Chinese female colleague had incurred the wrath of an international board member by **expectorating** very loudly and publicly at a press conference over which they were presiding!

3 Less well known, perhaps, is the way that many Chinese still **blow their nose** in public: by stopping one nostril with their fingers, and blowing down the other without the benefit of a handkerchief!

Evaluation

4 Consequently, you are potentially at risk from flying **sputum** and **mucus** in public places.

5 Perhaps you remember the British comedian Tony
Hancock singing '**coughs** and **sneezes** spread diseases,
catch them all in your handkerchief' to the tune of
Josef Haydn's *Austria* in the sketch *The Blood Donor*.

Control

6 The authorities are trying to outlaw **spitting** in major
cities (e.g. Beijing); and, in the wake of SARS, have
even formed **anti-spitting squads** in Guangzhou.

7 Meanwhile: watch your step!

Passive smoking

Identification

1 If spitting is the national sport, **smoking** ranks a close
second!

EXAMPLES

1 In 1997, at the very first meal that I hosted for a visiting delegation in
London, even a Chinese colleague was amazed by how many of her
compatriots managed to smoke between courses, using their plates as
ashtrays.
2 In 1998, a local representative of British American Tobacco (BAT), told
me that China generated about 50% of the company's income.

Evaluation

2 Thus, you may be exposed to **passive smoking** in
confined public spaces.

EXAMPLE

My wife and I once stayed in a first-class Chinese (rather than
international) hotel in Guangdong Province, where our suite was so

impregnated with **tobacco smoke** that not even a whole spray-can of pungent deodorant ('Old Spice', I think) could obscure the smell.

3 Nevertheless, at **formal business meetings** – as opposed to banquets – with the Chinese (described in Chapter 12) I have never seen anyone smoke.

Control

4 Always ask for **non-smoking rooms** in hotels, **non-smoking areas** in restaurants, etc, as you might in any other country.

5 Insofar as you are able to control anything that goes on in China, I recommend from personal experience that you designate your office, home and car **non-smoking areas**.

Tuberculosis (TB)

Identification

1 The most common and serious air-borne illness to which you may be exposed in China is probably **TB** – the containment of which is not helped by the way that many Chinese still discharge **sputum** and **mucus** in public, described above.

Evaluation

2 According to the most recent figures at the time of writing published by the **WHO** (*Global Tuberculosis Control*, 2003, pp. 69–72), in 2001:
   (a) China ranked second in the world with an estimated **incidence** of 113 TB cases per 100,000 inhabitants.

(b) The notification rate of **new cases** had almost quadrupled over 20 years to approximately 38 per 100,000 inhabitants (from ten in 1982).

(c) Just over 5% of new cases were **multi-drug resistant**.

3 Because TB disproportionately affects the country's 100 million-strong **migrants**, mentioned above, the WHO estimates that one-third of China's cases are never reported.

4 The situation is further exacerbated by a **health system** that 'focuses on how to maximize revenue, not coverage' (WHO Beijing, quoted in *Time Asia*, op. cit.).

5 On a personal note I find these statistics very disturbing, since my late father was one of the leading scientists who collaborated with the WHO during the third quarter of the 20th century to develop anti-TB drugs.

Control
6 Ensure that you are properly **inoculated**.

COMMUNICABLE ILLNESSES
At the time of writing, the WHO lists the following illnesses as being obligatorily communicable to itself by the responsible health authorities.

Influenza

Identification
1 In 2002/2003, an outbreak of **atypical pneumonia** in Guangdong Province was notified to the WHO by the

Beijing authorities as having no link with the parallel outbreak of **influenza** in neighbouring Hong Kong.

2 In 2003/2004 **avian flu** was widely reported in the world media.

Evaluation

3 According to the US Centre for Disease Control (CDC) at the time of writing (*Update on SARS and Avian Influenza A (H5N1)*, 10 Jun 2004, listed in the Bibliography):
   (a) 'There currently is no evidence of efficient human-to-human transmission of **avian influenza** A (H5N1) viruses.'
   (b) 'The degree to which' outbreaks of **avian flu** in China 'have been controlled remains uncertain.'
   (c) 'On the basis of current information, human infection with **avian influenza** A (H5N1) viruses remains a public health risk' in China.

Control

4 As in your home country and anywhere else in the world, depending on your age and circumstances, you may consider in general:
   (a) **Vaccination** (such as encouraged for the elderly in the UK by a television (TV) campaign featuring the ex-boxer, Sir Henry Cooper).
   (b) Suitable **anti-viral drugs**.
   (c) Avoiding **crowded enclosed spaces** and close contact with people suffering from **acute respiratory infections**.

5 Specifically as regards **avian flu**, the DOS (*Avian Flu Fact Sheet*, 29 Jan 2004) recommends that you:

(a) 'Avoid **poultry farms**, contact with animals in live food markets and any surfaces that appear to be contaminated with feces from poultry or other animals.'

(b) Follow '**good hygiene** practices during handling, including hand washing, prevention of cross-contamination and thorough cooking of poultry products.'

Poliomyelitis

Identification

1 '**Polio** virus has been shown by reliable data to have been **completely interrupted** since 1994 through eradication programmes' – according to British United Provident Association (BUPA) International's website.

2 At the end of 2002, China was certified by the WHO as **polio-free**.

Evaluation

3 Previously, the last reported case of **polio** was in late 1999, involving an unregistered and, therefore, unvaccinated infant of the Sala minority group in Qinghai province – to which the authorities responded with an immunisation and surveillance programme, not only amongst the target group but also across several provinces.

Control

4 Ensure that you are properly **inoculated**.

Severe acute respirarory syndrome (SARS)

Identification

1 That **SARS** originated in mainland China (Guangdong Province) in November 2002 is well known, as subsequently widely reported in the world press.

Evaluation

2 At the time of writing: 'No...cases of SARS in China or anywhere else in the world have been reported since April 29, 2004. On May 18, the World Health Organization...reported...that the outbreak in China appears to have been contained' (CDC, *op. cit.*).

Control

3 If you are concerned about SARS:
   (a) Ensure that you are properly **inoculated** and consider carrying a proprietary '**SARS kit**' (akin to an 'AIDS kit').
   (b) See the guidelines published by **Dezan Shira & Associates**, included by kind permission as Appendix 4.

FOOD AND WATER-BORNE ILLNESSES

Contamination and pollution

Identification

1 'Many of China's **rivers** and much of its **groundwater** are seriously **contaminated**; and local **public water supplies** should always be regarded as suspect' (*China Business Handbook 2003*, p. 46).

2 Hence, a number of illnesses are caused by:

(a) **Ingesting contaminated water** and **food**.

(b) **Bathing in contaminated water**.

Control

3 The best prevention, therefore, is **scrupulous personal** and **culinary hygiene** (detailed below).

4 'Always be aware of the quality of what you **eat** and **drink** when you are travelling' (*Cholera: Basic Facts for Travellers*, WHO, 2001).

5 **Lactating mothers** may be advised to stop breast-feeding, so as not to transmit to babies.

EXAMPLE

This was the advice given to my wife when she suffered from amoebic dysentery shortly after the birth of our second son in Colombia.

6 **Swim** only in well-chlorinated and maintained **public pools** – not in **fresh** watercourses. **Salt water** is usually safe.

7 Where such illnesses result in diarrhoea **fluid replacement** is essential (detailed below).

Cholera

Identification

1 According to the WHO (*Special Focus: Communicable Disease Surveillance and Response Strategy – Overview*, 2003):

(a) **Since 1994**: 'the number of **cholera** cases have been steadily decreasing' in general.

(b) **In 1998**: 'the number of reported cases significantly increased in several countries, including China'.

(c) **In 1999**: 'significant numbers of cases were reported from China'.

Evaluation

2 According to BUPA *(op. cit.)*, at the time of writing:

(a) 'A strain of **Bengal cholera** has been reported in western areas.'

(b) '**Cholera** is a slight risk (especially in the South) ... and precautions should be considered.'

Control

3 Proof of **cholera vaccination** is not required to enter China, in accordance with the 1973 ruling of the WHO World Health Assembly.

4 Should the situation change in China in the future without due warning, requiring your being vaccinated at the border, you can avoid **infection** from **non-sterile needles** and **syringes** by carrying your own **sterile medical equipment pack** (detailed below).

5 Meanwhile, WHO sources seem to suggest that there is some doubt about the efficacy of **vaccination**.

6 From personal experience, be warned that the experience may not be a pleasant one! When I was vaccinated in Spain (mentioned above), my arm felt like a lead pipe for several hours afterwards!

7 Since **cholera** often follows **flooding**, which is usually widely reported avoid **flooded areas** (mentioned in Chapter 3).

Diarrhoea or 'Chinese tummy'

Identification

1 Between about a third and a half of all travellers from Western to developing countries may expect to suffer to a greater or lesser extent from some form of **bacterial** or **viral gastro-enteritis**, characterised by **vomiting** or **watery diarrhoea** caused by a **change in diet** and/or **water** – particularly during the first few weeks of their stay.

Evaluation

2 Although the WHO does not have available at the time of writing any figures for the incidence of **acute diarrhoea** in China (*Emergency and Humanitarian Action: Baseline Statistics for China*, Mar 2001, listed in the Bibliography), I understand that the risk of **travellers' diarrhoea** (TD) (commonly called '**Chinese tummy**') is only moderate.

Control

3 Nevertheless, to **reduce the risk** further, follow the general guidelines for **culinary hygiene** described in detail below.

4 Should you experience TD: **fluid replacement** is essential and should be started immediately – as follows:
   (a) Drink plenty of **non-alcoholic fluids**.
   (b) Ingest **oral rehydration salts** (ORS): these can be bought at most local pharmacies in the West and are particularly useful for **children** who dehydrate more quickly in hot countries.
   (c) Before taking any **anti-diarrhoeal medicines** always

check the instructions for **contra-indications** – such as in the case of **cholera**, when the WHO does not recommend their use (*Cholera: Basic Facts for Travellers*).

(d) If you are hungry and can keep food down carry on eating, but avoid **fatty foods** and **dairy products**.

EXAMPLES

In the early to mid-1970s:

1 In **Colombia** when my son and I ran the risk of dehydrating, the local doctor prescribed **Coca Cola** as an **ORS**.
2 In **Spain** to counter 'Spanish tummy', I used an **antacid solution** to line my stomach before eating.

---

5 Always seek **medical attention** if:
   (a) Your **diarrhoea** lasts for **longer than a few days** (say three to four).
   (b) You have:
      ♦ a **temperature** of 38°C or higher;
      ♦ **blood** or **mucus in the stool** (which may be a sign of **dysentery**, described below);
      ♦ **very frequent watery bowel movements**.
   (c) You are **repeatedly sick**.
6 **One word of caution** (from personal experience): do not forget that **TD works both ways**. That is, once you are accustomed to Chinese food and drink, you may well find that, conversely, your stomach becomes less tolerant of Western food back home!

EXAMPLE

In the 1970s, my late father – an eminent senior consultant pathologist – kept me supplied with **anti-diarrhoeal tablets** to combat '**English tummy**' during our UK home leave!

Dysentery

Identification

1 '**Dysentery** may be simply defined as **diarrhoea** containing **blood**' (*Fact Sheet 108*, WHO).

Evaluation

2 At the time of writing, I can find no authoritative data regarding **dysentery** in China, other than a general statement by the WHO that 'incidences of other **diarrhoeal diseases**...are also high and they pose a major public health threat in the (West Pacific) Region' (*Special Focus: Communicable Disease Surveillance and Response Strategy – Overview*).

3 On the other hand, when we lived in South America (in 1974):

(a) **Amoebic dysentery** was a fact of daily life, from which most people and classes of society suffered, and to which they seemed to pay little attention.

(b) Ironically, I was unaffected, despite much business entertaining; whereas my wife, who mainly ate at home – where she supervised the food preparation – did suffer!

(c) Back in the UK, the family doctor could not understand our lack of concern; and wanted to refer my wife to the London School of Hygiene and Tropical Medicine.

Control

4 According to my wife, although **amoebic dysentery** is particularly unpleasant, the six-weeks course of **drugs** that she had to take made her feel temporarily worse than the illness itself!

Giardiasis

Identification

1 'The **giardia lamblia** parasite...seems to be particularly prevalent in China...

Evaluation

2 It appears to cause few symptoms among locals. Visitors, however...can become quite ill, with chronic **abdominal pain** and recurring **diarrhoea**...

Control

3 **Giardia** can be difficult to eradicate from a **restaurant** kitchen' *(China Business Handbook 2003,* p. 45*)*.

Hepatitis A and E

Identification

1 **Hepatitis A** is quite widespread in China.

2 **Hepatitis E** is prevalent in North-East and North-West China.

Evaluation

3 The risk of **hepatitis A** 'is particularly high for (non-immune) travellers exposed to poor conditions of **hygiene**, **sanitation** and **drinking-water** control' *(International Travel and Health,* WHO, p. 52, listed in the Bibliography).

4 **Hepatitis E** may be particularly harmful to **pregnant women**, especially during the third trimester *(ibid.,* p. 54).

Control

5 At the time of writing, there is only **vaccine** available for **hepatitis A** – but not **E**, for which the only antidote is a **clean** and **safe diet**.

Schistosomiasis

Identification and evaluation

1 According to the WHO, **schistosomiasis** (spread by the parasitic worm *schistosoma japonicum*, whose vectors are **water snails**) is the world's second most debilitating parasitic disease, after malaria. This is the illness that His Royal Highness Prince William is said to have caught whilst bathing in Africa in 2003.

2 At the time of writing, according to BUPA *(op. cit.)*, '**bilharzia** (**schistosomiasis**) is endemic in the central Yangtze river basin', contracted from bathing in **water contaminated** with **human sewage**.

3 In 2002 'according to statistics from the (Chinese) Ministry of Health, 810,000 people contracted **schistosomiasis**, more than double the number of cases in 1988. But experts caution that the real figure is much higher and could spiral further upward upon completion of the Three Gorges Reservoir, which might cause the snails' – the vectors – 'to spread eastward' (*Time Asia*, op. cit.).

4 This increase is attributed to anti-**snail-fever** bureaus having to find alternative sources of revenue (such as from treating STIs) once the government withdrew its funding for **schistosomiasis** (in the early 1990s) after successfully reducing it from 12 to 2.5 million during

Mao's rule (1949–1976), and to 400,000 by the late 1980s.

Control

5 **Swim** only in well-chlorinated and maintained **public pools** – not in **fresh** watercourses. **Salt water** is usually safe.

Typhoid

Identification and evaluation

1 **Typhoid** is not commonly found in China, except in **small towns** or **rural areas** with **poor hygiene** standards.

Control

2 Ensure that you are properly **inoculated**.

Worms

Identification

1 Infected food, especially **undercooked meat** and **salad**, may contain **tapeworm cysts** (which appear to be endemic in China).

2 You may be able to **self-diagnose** by stool examination.

Evaluation

3 Apparently (having been spared myself), worms are **unpleasant** but **not normally dangerous**!

Control

4 See the sections in Chapter 5 on Food Preparation and Eating Out.

5 Alternatively, include **worm tablets** in your medical kit.

Other

Identification
1 At the time of writing, according to BUPA *(op. cit.)*:
   (a) '**Brucellosis** also occurs', from consuming **unpasteurised milk** and milk-products.
   (b) 'Oriental **liver fluke** (*clonorchiasis*), oriental **lung fluke** (*paragonimiasis*) and giant **intestinal fluke** (*fasciolopsiasis*) are reported', from eating **contaminated food**.

INSECT-BORNE ILLNESSES

Overview

Identification
1 A number of organisms are carried and spread to humans by **insects** (such as mosquitoes, fleas, bed bugs, ticks and sand flies) that **bite** from dawn to dusk.

2 Such organisms may be injected into you by the female of the species when she pierces your skin to draw the blood needed to complete her breeding cycle.

Control
To avoid being bitten by insects, I recommend from personal experience (except of 3e and 8) that you:

3 Use an effective **insect repellent**; and apply it regularly on exposed skin, especially between dusk and dawn, as follows:

(a) The most effective are those that contain **DEET** (*diethyitolumide*) – a preparation not, however, suitable for **infants**.

(b) Do not:
- spray **wounds** or **broken skin**;
- **inhale** or **swallow** repellent sprays, or get them into your **eyes**.

(c) To apply spray products to **your face**:
- **first** apply to your hands;
- **then** rub your face with your hands, avoiding eyes and mouth.

(d) To protect **young children**, do not:
- allow children under (say) 10 years old to apply repellent to themselves – an **adult** should do it for them;
- apply to their **hands**, or around their **eyes** and **mouth**.

(e) DEET-impregnated **wrist** and **ankle-bands** are also available.

4 Wear **long-sleeved shirts**, **long trousers** and a **hat**, especially in the evening, and between dusk and dawn; and spray the material with a repellent or insecticide to give added protection – but 'take care with artificial fibres/plastics, as DEET is known to have solvent problems' (*Holiday Essentials Catalogue*, Medical Advisory Service for Travellers Abroad [MASTA], 2003, p. 3).

5 Clear your bedroom at night with a knock-down **insect spray**, including inside any bed net you may be using, as follows:

(a) Do not **inhale** or **swallow fly sprays,** or get them into your **eyes** for which reason...

(b) Spray your bedroom, shut the door and stay outside for (say) 20 to 30 minutes before re-entering.

6 Alternatively, use:

(a) **Indoors: plug-in insecticide vaporisers,** which are equally effective.

(b) **Outdoors:** insecticide-impregnated **smoke coils,** which are readily and cheaply available in China.

7 **Air conditioning** found in most if not all accommodation aimed at the expatriate market is also an effective deterrent.

8 Alternatively, use an insecticide-impregnated **mosquito bed-net,** as follows *(ibid)*:

(a) '**Check inside** the net on entry for unwelcome visitors.

(b) **Repair** holes in the net immediately.

(c) Make sure the net is **tucked in** carefully.'

9 Wear **boots,** with **trousers tucked into socks,** in long grass; and generally do not go **barefoot** outside to avoid **snake** and **tick bites** and other **parasitic infections**.

Note: The most effective way to **remove a tick** is to use a pair of **tweezers** to pull it out by the head, not the body (which may leave the head still engaged).

10 Shut **windows** at dusk; and, where possible, fit the windows of your home with **fly screens** (which we did), for which an '**emergency repair** can be effected by pushing cotton wool into the tear with a matchstick' *(ibid).*

Dengue (break-bone) fever and dengue haemorrhagic fever (DHF)

Identification

1 'The southernmost provinces (of China – that is: Guangdong, Guangxi, Hainan and Yunnan) have endemic **dengue**, but not on a dramatic scale' (*Dengue*, WHO, 1999).

Evaluation

2 According to the most recent figures (at the time of writing) published by the WHO:

(a) During the ten years from 1991 and 2000, some 9,800 cases but only three deaths were reported in mainland China (*ibid*; and *Summary of the Dengue Situation in the Western Pacific Region – An Update*, Aug 2001).

(b) **Dengue** was reported for the first time in the Special Administrative Regions of **Macau** (some 2,100 cases) and **Hong Kon**g (less than 40) in 2000 and 2001, respectively (*Combating Communicable Diseases: Dengue*, 2002).

3 **Dengue** tends to be at its peak during June to November.

4 'The risk for contracting **dengue** is:

(a) **Greater in urban areas**

(b) **Lower** in rural areas and areas at **high altitude** (above 4,500 feet [1500 meters])'.

(*Notice: Dengue Fever: Tropical and Subtropical Regions*, CDC, Jul 2003).

5 Unlike her **malaria** counterpart, the **dengue-carrying mosquito** is **diurnal**, being especially active during the

first and last few hours of daylight.

Control

6 You should follow the general advice (above) to avoid **mosquito bites**, since there is currently no **vaccine** – although the WHO is hopeful that there will be in several years time (*Fact Sheet 117*).

Japanese encephalitis (JE)

Identification

1 **JE** is:
   (a) Endemic to China.
   (b) Spread by **mosquitoes** that breed in **stagnant water** and visit farm animals such as **pigs**.

Evaluation

2 JE tends to be:
   (a) **Seasonal**, in **summer** and **autumn**, but **not predictable** – for which reason some commentators estimate from April to October; and others June to September.
   (b) Confined to **rural areas** (where the mosquito breeds in **rice fields**).

3 Outbreaks in Guangdong in 2003 are thought to have originated amongst the large at-risk **migrant population** mentioned above.

Control

4 If you live or work in **rural areas** consider **immunisation**.

Malaria

Identification

1 According to the WHO (*International Travel and Health,* 2003, pp. 157–158):

   (a) **Malaria** risk – including the **malignant** form – occurs in Hainan and Yunnan.

   (b) **Multidrug-resistant malignant malaria** has been reported.

   (c) Risk of **benign malaria** exists in Fujian, Guangdong, Guangxi, Guizhou, Hainan, Sichuan, Xizang (only along the valley of Zangbo river in the extreme south-east) and Yunnan.

   (d) **Very low malaria risk** exists in Anhui, Hubei, Hunan, Jiangsu, Jiangxi, Shandong, Shanghai, and Zhejiang.

Evaluation

2 Where it does exist, **transmission** occurs as follows:

Altitude	Period		Latitude	
	From	To	North of	South of
below 1,500 metres	July	November	33°N	
	May	December	25°N	33°N
	January	December		25°N

3 There is **no risk** in **urban** or **densely populated plain** areas.

Control

4 Only if you plan to visit **remote rural areas** in the provinces listed above do you need to take **malaria prophylaxis** such as in:

(a) **Risk areas**: chloroquine.

(b) **Hainan and Yunnan**: mefloquine.

5 Whatever **anti-malarial precautions** you take, always:
   (a) **Before going to China**:
   - consult your own physician or travel health adviser;
   - ensure you have an ample supply for your whole time in China (since it is not generally advisable to change **anti-malarials** mid-visit).
   (b) **Whilst in China**:
   - Complete your full course of medication.

6 According to the *Occupational Health Magazine* of June 1994 (*Travel Management – Advice for business travel: the wider picture,* Kate Goodwin and Daragh Brennan):
   (a) '**Prevention** of malaria is becoming more difficult because of the increasing resistance of the parasite to **antimalarial drugs**.
   (b) **Business travellers** often consider lengthy **chemo-prophylaxis** inconvenient for short, frequent trips and coupled with the uncertainty of their effectiveness may cease to think they are necessary.
   (c) The importance of taking the full course of **malaria prophylaxis** should be stressed.'

Yellow fever

Identification and evaluation

1 **Yellow fever** does not exist in China, but the **mosquitoes** capable of carrying the illness do.

Control

2 Anyone entering China within six days of leaving a **yellow fever** infected country (such as parts of Africa and South America) is required to produce a **certificate** proving that they have been **immunised** against the illness.

Other

Identification

1 At the time of writing, according to BUPA *(op. cit.)*:
  (a) '**Bancroftian** and **brugian filariasis**' – otherwise known as **elephantiasis** – 'are still reported in southern China', spread by **mosquitoes** and **black flies**.
  (b) '**Visceral leishmaniasis** is increasingly common throughout; and **cutaneous leishmaniasis** has been reported from Xinjiang', spread by **sand flies**.
  (c) 'There is some risk of **plague**', spread by **flies**.
  (d) '**Mite-borne** or **scrub typhus** may be found in **scrub areas** of South China.'

TRANSMITTABLE ILLNESSES

Overview

Identification

1 There is a risk of acquiring **transmittable illnesses** from:
  (a) (Re-)using **non-disposable** and **non-sterilised equipment** (e.g. needles, syringes and blood-transfusion lines).
  (b) Using **non-screened blood** and blood products.

(c) Practising **unsafe sex**.

Control

2 If you are worried about the hygiene of Chinese medical practitioners, I suggest that, like us, you take to China a **sterile medical equipment pack** (commonly known as an '**AIDS kit**'), containing a selection of surgical and dental needles and syringes for personal use (as recommended below).

(a) To allay any suspicions that the Chinese customs and immigration authorities may have, you must provide proper accompanying documentation. Otherwise, you run the risk of being arrested for drug trafficking (as mentioned in Chapter 3).

3 If going to a **rural** or **remote area** of China, you might consider supplementing the pack with:

(a) Fully screened and tested **blood** and blood products.

(b) Sterile **transfusion equipment** such as available (in the UK) from **The Blood Care Foundation**.

4 It goes without saying that you should practice **safe sex**, as appropriate.

Hepatitis B, C and D

Evaluation

1 **Hepatitis B** 'is congenitally acquired by 15–20% of the population' of China *(China Business Handbook 2003,* p. 45*)*.

2 Other sources suggest that:

(a) 10% of Chinese are **carriers**, compared with less than 1% of Americans.

(b) 20% of those receiving **blood transfusions** are at risk of contracting the illness.

3 One reason may be that 'China has had a cheap **vaccine** for **Hepatitis B** available since 1985; but local health bureaus were loath to offer it free of charge, because the vaccine was a crucial source of income' (*Time Asia*, op. cit.).

Control

4 **Hepatitis B vaccination** is a must for socially (including sexually) active young people.

5 At the time of writing, there are no **vaccines** for **hepatitis C or D** – for which the only antidote is a **clean** and **safe lifestyle**.

Acquired immune deficiency syndrome (HIV)/ AIDS and other STIs

In January 2003, the *China-Britain Trade Review* (pp. 21–22, *Tackling the Aids Challenge*, Heather Xiaoquan Zhang and Lin Gu) reported as follows.

Identification

1 Many Chinese have long assumed that **HIV/AIDS** is a Western illness, the result of a decadent bourgeois lifestyle characterised by **sexual promiscuity** and an obsession with **sex** – against which traditional Chinese culture (based on Confucianism) and the official ideology of the Communist Party of China should prevail.

2 Sadly, the truth belies this view; and 'China now faces a serious epidemic that threatens to erode the remarkable growth and reverse the progress in human development

achieved over the past two decades' as a result of **'illegal blood banks** and their regulators, as well as an increasingly **deregulated health sector'**. Only recently has China introduced **blood screening** for **HIV** as a standard medical procedure.

Evaluation

3 **Estimates for 2002** put the number of people with:
  (a) **HIV**: at **over 1.5 million** (source: United Nations and WHO).
  (b) **Full-blown AIDS**: at **200,000** – of whom probably more than 50% have died.

4 Based on these figures, and unless something is done to combat AIDS, **projections** for **HIV** infections during the first decade of the 21st century would be:
  (a) **2005:** 5 million.
  (b) **2010:** 10 million.

5 Since then, however, in the autumn of 2003 – as was then widely reported in the news – the Chinese authorities admitted for the first time that their published figures were grossly underestimated.

6 Apart from the government's refusal, until recently, to face up to the **sexual revolution** in China (as mentioned in Chapter 2), **ignorance** is a major factor in the spread of **HIV/AIDS**.
  (a) For example, a survey conducted in 2002 by the *Guangming Daily* indicated that:
    ◆ less than 4% know how **HIV** is transmitted;
    ◆ about 50% believe that they can catch **HIV** from chopsticks previously used by someone who is HIV-positive.

Control

7 The most effective ways to avoid **STI**s include:

    (a) Practising '**safe sex**' (too well known to need to detail here).

    (b) Providing your own, and not sharing others', **needles** and **blood**.

OTHER ILLNESSES

Altitude sickness

Identification

1 If you are not used to living at **high altitudes** (say above 2,500 metres), you may experience difficulties due to **lack of oxygen**.

Evaluation

2 Apparently, '**altitude sickness** can be a problem in parts of Tibet, Qinghai, Xinjiang, Sichuan, Yunnan and Gansu' *(*BUPA, *op. cit.)*.

Control

3 From personal experience (of living at c. 9,000 feet in Bogotá, and having had to attend umpteen business functions and deal with several visiting foreign 'macho' businessmen) I suggest that – until you have become fully acclimatised – you:

    (a) Drink **alcohol** (especially spirits) in moderation, unless it is also so hot that your body sweats out the alcohol faster than it can absorb it.

EXAMPLES

In **Colombia**:

1　We had to cancel a social engagement for a visiting colleague, whose capacity for alcohol was legendary, when he became so ill that he had to admit – possibly for the first time in his life – that he had drunk too much!

2　On the one occasion that I drank a glass of vodka at a reception, I became so 'woozy' that a friend had to take me home at once.

3　On the other hand I spent a very sober afternoon in the Colombian 'hot country' (c. 40°C plus) sharing a bottle of the local fire-water with my Caleño host.

(b) Refrain from (for you) **abnormal physical over-exertion**.

EXAMPLES

In **Bogotá**:

1　When still young, and relatively fit, I tried **skipping** for some light exercise, but soon felt quite dizzy.

2　**Running upstairs** was inadvisable. And when the lift in our office building broke, and we had to walk up four flights, we used to arrive quite exhausted!

(c) May need to carry warm and cold weather clothes in **tropical areas**, where **changes in altitude** are accompanied by **variations in temperature**.

EXAMPLES

In **Colombia**:

1　When driving up and down country from Bogotá, road signs encouraged us to stop and change into warmer and cooler clothing, respectively.

2 When flying down country from Bogotá on business, we would have to carry a semi-tropical suit to change into immediately on arrival.

Chinese restaurant syndrome

Identification

1 **Chinese restaurant syndrome** is the aptly-named term – that I only came across whilst researching for this book – to describe the unpleasant consequences of **monosodium glutamate** (MSG) ('*weijing*'), with which Chinese food is often laced in order to make you feel full by swelling inside you.

Evaluation

2 Depending on your general health, you may react unfavourably to **MSG** in one of two ways:
   (a) **Hot flushes**.
   (b) **Upset stomach**.

Control

3 If you do react badly to it – as my wife did – try asking in Western-style restaurants for **food without MSG** (*qing gei wo mei you weijing*).

Cold

Identification

1 In winter, some parts of China (detailed in Chapter 9) may get very **cold** and/or accommodation be unheated.

Control

2 **Dress** appropriately (as suggested in Chapter 9); and do not stay **outside** longer than necessary.

EXAMPLE

The temperature at mid-day in January in Beijing was often ten or more degrees Celsius below zero, which quickly proved too much for me when walking the dog in the country.

Heat

Identification

1   In summer, some parts of China (*ibid.*) may get very **hot**, when the loss of body fluids can lead to **dehydration**, especially in children and the elderly.

Control

2   Dress appropriately (*ibid.*).

3   To avoid **dehydration** increase your **fluid intake** and **salt consumption**, when, as a rough guide (according to *Living and Working in China*, Employment Conditions Abroad Ltd, UK, 1996, p. 31) 'in every 24 hours you should:
    (a) Drink a basic 2 litres, adding 1 litre of **liquid** for every 10°C (i.e. if the temperature registers 30°C, the daily liquid intake should be 5 litres).
    (b) Take an extra 15 grams of **salt**.'

4   Also take normal measures to protect your skin and head against the **sun**.

Rabies

Identification

1   At the time of writing, '**rabies** is present, although the government policy which banned **dogs** and **cats** from

main cities' – mentioned in Chapter 8 – 'makes this less of a risk in these areas' *(BUPA op. cit.)*.

2 According to the WHO *(Fact Sheet 99)*: 'Dramatic decreases in **human cases of rabies** have...been reported during recent years in China...following implementation of programmes for improved post-exposure treatment of humans' – estimated in its *1998 World Survey of Rabies* at some 5 million annually – 'and the **vaccination of dogs**' (mentioned in Chapter 8).

Evaluation

3 Since **rabies** is not a reportable illness in China, reliable figures are scarce, as follows:
   (a) **1998**: 208 human deaths *(ibid)*.
   (b) **2001**: ten people are said to have died in Guangdong Province in early 2001 (MASTA, Health Brief for my wife and self, Jan 2002).

Control

4 **Pre-exposure vaccination** is advisable if:
   (a) You plan to spend any length of time in **risk** or **rural areas**.
   (b) Your job may bring you into (regular) contact with **animals**.

3 Otherwise, you will need a full course of **post-exposure vaccinations**.

4 If you should be bitten or scratched by a **suspect animal** (especially dogs, cats and monkeys): do seek medical attention immediately. Even if you have been vaccinated, you will need a **post-exposure booster**.

5 Take special care with **children**, who may be tempted to play with 'adorable' puppies or kittens, suffer a bite or scratch, and not bother to tell you immediately

---

EXAMPLE

In the late 1990s, because my job required me travel to risk areas, I was vaccinated against rabies. Thankfully, the vaccination is now into the arm – not the stomach, as it used to be!

Other

1 **Haemorrhagic fever** with renal syndrome is endemic.

2 **Meningitis** occurs frequently in China, and **vaccination** is advisable.

⑤

Healthcare

In China, in addition to the **illnesses** described in Chapter 4, your health may be at risk from **poor medical treatment** due to:

- **shortage of** basic, let alone modern **equipment**;
- **emigration of doctors** to the West;
- **fake medicines**;
- **high fees** demanded of foreigners by local hospitals in cash up front.

OVERALL CONTROL

I suggest that you follow the recommendations described below, arranged in the order in which they occur:

- before going to China;
- en route to China;
- whilst in China;
- culinary hygiene;
- personal hygiene;
- after leaving China.

BEFORE YOU GO TO CHINA

Based on the premise that prevention is better than cure, before going to China, you should:

1 Obtain a **health brief** from a reputable organisation such as one of those listed in the Bibliography.

2 See your family or company doctor, dentist and optician for a **medical**, **teeth** and **eye check-up**, respectively, in order to minimise potential medical, dental and ophthalmic emergencies.

3 Have an **AIDS test** and **chest X-ray**; and your **blood group** analysed.

    (a) Whilst all or some of these may be required to obtain a **visa** and/or **driving licence**, be aware that some Chinese officials may *not* accept a **foreign medical certificate**, even if translated and notarised, but insist on further tests locally. If in doubt: check with your **local Chinese Consulate**.

    (b) Unfortunately, it is said that you are likely to be infected by the needles used in Chinese state clinics (unless you are able and allowed to provide your own, as intimated below).

    (c) Consequently, many expatriates prefer being driven (rather than driving themselves) to exposing themselves to the practices – real or imaginary – of such clinics in the course of obtaining the necessary licence.

4 Have all the **vaccinations** recommended in your health brief (as mentioned in Chapter 4) or by your family or company doctor.

5 Arrange **health insurance** – unless your employer has already done so for you – preferably with an organisation that has representation in China, such as **AEA International**. See also below: *Expatriate Health Insurance*.

What to take with you

From personal experience, I recommend that you take with you to China any or all of the following **medical kits** and **supplies** – which should be readily available from your normal practitioners or otherwise from one of the suppliers listed in the Bibliography.

1 **First aid kit** – as comprehensive as possible, but containing at least: **plasters, bandages, antiseptic spray, scissors, tweezers** and a **thermometer.**

2 **First aid manual** (preferably symptom-based) – since the kit will be of little use if you do not know how to use it!

3 **Sterile medical equipment pack** (commonly known as an **AIDS kit**) – containing a selection of **surgical** and **dental needles** and **syringes** for personal use.

4 **Emergency dental kit** – designed primarily to self-administer temporary fillings.

5 **Prescribed medicines** (see below) and any others that you may think necessary – nearly all mentioned above or below – such as:
    ◆ **analgesics**;
    ◆ **anti-diarrhoeal** tablets;
    ◆ **anti-malarial** drugs;
    ◆ broad-spectrum **antibiotics**;
    ◆ **insect** repellent, spray and bite treatment;
    ◆ **oral rehydration salts**;
    ◆ **sterilising** solution – such as chlorine or iodine-based or Milton;
    ◆ **travel sickness** remedies.

6   Spare **spectacles, contact lenses, hearing aid, dentures** and similar.

7   Medical, ophthalmic and similar **prescriptions**.

8   Copies of medical, dental and similar **records**, including a card showing your **blood group** and **allergies**, preferably with a summary in Chinese.

9   **Contact details** of your doctor, dentist, optician, next of kin and similar (see below).

EXAMPLES

1 In the 1970s, in **Europe** and **South America**: my late father whilst Director of Medical Research at Pfizer Pharmaceuticals (UK) kept me well supplied with that company's brand of broad-spectrum antibiotic.
2 In the late 1990s, for **China**: my employer's Chief Medical Officer supplied my wife and self with much of the above, some of it sourced from MASTA.

Airline security caution

To comply with international airline security requirements you should pack all **sharp implements** (such as tweezers, scissors and needles, mentioned above) in your consigned – not hand – luggage.

SARS kit

1   Depending on the risk of SARS at the time of travelling, you may wish to consider a **SARS kit** containing such items (according to *SARS: What Sells?*, Charles Chaw and Paul Mc-Cabe, China Knowledge Press) as:

- vitamins B, C and E; garlic and zinc tablets; and other nutritional supplements and products believed to build immunity and reduce the duration and severity of colds;
- products to strengthen lungs and balance pH;
- surgical masks and protective clothing;
- alcohol swabs, soap or other hand cleaner, Dettol or other disinfectant, and bleach;
- digital thermometer;
- personal electrostatic air purifier.

Prescription drugs

In view of the penalties for **drug offences** in China, mentioned in Chapter 3, it is worth my repeating the following advice.

1 Carry a **prescription** and **explanatory letter** from your doctor, in English and Chinese, justifying any **prescribed medications** for personal use.

2 Leave **medications** in their **original labelled containers** (so that they coincide with the corresponding prescriptions).

3 Check with your **local Chinese Consulate** that any prescription medicines you intend taking with you are free of restrictions.

Moreover, according to BUPA (*On The Move*, p. 12):

4 'Medicines that are widely available in the UK will not always be available abroad. In **China** for example...western medicines may be unavailable.'

5 It is important, therefore to organise any necessary **repeat prescription**.

6 'The website *www.prescriptions.ltd.uk* ensures that British nationals who are living abroad can organise a long-term supply of any medication they will need. The prescribed drugs are all prepared and dispatched according to the UK's strict regulatory controls.'

Emergency medical records
MedicAlert® (listed in the Bibliography):

1 Operates a 24-hour response centre where members' **records** can be freely accessed from anywhere in the world by emergency medical services. The centre will also contact your family.

2 Can also supply **bracelets** identifying your specific allergies and/or reactions to certain drugs.

Both services are particularly useful if you cannot speak the language and/or are unconscious.

Disabilities
1 'Regulations and care for those with **physical** or **mental disabilities** vary greatly from country to country...Schools, for example, may not have adequate facilities or programmes for students with **physical limitations** or **learning difficulties**' (BUPA, *op. cit.*, p. 13); or offices, hotels or other public buildings, for example, offer suitable **wheel-chair access**.

2 Check beforehand with your **local Consulate** in China.

3   Meanwhile, you may be pleasantly surprised. Since Deng Xiaoping had a physically disabled son, it is said that China is better prepared than some other countries in accommodating disability, but I have no corroborative evidence.

Rare blood groups

Apparently – since, as in other parts of Asia, it is not indigenous to China – Chinese blood banks do not store **rhesus negative blood**.

Should you belong to this group, therefore, I suggest that you contact **The Blood Care Foundation** (listed in the Bibliography) for advice.

ON YOUR WAY TO AND FROM CHINA

Jet lag

Identification

1   **Jet lag** is the name commonly given to the disruption of the sleeping and waking cycle caused by your **body-clock**'s slowness in adapting to flying across several (say more than three) times zones and whose **symptoms** are too well known to merit description here. The **effects** are nevertheless too often under-estimated and, hence, overlooked and ignored.

Evaluation

2   'Symptoms tend to be worse after an **eastern** rather a western transition' – that is: when you fly to a time-zone ahead of your point of departure (such as from **Europe to China**).

3   The problems of jet lag increase with **age** and **distance**.

Control

4   'Flights should be arranged to **arrive** at the final destination in the **evening**' – whereas, in practice, many flights from Europe to China arrive early in the morning

5   '**Time zone adjustment** is promoted by immediate involvement in the new time zone routines, such as meals and sleep' – which, given the pace at which most foreigners seem eager to do business in China, should not be too difficult!

6   'After long haul flights, **business travellers** should allow three days to elapse before making important decisions' – whereas, in reality, many:
    (a) Fly into China one morning.
    (b) Attend several meetings and banquets the same day.
    (c) Become instant China experts overnight.
    (d) Make snap decisions the following day.
    (e) Leave after 36 to 48 hours.

7   To reduce the effects of **jet lag** for your particular circumstances, try using the MASTA on-line **jet lag calculator** (listed in the Bibliography) which works on the principle that the **body clock** can be made to adjust faster by exposure to bright and dim light at appropriate times.

EXAMPLE

See Appendix 5.

All of the above may explain why some Chinese are so successful at turning senior Westerners' business schedules to their advantage.

(Quotations from *Occupational Health* magazine, June 1994, *op. cit.*)

Deep vein thrombosis (DVT)

The following comments are made without prejudice to, or implication of liability of, any airline.

Identification

1 There have been many reports over recent years in the world media about **DVT** – a blood clot that usually develops in the leg after sitting still for hours, *and not just in aeroplanes* – with which I can readily identify, having been operated on for an inherited **blood-circulation** problem in one leg.

Evaluation

2 According to the *Daily Mail,* London, 28 Jun 2003 (summarising a report by Professor Belcaro, of D'Annunzio University (Italy) at a scientific forum in Lisbon that same month):

(a) 'Many (**blood clots**) cause no ill-effects but some can travel to the lungs with fatal results.'

(b) '**Long-haul flights**...can lead to **sluggish circulation** and **swollen ankles**, as fluid collects in the lower limbs, and changes occur in the state of the blood which can promote clotting.'

(c) The **risk** of developing a **clot** after a **long flight** is about:

◆ 1% for those at a normal to low risk of **DVT**;

- 2% for those at medium risk;
- 5% for high-risk groups.

(d) The **high risk** group includes those with:

- previous incidences of **thrombosis, blood-clotting** problems, and **circulatory problems** in the legs (like me);
- a significant **weight problem**.

(e) Women on **Hormone Replacement Therapy** (HRT), **cancer** patients, and anyone who has had **recent surgery** are also at risk.

(f) For the high-risk group, even a **3-hour flight** (such as Beijing to Guangzhou or Hong Kong) could contribute to **DVT**.

Control

3 From personal experience (and the example of my late father), I have found that the following precautions seem to help my legs:

(a) Wearing **support hose** (aka '**flight socks**') which, according to the *Daily Mail* (op. cit.), can dramatically reduce the risk: 'air travellers who do not wear **compression socks** are six times more likely to develop a potentially fatal blood clot.'

(b) Regularly **wiggling my toes**, and frequently **walking** along the aisle (such as to/from the toilets).

(c) Requesting **seats with ample leg-room** (unless travelling in business or first class accommodation with already suitable seating arrangements) – either at extra cost or by persuading the travel agent of my genuine need. Not for nothing is **DVT** dubbed '**economy class syndrome**'.

(d) Many airlines now include in their in-flight magazine suggested exercises and such precautions as:

- ◆ drink plenty of **water**;
- ◆ avoid **alcohol**, **tea** and **coffee**;
- ◆ wear **loose fitting clothes**;
- ◆ avoid crossing your legs or ankles.

EXAMPLE

In the 1960s, when aeroplanes were less capacious and comfortable, even for non-economy class passengers, my late father's employer paid for him to have three seats on a flight from the UK to Japan so that he could stretch out his **phlebitic legs**!

Stroke

Again, without prejudice to, or implication of liability of, any airline.

Identification

1 The very day that I was due to send the final draft of this chapter to the publisher (29 Mar 2004), the *Daily Mail* carried an article claiming that 'passengers could be at risk of a **stroke** after **long-haul flights**...of eight hours or more...brought about by **cramped seating** which restricts movements.'

Evaluation

2 According to one expert source quoted: 'it could be extremely rare or...more common than we imagine'. However, 'people must not be scared – there is a smaller risk than of getting **DVT**'.

3   'Passengers at **risk** from the syndrome – labelled '**economy class stroke syndrome**' – are those with a **small hole in the heart** which failed to close during childhood' (most of whom 'are unaware of it because the hole is not large enough to cause problems'), through which a **blood clot** – that could form in the legs – might slip and reach the brain.

Control
4   In the absence of any specific advice, I suggest the same precautions as for DVT.

Flight phobia

Identification
1   In these days of modern aeroplanes, package-holidays and high-risk sporting pastimes, it may be hard to imagine that many people are still **afraid of flying**. Thirty or 40 years ago, perhaps: but not in the 21st century, surely?

Control
2   I am not aware of any **textbook remedy**, although apocryphal stories abound of **unconventional cures**.

EXAMPLES

1   One late friend of mine, a 'macho' Spaniard who climbed, dived, sailed, skied, drove fast cars, etc, was so **afraid of flying** that, after a particularly for him bad flight, he would ask the pilot's name so as to avoid flying with him again (he was that well connected or *enchufado* with the right *guanxi*!). Quite inadvertently, he was cured by my giving him a lift one day to the airport in my Mini Cooper – when he commented that the experience was even worse than flying, since I did not drive fast but flew low!

2 At training events, I have heard of people who have allegedly cured their **fear of flying** by bungee-jumping or doing a sponsored parachute jump for charity!

3 If you are worried about flying, try talking to your employer and jointly devising a suitable coping strategy, however bizarre!

Travel sickness

Control

If you anticipate being a **frequent flyer** in China include a sufficient supply of your usual **travel sickness remedy** in your **medical kit**.

DURING YOUR STAY IN CHINA

Your first week in China

During your **first week** in China, you should:

1 **Locate** and 'suss out' the nearest **pharmacies, doctors, dentists, hospitals**, etc.

2 Ask other **expatriates** what they think of these **local healthcare facilities** and which (other) ones they recommend.

3 Exchange information with other **expatriates** about any **peculiar medical problems** you may have (such as rare blood group, allergies, etc.).

4 Register with your **local Consulate** so that they can contact you in the event of an epidemic (as already mentioned and illustrated in Chapters 3 and 4).

Your first year in China

During your **first year** in China, like many expatriates in any foreign country (including some members of my family), you may find that you are ill more often than usual.

This could be for any of the following reasons:

1   Your body will not yet have become **immune** to the bugs in the **food, drinking water** or **air.**

2   You will need some time to adjust to the **climate.**

3   Settling into any **new environment** – whether at home or abroad – causes **stress**, which in turn will weaken your body's power of resistance.

4   All those **simple household remedies** for curing minor ailments that you always have handy at home may not be immediately available; and it will take you some time to find local alternatives.

5   If you are unfamiliar with the **local healthcare system, medicines** and **language**, you may be tempted to put off seeking medical attention until you are really ill.

6   To save or build **face** (your own, employer's and home country's), you may be tempted to impress your Chinese colleagues with your strength and stamina by returning to work too soon after being ill and before you have fully recovered – with the attendant risk of a more serious relapse.

Certainly I can personally identify with most, if not all, the above!

Chinese traditional medicine (CTM)

CTM is too well known throughout the world for me to dwell on it at any length here.

Suffice it to say that probably the believers will swear by, and the sceptics 'pooh-pooh', **CTM**. Nevertheless, the Chinese certainly believe that it works for them, so why not give it a go?

EXAMPLES

In 1998:

1 In **Beijing**, ten one-hour sessions of combined **aromatherapy, osteopathy, massage** and **acupuncture** seemed to cure my wife of a **back problem** – although my main recollection is of screaming coming from the bedroom.

2 In **Hong Kong**, an obscure **homeopathic cream** from a local pharmacy cured a **rash** from which I had suffered for several years (after falling in a river), despite proprietary Western treatments.

Pregnancy

For the **health** and **safety** of mother and child (as well as to avoid problems of **dual nationality**, mentioned earlier in Chapter 3), the general advice seems to be: **give birth in your home country**.

EXAMPLE

That said, my wife and children probably received better **maternity** and **post-natal care** in the expatriate hospitals in Spain and Colombia in the early 1970s than in the UK some ten years later.

If you need medical attention

If you need to visit a **doctor** or **dentist** (see below: Expatriate Healthcare Providers):

1   Take with you an **interpreter** whom you can trust to be discrete.

EXAMPLE

We always took my bilingual Chinese Personal Assistant with us, unless we were 100% certain that the medical staff spoke English.

2   Remember to take your **AIDS kit** with you; and do not be afraid to ask the doctor to use it. It is better to be safe than sorry.

EXAMPLE

As a matter of course, when **booking a doctor's or dentist's appointment**, my bilingual Chinese Personal Assistant would ask if I should take my **AIDS kit** – sometimes to the amusement of the practitioner who, nevertheless, always understood why.

3   Remember to take your **medical records**, and any **prescriptions** or **prescribed medicines** – preferably in English and Chinese.

PERSONAL HYGIENE

As elsewhere in the world, always **wash your hands** thoroughly:

1   After: using the **toilet** or such potentially 'unclean' activities as **gardening, fishing**, attending to **domestic animals** and similar.

2   Before: eating and preparing **food**.

And make sure that the **towel** you use to dry your hands is **hygienic**.

> **EXAMPLE**
>
> My paternal grandfather was most fastidious about washing his hands after touching our dog. My mother just did not have the heart to tell him that the towel on which he dried his hands was the one she used to dry the dog!

Public toilets

Despite the many horror stories with which returnees from China may try to shock you, I can assure you from personal experience that Chinese **public toilets** are improving, with an abundance of western-style 'sitters' in places visited by foreigners.

> **EXAMPLE**
>
> Having visited both France and China in recent years, I would say that their **'squatters'** are of similar standard.

CULINARY HYGIENE

As described above, some illnesses are caused by ingesting **contaminated food** and **water** against which the best prevention is **scrupulous culinary hygiene**, as follows.

Drinking water

1   Drink **bottled water** in preference to any other:
    (a) The management of most foreign housing complexes can arrange for **carboys of bottled water** to be delivered on a regular basis.
    (b) Ensure that the **seal on bottled water** is intact when you purchase it.

2   Otherwise, drink **boiled water**:
    (a) Bring the water to the boil – contrary to the advice

in some books **continuous boiling is not necessary**.

3 Or **purify the water**, as follows (according to MASTA, *op. cit.*):

(a) 'Use an **iodine resin water purifier** – these do not leave a strong after-taste.

(b) Use a **basic water filter** and then treat with **iodine tablets** or **drops**.'

(c) Be aware that 'many **basic water filters** are often unable to clear viruses.

(d) Ensure that you use a filter that combines an **iodine treatment**.'

(e) Alternatively, 'treat the water with **iodine drops** or **tablets** afterwards.

(f) **Chemical treatments** used alone may not inactivate **parasitic cysts**.'

(g) Leave water treated in this way for about 15 to 20 minutes before drinking.

4 Do not use **tap water**:

(a) Like my wife, you should use only 'safe' (i.e. bottled or boiled) water for **cleaning teeth** – although I survived using tap water!

(b) Use only 'safe' water for preparing **salads** and **raw vegetables** (as described below).

5 Avoid **ice cubes** in drinks, unless you are certain that they are made from 'safe' water.

6 Avoid **fountain drinks**.

7 **Tea**, **coffee** and **bottled drinks** (especially fizzy ones) are usually safe.

Nevertheless:

8   In **Beijing**, according to the *China Business Handbook 2003*: 'the **public water** supply appears to be bacteriologically safe, and can certainly be used for **brushing teeth**. Locals drink it without any apparent consequences, but due to lack of information about its chemical content, most foreign doctors are reluctant to advise visitors to consume it regularly.'

Food preparation

At the risk of repeating some of the previous advice by applying it to the specific context of **storing** and **preparing food**:

1   Whenever possible and practicable:
    (a) **Cook everything thoroughly** for at least ten minutes.
    (b) Ensure that food is **freshly cooked** and **served piping hot**.

2   Fruit with an outer removable peel – such as **bananas** and **citrus fruit** – is safe to eat.

3   All **other fruit** must be both thoroughly **washed** with boiled/bottled water or a chlorine/iodine solution (which destroys many germs, but is not 100% effective) and **peeled**.

4   Salads and **raw** (leafy) **vegetables**:
    (a) May be grown on '**night soil**' from latrines.
    (b) Often carry **worms** and **diseases**.
    (c) Should, therefore, be **avoided in restaurants** at all times; and at home during the first few months of your stay.
    (d) Can be **prepared at home** by being both thoroughly

washed in the same way as described above for fruit and **peeled**, but there is still a risk.

EXAMPLE

We cleaned all our salad, fruit and vegetables in a proprietary baby bottle sterilising solution (Milton), even before cooking them.

---

5 **Shellfish**:

   (a) Tend to live near **sewer outfalls** and thus carry diseases.

   (b) Should, therefore, be **avoided** unless you know for sure that they have been cooked in hot water or oil for at least ten minutes.

   (c) If **raw** – however appetising they may look – should be politely refused in the interests of your health.

EXAMPLE

A favourite way of serving prawns is alive, marinated in alcohol. Hopefully comatose – but in our experience occasionally wide awake and 'hopping mad' – these are referred to as '**drunken prawns**'.

---

6 'Never eat **undercooked ground beef** and **poultry, raw eggs** and **unpasteurised dairy products**' (according to the CDC website, listed in the Bibliography), or **products containing raw egg** (such as **mayonnaise** and some **salad dressings**).

7 **Insects** can be removed by soaking in a **strong salt solution** for about ten minutes.

Food storage/fridge management

Keep three separate areas in your **fridge**, one each for:

- raw unwashed produce;
- raw but washed and disinfected produce;
- cooked food.

Eating out

I have often (and my wife to a lesser extent) eaten out in restaurants rarely if ever frequented by foreigners, normally in the company of my Chinese colleagues; and lived to tell the tale.

Basically, I trusted them, working on the premise that they would not have taken me were it not safe!

If you are alone, however, here are some recommendations.

1 Avoid food from **street vendors**. Otherwise, make sure that such food:
   (a) Is **thoroughly cooked** in front of you.
   (b) Contains **no uncooked ingredients**.

EXAMPLE

We bought food from **street vendors** very rarely, mainly because we did not fancy '**lizard on a stick**' or similar delicacies. On one occasion that we did, I managed to break my crown on a very large toffee-strawberry!

---

2 If you are concerned about the hygiene (such as cracks and chips) of the **crockery** and/or cleanliness of the **chopsticks** (unless you carry your own): clean them with **hot tea** and a **tissue**.
   (a) Such precautions are not necessary in Western-style hotels or restaurants, or at official banquets.

(b) Some up-market clubs (such as the China Club, Beijing) provide **silver chopsticks** – which are supposed to discolour on contact with poison.

3   When given **wooden disposable chopsticks**:
(a) Ensure that they are still joined at the head (a sign that they have not been used before).
(b) Separate them.
(c) Rub the tips together, to remove any **splinters**.

4   Consider carrying proprietary **anti-diarrhoeal tablets** with you.

EXAMPLE

In the 1970s a late ex-colleague of mine in Paris always used to call in at the local pharmacy for 'tummy settlers' on the way home after eating sea-food in a restaurant!

5   As elsewhere in the world, **pork** may carry increased risk.

6   Avoid **ice-cream** from unreliable local sources, which may well contain a high **animal-fat** content and/or be **contaminated** and cause illness.

7   In Western-style restaurants, ask for food without **MSG** (*qing gei wo mei you weijing*) if you react badly to it (see Chapter 4).

8   **If all this puts you off: there is always MacDonald's or Kentucky Fried Chicken!**

Summary
To quote CDC (*ibid.*): '**boil it, cook it, peel it, or forget it**'.

DIET

1 In view of the previous comments about potentially unsafe **dairy** and **salad products**, ensure that you maintain a sufficient intake of **calcium** and **iron** by alternative safe means.

2 In those areas of scant dairy products – which the Chinese tend to disdain as disgusting or for children only – **vegetarians** should ensure that they maintain a sufficient intake of **protein** by eating alternative suitable foods.

AFTER YOU LEAVE CHINA

See your family or company doctor, dentist and optician for a general **medical, dental** and **ophthalmic check-up,** respectively.

EXPATRIATE HEALTHCARE AND PRODUCTS PROVIDERS

From personal experience, I can recommend the **medical** and **dental facilities** at the following clinics, staffed by **foreign practitioners** (thanks to the 1993 change in the law allowing non-Chinese doctors to practice in China):

♦ **AEA International: Beijing International (SOS) Clinic,** www.international-sos.com/world-network/dir.cfm, which I had occasion to use in the event of a:
   – suspected fractured elbow;
   – root-filling and crown replacement;
   – suspected minor heart-attack.
♦ **Beijing United Family Hospital,** www.bjunited.com.cn, which I had occasion to use in the event of a course on stress management.

For an approved list of **English-speaking doctors trained to UK and US standards**, please consult:

♦ **International Association for Medical Assistance to Travellers**, www.iamat.org

In the UK, members of:

♦ **AXA PPP Healthcare** should consult the company's up-to-date Directory of Hospitals in China at: www.axappphealthcare.com/blue.htm?html/members/countries/china.htm

♦ **BUPA International** should visit the company's international home page at: www.bupa-intl.com/home/index.asp

If you have difficulty in obtaining any of the **medical products** mentioned above, try contacting:

♦ **Medical Advisory Service for Travellers Abroad**, www.masta.org

♦ **Farnham Castle International Briefing and Conference Centre,** www.farnhamcastle.com

Expatriate health insurance

In March 2004, *TimesTwo* – a supplement of the *Insurance Times* in the UK – carried an article on expatriate healthcare which included the following **health insurance brokers** and **providers**.

Specialist brokers

♦ **Medibroker Online**, www.medibroker.co.uk

♦ **PMI Health Group**, www.pmi.uk.net

International brokers
- **Aon**, www.aon.com
- **Marsh**, www.marsh.com

Providers
- **Allianz Worldwide Care**, www.allianzworldwidecare. com
- **Goodhealth Worldwide**, www.goodhealthworldwide. com
- **InterGlobal**, www.interglobalpmi.com
- **International Health Insurance** (IHI) **Danmark**, www. ihi.com
- **International Medical Group** (IMG), www.imglobal. com
- **MediCare**, www.medicare.co.uk
- **William Russell**, www.william-russell.com

Who pays?

Many **employers** pay for all their expatriates' **medical expenses**, for the following reasons.

1 You and your family are in China at their behest, where:
    - **local healthcare** leaves much to be desired by Western standards;
    - **internationally acceptable practices** are still at a premium.

2 It is in their best interests to protect their not inconsiderable investment in your posting by keeping you and your family healthy, otherwise:
    - **your performance** will decline
    - **their business** may suffer.

However, for some expatriates and their employers – especially the younger and/or less experienced ones – long-term health issues may unintentionally but understandably be ousted by such short-term concerns as settling into a new job and country, and finding a new home and school.

Thus if your employer is quiet on this subject, try using these arguments to persuade them to follow suit before you finally commit yourself and family to China.

(6)

Accommodation

For many years, Chinese government policy has been to **segregate foreigners** from the local population, and make them live in specially designated and segregated (i.e. walled-in or fenced-off) properties (e.g. **foreign housing complexes**) and 'pay through the nose'. Indeed, so rigid was such **segregation** that it also applied to the **Chinese wives of expatriates** who – rather than being allowed to house their Western husbands in their local accommodation – were obliged to relocate with them to foreign-designated properties and bring up their **mixed-race** children in a predominantly non-Chinese environment.

The reason has been:

◆ *Officially:* to prevent the local population from being 'contaminated' by the '**interlopers**', by quarantining the latter behind a miniature version of the Great Wall.

◆ *Unofficially:* to keep a close eye on the **aliens** in their midst. As mentioned in Chapter 2, one of the less pleasant aspects of a dictatorship is the **Big Brother** syndrome. Thus, for example, it is said of China that security guards in foreign housing compounds are the eyes and ears of the PSB.

EXAMPLE

In the late 1990s, whilst living in Beijing (Dragon Villas), the **security guard** assigned to our cul-de-sac of some half-a-dozen houses appeared to note down our movements each time we left home.

And who could blame them, after the way that the West treated the Chinese as foreigners in their own country after the **Opium Wars** under the terms of the **Unequal Treaties**? (As mentioned in Chapter 2.)

Thus, for many Westerners – even those 'with Chinese faces' – living a Chinese life-style in a **dream cottage** in the country or **period house** in the city might have remained just that ... a dream.

Now, however, the law is being gradually repealed, so that **expatriates** will be able to:

◆ not only live in
◆ but also rent or purchase

local housing on the same terms as the Chinese – at the time of writing in **Shanghai** and **Beijing** (since 2001 and 2002, respectively).

Caveat
Nevertheless, **foreign lettings** must still be **registered** with the PSB; and you should ensure that your **lease** is so registered. Otherwise tenants whose landlord refuses to register them (which is not uncommon, either through ignorance or distrust of the law) may be summarily **evicted** by the municipal authority if discovered during one of its periodic inspections.

OPTIONS

Expatriates may choose from a wide range of:

+ **hotels**;
+ **aparthotels** – serviced apartments in an hotel;
+ **apartments** – or flats, whether serviced or not;
+ **houses** – whether detached or linked (i.e. terraced, semi or link-detached), with small gardens.

Occasionally, Chinese **courtyard housing** may be available – such as that rented out by the PICC in North-West Beijing or individual government officials in the city-centre, which we viewed in the late 1990s.

Design and decoration

Western **designs** abound, including European and Spanish villas, Californian houses and neo-Georgian mansions; all built to **western standards** using **imported materials** (e.g. hard-wood floors, Italian tiles and German air-conditioning) although, in some cases, what constitutes 'western' is imaginary rather than real! (See Figures 3 and 4.)

As mentioned in Chapter 9 in the context of clothing, the Chinese have a very different sense of **colour** from the West, and **architecture** is no exception. Personally, I find that the vista of urban China is enhanced by its gamut of **coloured building materials**; but you may not relish yellow bricks and pink pebbledash (in which our houses were clad – severally, and not in combination!).

Rent or purchase?

From experience, it is probably **better to rent** than purchase, because of the:

Examples

Fig. 3. Our first house at Dragon Villas, Beijing.

Fig. 4. Our second house at Greenland Gardens, Beijing. Note the
high-rise security camera to the right of the house.

1   **Superficial build quality** of unscrupulous developers.

2   **Poor maintenance** of unskilled or unsupervised trades-men.

3   **Restrictions** that may or do apply to **foreigners** who **purchase** property, including:
    (a) **Which foreigners** (e.g. overseas Chinese or Hong Kong residents).
    (b) **What type of property** (e.g. detached).
    (c) The **state ownership of all land**, by virtue of which all property is **leasehold only** and reverts to the state after 75 years.

True: **purchasing** should automatically confer a **permanent residence visa** – but only in theory and not necessarily in practice, given China's fluid **legal system** (as mentioned in Chapter 2).

New or old?
From experience, it is probably **better to choose new property** – even though, as mentioned above, standards of construction and finishing may be only superficially acceptable – since **older property** may:

◆ not only have **sub-standard public utility** supplies and installations (i.e. heating, electricity, water, plumbing and gas);
◆ but also need **constant repair**.

Indeed, given that most engineering effort appears to be channelled into building rather than maintenance, the secret is not to stay around long enough to watch property decay!

EXAMPLES

Both the brand-new houses where we lived, of which we were the first occupants, suffered in the **rain**:

1   At one the **rain** stripped the paint on the front door; and the dog that on the lamppost.

2   At the other **rain** running off the balcony stained the brickwork below.

One explanation for this **dereliction of older property** seems to be that the Chinese who can afford it 'want to buy new and specify their own fixtures and fittings. No one in China would want to live in the old houses in London – in China they would be museums. Even housing built before 1990 is considered too old, and will be pulled down...' (*China-Britain Trade Review*, Mar-04, p. 7).

Furnished or unfurnished?

Except for hotels and serviced apartments, **rented property** tends to fall into one of the following three categories:

1   **Unfurnished**.

2   **Hard-furnished** – and should include all:
   (a) Main **white goods** (e.g. cooker, fridge, dishwasher, washing machine, tumble dryer).
   (b) Major items of large **furniture** (e.g. lounge, dining and bedroom suites), which may be imported, and of colonial or Mediterranean style.
   (c) **Curtains**, fitted **carpets** and **light fittings**.
   (d) **Television** (linked to the complex's receiver, supplying international foreign language programmes).

3 **Furnished** – and should also include:
 (a) Microwave, vacuum cleaner and iron.
 (b) Cooking utensils, crockery, glassware, and cutlery.
 (c) Possibly table linen, bedding and lamps.
 (d) Some occasional furniture.
 but probably not floor rugs, towelling or bed linen.

Whichever option you choose, most purpose-built accommodation for foreigners should have:

 ♦ **central heating**;
 ♦ **air-conditioning**;
 ♦ two **telephone lines**: one for **voice**, and the other for **fax/data**;
 ♦ connections to the complex's **television receiver**.

City centre or suburb?

In choosing whether to live in the **city centre** or the **suburbs**, I suggest that the main considerations for and against each include the following.

Location	City centre	Suburbs
For	Convenience (i.e. proximity to work and school)	Quality of life (e.g. fresh air and green spaces)
	. Amenities	Cheaper
Against	Noise	Travel time and traffic congestion
	Pollution	Isolation
	Expensive	Lack of amenities

We first lived at Dragon Villas on the **outskirts of Beijing,** a car journey of initially 45 minutes – that became an hour within six months, even with a driver who could rival the Schumachers – from the city-centre along a freeway dubbed '**death alley**' by the expatriate community, on account of the virtually **daily fatal accidents**, the evidence of which was not always scraped off the road until some time later.

Eventually we moved to Greenland Garden in the **suburbs**, some 30 minutes closer, for the following six reasons:

1   Despite our previous experience of traffic accident victims being displayed at the side of the road in Colombia (South America), the regular **sight of mangled bodies** was too much to stomach, and we moved into the city.

2   Although:
    (a) we had sole and unlimited use of a company car and personal driver 24 hours a day, seven days a week;
    (b) our working hours tended to be such that we could both be driven to and forth quite separately and independently;
    there were inevitably times when one of us had to:
    (c) **readjust our movements** to suit the other;
    (d) **use third-party transport**.
    For example – when our teenage son returned to China from the UK during the school holidays.

3   Apart from begging a lift from a friend, until the management of Dragon Villas introduced a taxi service, the only other means of transport was their fleet of **shuttle-buses** – a ride on which was a death-defying experience not for the faint-hearted (as mentioned in Chapter 3).

4   Although the drive to work afforded **quality quiet time** (for example to think, read and write reports and prepare for the day ahead), and the journey home: was an opportunity to **unwind** and **sleep**, the enjoyment of and enthusiasm for **social activities** (such as evening banquets, weekend shopping and church attendance) could be dampened by a further two hours dead time travelling.

5   By the same token, friends and colleagues (especially those who lived on the other side of Beijing or did not have their own transport) might similarly baulk at the journey.

6   Being so far outside Beijing, and in an area mainly restricted to foreigners, some personal and most **taxi-drivers** did not know where it was.

For us, as **dog-lovers**, the main down-side of the move was the legal restriction imposed on our dog outside the complex (as described in Chapter 8) after the relative freedom previously enjoyed in the countryside.

AMENITIES AND FACILITIES

From experience, **purpose-built accommodation** for **foreigners** often includes:

♦   master bedroom with en-suite bathroom (with two hand-basins, shower cubicle and bath or – as in our first house – jacuzzi);

♦   family and guest bedrooms and bathroom(s);

♦   lounge, dining room and cloakroom;

♦   family room and study (usually a converted bedroom);

- kitchen, utility room, and maid's quarters (bed-sitting room with toilet and shower);
- garage, balcony and storage area (attic or basement).

Status or face

The **status** (i.e. type, location, size, furnishing, etc) of your accommodation may be interpreted by others (Chinese and foreigners alike) as an indication of not only your **own worth** to your employer but also your **employer's worth** as a business.

In other words just as you are an 'ambassador' for your employer so is your accommodation its 'residence' or public 'face'.

Thus, for the sake of **face** – so important to and beloved of the Chinese (as mentioned in Chapter 2) – I recommend that your accommodation should:

1   **Correctly reflect** your:
    (a) **Personal worth** to your employer.
    (b) **Employer's worth** as a business.

2   **Bear favourable relation** to the accommodation provided by other comparable employers (e.g. neither significantly larger or smaller nor more or less ornate than theirs).

EXAMPLE

I had to submit to my international head office details of accommodation provided by other major Western companies in the same line of business for my opposite numbers.

Even if you are not status conscious, your Chinese employees certainly will be; and expect you, as the boss or *laoban* (as mentioned in Chapter 2), to live in accommodation of such splendour that they can bask in its **reflected glory** and take pride in (if not show off about) working for an obviously so successful foreign employer.

EXAMPLES

This **reflected glory** explains why:

1 Some Chinese colleagues, when I was house-hunting, appeared more interested in the **corporate status** rather than the **personal suitability** of some properties (such as living in the same apartment block as Deng Xiaoping's daughter)

2 My driver and PA seemed only too happy to help us shop for furniture and household goods that they could never have afforded 'in a month of Sundays'.

Security

For recommendations regarding **home security**, see Chapter 3.

Other 'unwelcome visitors' include **winged insects**, best deterred by fitting **fly-screens** and other methods described in Chapter 4.

Facilities and amenities

Foreign complexes and apartment-blocks often claim to include:

1 **Shops** such as:
   (a) Western supermarket;
   (b) clothes boutique, laundry and dry-cleaning;
   (c) hair, beauty and massage salons;

(d) newsagent and book-shop;

(e) bank and post office;

(f) gift shops, and arts and crafts centres.

2 **Eateries** and **watering holes** such as:

(a) restaurants, both Chinese and Western;

(b) cafes, tea houses and bakeries;

(c) bars.

3 **Child-minding** facilities such as a crèche.

4 **Clubhouse** or **recreational facilities** such as:

(a) gym and aerobics studio;

(b) tennis and squash courts;

(c) sauna, jacuzzi and swimming pools;

(d) table tennis, snooker, billiards and pool tables;

(e) ten-pin bowling alley;

(f) electronic games arcade;

(g) mah-jong, bridge and chess rooms;

(h) children's play area.

The use of these – and especially the last – may be:

- either automatically included in the rental;
- or optionally and additionally payable.

Additionally:

5 Mention has already been made (above and elsewhere) of the **shuttle-buses**, some of whose drivers are the worst in the world: you have been warned!

6 The property management normally has a small army of **tradesmen** and **gardeners** of indifferent ability at its disposal: thus, do not be surprised if your lawn is cut by a platoon of 'coolies' using hand-shears!

Moreover:

7 Preparations for the **2008 Olympics** in Beijing are spawning bigger and better property projects, serviced by improved general urban and specific transport infrastructure.

8 The relaxation of China's regulatory regime following her entry to the **WTO** has stimulated Foreign Direct Investment (FDI) in so many new residential building projects to such an extent that they will need to provide an ever-increasing range of facilities and services to outdo the competition and survive.

Utilities and services

From personal experience, I recommend that you:

1 Ensure that all **utilities** and **services** are connected and working before, and as a condition of, moving in. There is less urgency for the property company to complete once the residents are installed.

2 In particular, check that the **mains gas** and **water** pressures are sufficient to meet **peak demand**. (For example: on Sundays or at Christmas, and in the summer, respectively.)

3 Take note that **electric plugs** and **sockets** are of varying quality, shapes and sizes (but normally 5-amp 2-pin flat) for which reason:
   (a) Use only the most expensive **plugs**, **sockets**, **adaptors** and **wiring** as also being the safest. (The supply is 220 volts, 50 cycles AC.)
   (b) Stock up on locally-available **adaptors**.

4 Do not drink the **tap water** – rather...

    (a) Arrange (normally via your property management) regular deliveries of carboys of **drinking water** – for the ease of use of which...

    (b) Purchase a freestanding hot-and-cold **water dispenser** to connect to the carboys.

Helpful hint

If your house or apartment has **wooden floors**, to protect them:

    (a) Insist that everyone enters via the **hall**.

    (b) Provide an assortment of 'flip-flop' **slippers** in different sizes for them to change into.

COSTS

The following **costs** are based on the most recent publicly available information from the sources quoted at the time of writing.

Updated figures will be available from Minim Consulting at www.minim.biz

Rentals

Rentals tend to be for a minimum **period** of 12 months, renewable annually, whilst:

♦ **short-term tenancies** may be available at a premium;

♦ **long-term tenancies** should provide for earlier termination.

A **security deposit** is required, normally equal to three months' rent (but may be less for unfurnished accommodation).

Rent is normally:

- **non-negotiable**, though extras may be (e.g. club membership);
- **payable in advance**, monthly or quarterly, usually in US$.

Unfurnished accommodation may be cheaper than **furnished**, but not necessarily; and **suburban** rents than in the **city**.

Despite the changes in the law (mentioned above) and greater choice and quality of accommodation, **expatriate executives** may still be expected to pay **exorbitant rents** for the following three reasons:

1 They constitute a **captive market of wealthy clients** (see next point) chasing a finite supply of good quality Western-style accommodation although supply is now catching up with demand.

2 They are perceived as being **sufficiently affluent to afford high rents** particularly those whose accommodation costs are known or assumed to be borne by their employer.

3 Real estate in Beijing and Shanghai is amongst the most expensive in the world although prices are gradually falling, as supply catches up with demand and in the wake of the Asian crisis.

By way of illustration: according to Colliers International (*Quarterly Research Report – Greater China – Residential Market*, Apr 2004, pp. 4–5), the average **rentals for luxury**

residential properties (as defined) per square metre [m^2] per month during 2004 are forecast to be:

Location	US$ per m^2/month	Definition
Beijing	19.78	High quality apartments in prime locations with good management
Shanghai	23.12	Serviced apartments in prime locations with modern comprehensive facilities
Guangzhou	19.30	High quality serviced apartments of 1,000 square feet or more in a prestigious location with good management
Shenzhen	12.30	High quality serviced apartments of 1,000 square feet or more in a prestigious location with good management in the Shenzhen Economic Zone (SEZ)

Purchase

By way of illustration:

1   *Beijing*

    (a) 'Since the foreign and domestic housing markets merged' (in 2002) 'all properties have become available to individuals and organisations from overseas. This change in policy provides a wider range of options to potential home buyers and investors who are holding non-PRC passports' (*Residential Briefing – Beijing*, FPD Savills, 15 Jan 2003, p.7).

    (b) During the last quarter of 2003 (*ibid*, 22 Mar 04, p. 2), the average **sale price** per m^2 for Grade 'A' properties (apartments and villas) was in the range US$ 2,000/US$ 2,1000.

2   *Shanghai*
    (a) In mid-2003, the average **sale price** per m² was RMB 5,485 as compared with RMB 4,626 per m² 12 months earlier.
    (b) This increase (of nearly 20%) was primarily due to the fast growth in the luxury residential sector, especially in properties valued at over RMB 5,000 per m² with those over RMB 7,000 per m² almost doubling their share of the market in the same period (*Residential Briefing – Shanghai,* FPD Savills, 18 Dec 2003, p.3).

3   *Guangzhou*
    (a) In 2002 'Although developers continued to focus on quality, brand and enhancement of management to differentiate themselves from competitors, price competition remained intensive. Discounts on prices and rebates were common.
    (b) For example, the average selling prices of standard units in xxx were reduced to RMB 9,500 from over RMB 10,000 per square metre. Other developers also offered furnishing rebates up to 5–10% of the selling prices' (*Greater China Property Index*, Jones Lang LaSalle, Jan 2003, p.16)

Beijing property bubble

Despite the strong and rapid growth in the **Beijing property market** (stimulated by the successful bid for the **2008 Olympics** and China's entry to the **WTO**, mentioned above), 'a **price** and **construction bubble** is not likely to appear in the foreseeable future', according to Jones Lang LaSalle (*Beijing Economic Insight*, 17 Mar 2003) as follows:

1   'In general, a **bubble** forms when the level of price or construction is deemed to be unsustainable with respect to the affordability of the end users, or the overall market demand.'

2   '**Prices** (and to an extent **rents**) in...the luxury residential' sector 'have been steady over the last two years. Relative to the improvement in income and corporate profitability, affordability of property should have improved. A **price bubble** is not currently recognisable in the luxury...residential sector.'

3   '**Supply** of luxury residential' property 'will be high in the forthcoming years compared to previous years.'

4   However, **demand** is expected 'to expand on the back of WTO-related relaxation of the regulatory regime. Increasingly foreign companies are eyeing the domestic market in addition to utilising China's low cost resources to serve the global market.'

5   Assuming that demand remains as strong as predicted, 'then the scope for a construction bubble will remain limited.'

6   Moreover, 'seemingly aware of the potential risks, the **government** is implementing measures to slow down the development of the luxury residential market' (not only in Beijing but also **Shanghai**).

Utilities and service charges

Utilities (i.e. electricity, gas, water, telephone) and **service charges** (e.g. management, cleaning, gardening, waste disposal, use of communal facilities, club membership, etc) are usually:

1 **Additional** to, and not included in, the rental.
2 Payable in RMB or US$.

From figures published by FPD Savills, **utility costs** in Beijing during the 1st quarter of 2002 averaged:

Electricity	Gas	Cold water	Hot water	Heating
RMB 0.75	RMB 2.30	RMB 2.50	RMB 7.35	RMB 6.70
per kwh	per m^3	per ton	per ton	per m^2

HOUSEHOLD GOODS

In order to **import household goods** from your home country, you will need a **residence permit**.

For reasons outside the scope of this book, we never obtained such a permit and, hence, have no direct experience of importing household goods. However, from many expatriates who did, I understand that the process differs little from what we experienced elsewhere in the world, including into the UK; and can be summarised in two words: 'straightforward' and 'bureaucratic'.

What to take with you to China

Not being able to import goods from home was only a minor inconvenience because as mentioned below there was really no need to take anything, apart from personal possessions, since, contrary to many foreigners' perceptions (as mentioned in the Introduction), China is fast becoming a modern country with a thriving consumer economy ('**market economy with Chinese characteristics**') in response to demand by '**Chuppies**' and '**dinky**' couples for Western fashions (as mentioned in Chapter 2).

Consequently, most **everyday items** (both imported and locally manufactured) are readily available in China's **modern urban department stores** (see Figure 5) and **shopping malls**, from a wide range of qualities and prices to suit all tastes and pockets.

Examples

Fig. 5. Inside Number One Department Store, Shanghai, February 2003. Notice the international trademarks of (from left to right): Lancôme, Levis, Adidas and Jack Jones.

Thus, apart from **clothes** and other **personal items** such as anyone would pack for holiday, we only *needed* to take with us small items that were:

1 **Personal** – such as: photographs, ornaments, books and hobbies.

2 **Difficult** or **impossible to obtain locally** – such as: a cheese knife, ice-cream scoop, tea strainer, picture hooks and cranberry sauce.

3 **Available locally** but of **poor quality** – such as: a potato peeler, cutlery and barbecue utensils.

(For a full list, see Appendix 6.)

Fortunately, between business trips and visits by and to our several sons (for school holidays, a wedding and the births of two grandchildren), we were able to transport all such items quite quickly and easily on the airplane; and only once had to pay for excess baggage.

Subsequently (from observation during our visit to Shanghai in early 2003), the local availability and/or quality of some of those items has much improved, particularly kitchen and tableware (e.g. cutlery).

Furniture

As intimated above, **unfurnished accommodation** can be fully kitted out locally, and not just at the main Department Stores. Thus, there is really no need to take anything from the home country, apart from personal possessions. (See Figure 6.)

For the patient bargain-hunter and seasoned haggler, good-quality **antique Chinese furniture** – both **genuine** and **reproduction** – is readily available at acceptable prices, and makes excellent souvenirs back home at the end of the posting (subject to export restrictions, as explained below).

The main alternatives tend to fall into the following three categories, according to origin, quality, style, taste and price.

1 **Imported** or **locally-made tasteful** but **expensive copies** of **colonial furniture**, suitably and thankfully some-

times optionally 'aged' or 'distressed'.

♦ For example: in '**public**' areas used for **formal entertaining** such as the lounge and dining room.

2 **Locally-made plush**, ornate, even gaudy **new** furniture of **varying quality** and **price**, in an attempt to **emulate Western taste.**

♦ For example: in '**semi-public**' or '**semi-private**' areas used for entertaining **friends** and by members of the **household** only such as as the family room, study or den, and guest suite.

3 **Locally-made inexpensive** and **simple** yet **attractive**, acceptable and some even hard-wearing **modern Chinese** furniture.

♦ For example: in '**non-public**' or '**private**' areas reserved for **family** use only such as your bedroom, the children's play and bedrooms, and maid's quarters.

Example

Fig. 6. Inside our **hard-furnished** house at Dragon Villas, Beijing.

Whichever option you choose, I recommend from personal experience that you:

- Ensure that the **drawers** work in locally-made modern furniture; and expect them not to in genuine antiques.
- Cut off the tassels and other **embellishments** from locally-made soft furnishings.
- Pay extra for reproduction colonial furniture **not** to be **distressed**.
- Remember that 'all is not gold that glitters' (Latin proverb) and check that what appears to be solid wood is not **stained fibre-glass** which nevertheless makes very good and impressive study furniture, for example, but only at the right price!

An alternative source of reasonably-priced good-quality household goods and furniture are **departing expatriates**, who advertise in the various foreign-language magazines and/or on the notice boards in foreign housing complexes and/or supermarkets in Western-style hotels.

EXAMPLE

In 1998 to furnish our **unfurnished house** with a mixture of all the above, including antiques, we were given a budget of US$30,000 by my employer.

In other words 'you pays your money and you takes your choice'.

Helpful hint
The closest source of hard-to-get quality Western goods is Hong Kong; and expatriates taking local furlough there

seem to be fair game as 'personal shoppers' for all and sundry. Do not be surprised, therefore, if your friends present you with a shopping list when you announce you are visiting Hong Kong; nor, conversely, be afraid of asking them to return the favour!

Exporting antiques

Exporting household goods, on relocation and/or repatriation, differs little from elsewhere in the world, including from the UK; and is basically the reverse process of their importation.

Peculiar to China, however, are the procedures for **shipping home** any **antiques** that you have bought in China – when you should arrange for them to be inspected by the **Antiquities Bureau**, as follows.

1 (Ask a Chinese-speaking person to) contact the Bureau about four to six weeks before your removal date. (In Beijing, their telephone number is +86-10-6401-4608.)

2 **Before the inspection**, ensure that you have:
   (a) A **letter** from your employer, in Chinese, confirming the dates of your arrival in and departure from China.
   (b) Your **passport** or residence card.
   (c) The corresponding **receipts**. (While not necessary, a low value may persuade the inspector that an item is too cheap to be a prohibited item).
   (d) RMB **cash** for the inspection and certification fees.

3 Arrange (for your driver) to:
   (a) **Bring** the inspector to your home.

(b) **Hand over** the letter from your employer.

(c) Afterwards **return** him/her to the Bureau.

4 The inspector will:

(a) **Allow** you to export only those items that (s)he deems no more than 150 years old.

(b) **Mark** such items with a red wax seal.

(c) **Note** them on a **Bureau of Antiquities Export Permit** (pictured in Figure 7).

5 Unless you can persuade the inspector otherwise, (s)he will *not* allow you to export items deemed **older than 150 years**, also noting them on the same Export Permit.

6 A **fee** is payable for the inspection (I paid RMB 150) plus a variable amount between RMB 5 and RMB 40 (approximately) per red wax seal.

7 You should retain the **Export Permit** for **customs clearance** purposes.

Moving notice and name cards

In China, a **change of address card** is usually called a '**moving notice**'; and, when appropriately designed, can also serve as a **personal name card**.

For example: ours (see Figure 8) was:

◆ Made of card.

◆ The size of a compliments slip, so that it fitted easily into a standard business envelope.

◆ Divided by a vertical perforation into two unequal portions (approximately 75% and 25%) the larger

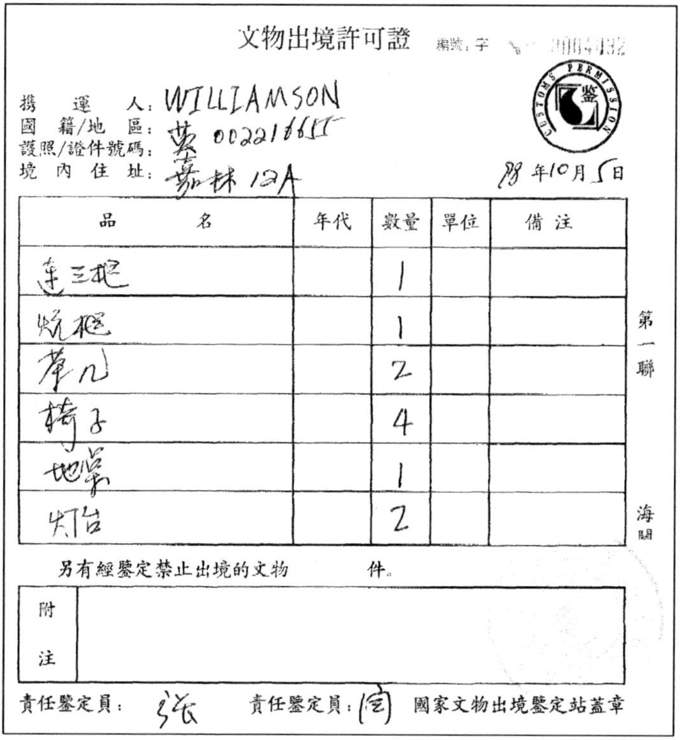

文物出境許可證 編號：字

攜運人：WILLIAMSON
國籍/地區：英
護照/證件號碼：002216655
境內住址：荔林 12A

98年10月5日

品名	年代	數量	單位	備注
连三柜		1		
炕柜		1		
茶几		2		
椅子		4		
地桌		1		
灯台		2		

第一聯　海關

另有經鑒定禁止出境的文物　件。

附注

責任鑒定員：张　責任鑒定員：信　國家文物出境鑒定站蓋章

Fig.7. Bureau of Antiquities Export Permit.

serving as the notice *per se*; the smaller as a (detachable) name card.

- Printed on both sides: one in English, the other in Chinese.
- Illustrated on the back of the name card portion with a sketch map, in English and Chinese, of where we lived.

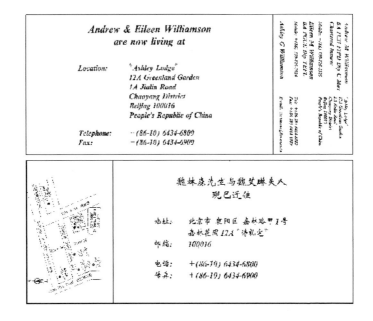

Fig. 8. Our moving notice and personal name card (front and back).

The purpose of such an arrangement is threefold – namely to:

1 Notify Chinese and non-Chinese speakers of your **new address**.

2 Provide both with directions for **personal** and **taxi-drivers**, who may not be familiar with areas primarily inhabited by foreigners.

3 Allow non-Chinese correspondents to stick a photocopy of the Chinese version as an **address label** on their mail to you, which the local postal workers can read.

Should you move without knowing your new permanent address (e.g. when you arrive in China, or move from one city to another, or return home), distribute cards with at least your **mobile phone number** and **e-mail address**.

Fig. 9. Our personal name card (for our visit to Shanghai in February 2003, staying in an hotel).

Musical note

In the late 1990s, my wife:

◆ Was unable to rent or purchase a decent **upright piano** at a reasonable price (approximately US$500 per month or many thousand US$, respectively).

◆ Did find a locally-manufactured full-size good-quality **electronic keyboard** (RMB 3,200, equivalent then to some £250 or US$400).

HELP!

To make sense of all the options and reach the optimum decision, it is advisable to:

1   Retain the services of a **property consultant** (normally for a fee of one month's rent) and **removal company** some of whom also offer **relocation services**, such as country briefing, cultural orientation and a local induction programme.

2   Talk to **other expatriates**, especially about the service level of the estate management.

3   Consult **Chinese colleagues**, particularly concerning the local infrastructure.

Below, I list the companies of which I have personal experience; and give their Beijing contact details, from where you can obtain specific local information.

Property consultants

Colliers International
1606 Capital Mansion
6 Xin Yuan Nan Road
Chaoyang District
Beijing 100004
Tel: + 86-10-8486-3099
Fax: + 86-10-8486-3789 V
E-Mail: Amanda.Goa@colliers.com
Web: www.colliers.com/Markets/China

FPD Savills
415 East Wing
China World Trade Centre
1 Jianguomenwai Dajie
Beijing 100004
Tel: + 86-10-6505-2351

Fax: +86-10-6505-2356
E-mail: mpurefoy@fpdsavills-bj.com
Web: www.fpdsavills-china.com

Jones Lang LaSalle
Room 408
4th Floor West Wing
China World Trade Centre
1 Jianguomenwai Dajie
Beijing 100004
Tel: +86-10-6505-1300
Fax: +86-10-6505-8133
E-Mail: caroline.moulin@ap.joneslanglasalle.com
Web: www.joneslanglasalle.com.cn

Removal companies
Crown Worldwide
Room 201
West Tower
Golden Bridge Building
A 1 Jianguomenwai Dajie
Beijing 100020
Tel: +86-10-6585-0640
Fax: +86-10-6585-0648
E-Mail: beijing@crownrelo.com
Web: www.crownworldwide.com

Domestic Staff

MAIDS

In China, every time something went missing in our house, the cry would go up: 'the *ayi* has lost so-and-so' – *ayi* being the Chinese word for 'auntie' used to address a maid. Not even for a split-second did we think that we had mislaid whatever we could not find. On such occasions, however, we were invariably right, since the *ayi* soon got into the routine of putting things away where they were more convenient for her, particularly in the kitchen. It probably never occurred to her that we would need, let alone know how to use, a particular piece of kitchen equipment.

This was because she:

♦ Not only thought that it was *infra dig* for **foreigners** to do any domestic work, which was her prerogative. (Once, she was horrified to find me washing up!)
♦ But also believed that all **foreigners** were stupid because, unlike her, they could not speak Chinese.

To overcome this last problem, we used **flash cards** – prepared by my personal assistant – with such useful phrases in Chinese (and English, so that we knew which was which) as 'please clean the windows today' or 'do the ironing tomorrow'.

Recruiting and training maids

Honesty before ability
Some items that the maid mislaid we never found. Did we really lose them or did she take them?

We do not know, but have our suspicions. If we had to choose between an honest and a capable maid, we would always choose the former. All maids start well, but soon deteriorate or lapse into bad ways. An honest maid, however, remains so.

It is just a pity that, in our experience, it is difficult to find an *ayi* who combines **ability** and **honesty**.

Sadly some maids have neither ability nor honesty, and they are best dismissed at once.

EXAMPLES

1 Our first 'chacha' (maid) in Franquist Barcelona in 1971:
   (a) Not only tried to remove the white flecks from the black marble bathroom floor with wire wool, thinking they were paint spots.
   (b) But also siphoned off our baby's cologne and refilled the bottles with water.
2 Worse still was the **security guard** who stole our things in Colombia in 1974, whilst being paid to protect us!

Training maids from scratch
Thus, thinking back over all the maids we have had in China and elsewhere after that first one in Spain, it was for their **honesty rather than ability** that we put up with them.

The only one who truly combined both was Pepa, who came to live with us in Barcelona in 1972 straight from school. At 16 she had not had time to develop bad habits – not in Franco's era – and so the only ways she knew were what she learned from us.

That experience taught us that **training maids from scratch** is by far the best way to guarantee mutual satisfaction for both parties, since she:

- does things your way;
- learns a trade.

It does not always work, however, as we found when we had to dismiss one maid very quickly in Colombia because she would and could not learn to flush her toilet. To be fair: it was not her fault since she had left the Amazon Jungle only two weeks earlier, and undergone an intensive induction at the hands of her urbanised aunt, a **maid broker**.

That experience taught us that **you should not trust recommendations by relatives** or **maid brokers**.

Choosing a maid
So how should you:

- First **choose** a good maid?
- Then **retain** her?

1   **Recommendation by a previous employer,** although essential, is not fool-proof since different mistresses have different standards, needs, rules, routines, backgrounds, etc including those who are:

- Out all day and/or always socialising in the evenings.
- Incapable of lifting a finger and/or stringing two words together of the local language.

2 When selecting a maid, therefore, it pays also to obtain **references on previous employers** especially any about to leave the country, for whom giving a glowing reference to a bad maid will have no backlash.

3 An **interview** is also essential; but again (irrespective of the prospective employer's interview ability) this is fraught with problems for the mistress who does not command the local language and/or understand the local culture.

4 To overcome this obstacle, I recommend using a **Chinese intermediary** (such as a colleague, friend, or other employee) who:
- speaks your language;
- is acceptable to both parties.

This practice is very common in China and should, therefore, not offend the interviewee (as mentioned in Chapter 2).

EXAMPLE

We always asked my Chinese bilingual PA to be present during interviews.

If ever we had problems later with the *ayi*, this practice had the added bonus that my PA was able to say to the maid something along the lines of: 'You remember that, at interview, we or you said or asked so-and-so? Well, things are not working out like that; so what we need to do to correct the situation is...etc.' That, at any rate, was the gist of what she said!

In the process, we also sadly discovered that one sure-fire way to motivate the *ayi* was to read her the riot act every so often. The home fax machine came in very useful here: my wife would ring my PA and explain the situation; and then my PA would speak to or fax back instructions in Chinese to the maid.

Probation

A period of **probation** of a few days at minimal wages is essential.

Although not long enough for the *ayi* to misbehave – since the prospect of full employment is probably sufficient motivation to guarantee good behaviour – a brief period of probation should give you ample opportunity to experience her cooking, ironing, cleaning, shopping and language ability.

State employment agencies

Maids should be employed through a state employment agency such as **FESCO** (Foreign Enterprise Service Company) which specialises in supplying Chinese workers of all types – professional and managerial as well as manual, and not just maids – to foreigners, since these are not allowed to employ Chinese people directly.

Thus, all employers should provide a **contract of employment** to FESCO, including for maids. Indeed, some branches of FESCO will provide a 'fill-in-the-blanks' pro-forma, stating duties and wages.

Domestic employment agencies

In recent years, as a result of rising **unemployment** (mentioned in Chapter 2) following the breaking of the **iron rice bowl** and reform of the **SOE**s, especially amongst **women** such as our office cleaner, mentioned below – a new generation of **professional domestic workers** and corresponding employment agencies has emerged, serving both Chinese and foreign households.

Before – during China's post-Imperial Communist iron rice bowl era – it might have been considered *infra dig* to render personal services. Today, however, the economic imperative and prospect of earning good money have allayed such qualms. In such ways has 'socialism with **Chinese characteristics**' evolved into a '**market economy with Chinese characteristics**'.

Managing maids

Discipline and dismissal

Some employers **fine** their maids for **poor performance**, but we never did: punishment may make the employer feel better, but it only tends to hide rather than improve poor performance.

Rather, since maids in China are two a penny, there is little point in tolerating a poor *ayi* who can be replaced immediately.

Thus, three words of advice:

1 **Dismiss** an incompetent and/or dishonest *ayi* instantly and without warning.

2 **See her off the premises** immediately, ensuring that she:

(a) Returns **your keys** and any other means of gaining access to your home (such as foreign housing complex identity card).

(b) Takes none of **your possessions** since she will probably think that you have too many things – by her standards – and may not be adverse to relieving you of some of them, either immediately or sometime later!

3 Use a **Chinese intermediary**, in the same way and for the same reasons as during an interview.

EXAMPLE

On the several occasions that we had to dismiss a maid, we would arrange for my Chinese PA suddenly to appear at home and, with my wife present, not only ask her to pack her bags but also check them before she left.

In the past era of the **iron rice-bowl**, such draconian measures might have offended Maoist sensibilities by denying a comrade the opportunity to reform and work. However, from my experience of asking local managers to deal with junior employees in similar manner, I believe that the new generation of Chinese employers are less sympathetic to and tolerant of **incompetent staff**.

EXAMPLE

Within only a couple of days of moving into new office premises and hiring a **cleaner**, a senior middle-aged Chinese colleague came to me with a 'sob story' of how the cleaner – who, with umpteen degrees after her name, had been made redundant from an SOE – could not work the shift pattern we wanted and had asked to change them. My reasoned response of 'change the cleaner' first surprised, but then made sense to, my colleague.

Supervision

Having referred several times above and elsewhere to my Chinese PA, it is probably worth clarifying here that her duties included acting as the maid's supervisor – a practice that saved face in difficult situations and we would thoroughly recommend.

Maids' duties

As to an *ayi's* duties: that is down to her employers' needs

---

EXAMPLES

1 As young parents in Spain and Colombia, we appreciated help with the **children** and **cooking**.
2 Twenty-five years later in China, we were looking for someone to **clean**, **wash**, **shop** and **walk the dog**, but not cook nor child-mind.

Child-minding and baby-sitting

Many parents rely on their *ayis* to look after the **children**, which is fine as long as the *ayi* really is capable. It also does wonders for the children's spoken Chinese.

EXAMPLE

As young parents in Spain and South America, with local friends in similar circumstances, we much enjoyed the social freedom that a ready-made child-minder/baby-sitter afforded, who also contributed to their natural acquisition of Spanish.

However, two words of warning.

1   Remember the Philippine maid in Hong Kong who, when asked by the parents to wash the baby, put it into the washing machine with fatal results. Not to mention the stories of **negligent nannies** elsewhere in the world that fill the newspapers from time to time.

2   From personal experience: **beware of young children who treat maids as their personal servants**, especially in countries (e.g. Colombia) where maids address children as 'you' and 'little master/mistress' and are addressed as 'thou' and by name. Proper respect for maids should be shown at all times – after all, it is in their country that we are living.

Maids as cooks

If you have visions of coming home every night to a sumptuous and appetising Chinese banquet cooked by your maid you may be in for a big disappointment!

Some maids have very fixed ideas about, for example, what you like to eat – generally, an exact match with their culinary skills and/or their previous Western employer's preferences!

EXAMPLES

1   The maid whom we inherited from my predecessor in Bogotá just assumed that we liked the same food, because we were both English, and continued cooking accordingly – whereas he had previously served in the Far East and we in Spain!

2   At the end of her probation, we quickly disposed of one *chacha* in Barcelona in 1975, who at some stage had been cook to the city's mayor. Despite my then allergy to mussels, she insisted on making a sea-food paella for which my politeness in eating it later paid dearly.

At least, however, she could cook what might be called bourgeois food, whereas **some Chinese *ayis* are only capable of serving up peasant dishes that taste awful**.

There is a world of difference between Chinese food in the West – which tends to be American-sanitised Hong Kong cooking – and authentic mainland China cuisine. Indeed, it is said that the Chinese 'eat anything that flies, except aeroplanes; anything with four legs, except tables; and anything in the sea, except submarines' – but more about that elsewhere (Chapter 12).

That is not to say that there are not maids who are superb **cooks**. Quite the opposite: some of our friends have them, whose cooking we have much enjoyed. However, they tend to be the 'old retainers' of long-term expatriates and/ or overseas Chinese who have trained them properly over the years.

Meanwhile, be warned that what the *ayi* is brewing in the kitchen may be reminiscent of the three witches in the opening scene of Shakespeare's Scottish play!

Love me, love my pets
The family dog (if you have one) is a valuable judge of character when it comes to choosing an *ayi*, as explained in Chapter 8; and a good *ayi* can be an invaluable **dog-sitter** and **dog-walker**.

Our longest surviving maids (in China, Colombia and Spain) were those who got on with our pets and vice-versa taking them for walks and looking after them when we were away, sometimes overnight.

Terms and conditions of employment

Living in or out?

Which raises the question: should the maid live in or out? When the children were small, we had **live-in maids,** precisely because it was more convenient than a constant stream of baby-sitters in a foreign country. However, the price we paid was our **privacy,** until such time as the boys could speak Spanish and were old enough to entrust to strange **baby-sitters**.

Even though maids may have their own quarters and try to be discreet, there is always the danger of your wandering into the kitchen at four o'clock in the morning for a glass of water wearing little or nothing at all only to bump into the maid.

In China, therefore, our maids always **lived out,** but had their own day-room (with sofa-bed and shower cubicle). I hate to think what would have happened had they lived in – although some of our friends' *ayis* did – since:

1   Chinese people in general, let alone maids in particular, have **little sense of privacy or personal space,** due to their crowded up-bringing and alleged big brother regime (as mentioned in Chapter 2).

EXAMPLES

This lack of sense for privacy manifests itself in the most unexpected ways:

1   One maid was quite surprised and offended when she was asked to wait on a number of ladies at a coffee morning, rather than – as she hoped to do – sit down with them.

2 Another maid was prone to hanging around the bathroom when we were trying to use it.

2 It is also rumoured that, **when the mistress is away,** the master is fair game – a sort of role reversal from Europe two centuries ago!

A living-in maid can also pose problems **while the family is away**, by which I do not mean just using the master bedroom and en-suite bathroom.

EXAMPLES

Even during Franco's puritanical dictatorship, Spanish maids managed to smuggle **boyfriends** into their rooms over the weekend when the master and mistress were out.

1 On one such occasion after their return, the mistress – a friend of my best Spanish friend – detected a peculiar smell coming from the maid's room, which worsened day by day. When, the following weekend, the maid went out and the mistress was able to enter the room to investigate, she found the corpse of the maid's boyfriend under the bed! Having died in a paroxysm of passion, the maid was too frightened to tell anyone, and had just hidden his body!

2 On another occasion with a different maid, the reverse happened: she died and had to be taken to hospital, with the embarrassed boyfriend still attached, to be prised apart!

Wages

The vexed question, of course, is: how much to **pay** an *ayi*?

The simple answer is: the **average going rate** that your friends and neighbours are paying since, if you pay:

- *over the odds:* you will soon lose your friends as their maids demand a raise;
- *a mere pittance:* the maid will soon leave.

For be assured that **maids' wages** are no secret between them.

At the time of writing, according to one of our Chinese friends who has employed the same maid for many years in Beijing and Shanghai:

- 'the average wage for an average (live-in) maid in an expat home in Beijing and Guangzhou has risen to US$200/month;
- however, the wage in Shanghai is much lower, it is only US$150 now;
- I'm not quite sure about the reason for the difference, but I'm guessing that it is due to the proximity of a big labour pool for maids around Shanghai (high-end labour pools).'

Of course: **hours**, **duties** and **perks** such as food and lodging come into the equation, but pity does not. Less than US$150/US$200 per month for a 35-hour week on top of a two-hour journey each way may seem little by Western standards, but do not be tempted to double or treble it: some graduate managers in Chinese companies may not even earn that much.

Bonuses and gifts
On top of the monthly wage, maids expect to receive a **bonus** and/or **gift** (such as moon cakes) at the **Spring New Year Festival** and **Autumn Moon Festival**, but this should

be regarded as a reward for good work rather than their right. However, it can be very embarrassing to receive a Festival gift from a maid that has cost her more than hers cost you!

And, while on the subject of **gifts:** be prepared for her to give your children a present too, and have one ready for hers.

EXAMPLE

When our son returned to boarding school in the UK at the end of his first holiday in China, the maid gave him the traditional gift of a (plastic) gilded boat.

Other **perks** you may legitimately consider giving a maid might include:

- a bicycle;
- television;
- sewing lessons;
- literacy classes.

This last was particularly pertinent in Colombia where our maid could not write down telephone messages or read instructions in Spanish. However, in China be warned that, however good your *pinyin* (the romanised spelling for transliterating Chinese), maids – like the vast majority of the normal population – only know characters.

Dress code

It is also a good idea to provide **working clothes,** such as a housecoat, in order to:

- avoid the embarrassment of **perspiration**;
- cover up the inappropriately **immodest** summer-wear;
- in the case of the Chinese who have an unusual dress sense: hide the loud and by Western standards **clashing colours**.

For **formal entertaining** (in Spain), we found that a smart dark dress with a white starched apron and hat made the occasion extra special, and motivated the maid to be on her best behaviour.

Days-off and holidays

As to days-off and holidays: again, follow the **local norms**.

Ideally, you should arrange so that the maid is only away when you are – unless required to dog-sit – and otherwise working. Provided you take adequate security precautions (as recommended in Chapter 3) and your home is within a managed foreign housing complex, there should be no undue risk in leaving your home empty for a short time – unlike Bogotá, where we had to employ a full-time guard and relief-maid.

If in doubt, in this as in all aspects: *do ask the local people rather than the foreigners.*

Social security

The Chinese authorities will expect the:

- *employer:* to pay **social security** for the maid;
- *maid:* to make a small contribution.

Beware of those maids, therefore, who:

- try to persuade you that this is not necessary;
- do not pay their share.

In the case of expatriate employers living in accommodation designated for foreigners, it is very easy for the local government officials to:

- **visit** the property management and individual homes;
- **enquire** which maids are registered with the competent authority or not;
- **check** that they comply with the social security requirements;
- **sanction** those maids and employers who are in breach.

Taking liberties

The greatest **liberty** any of our *ayis* took, apart from using the phone – which is a hazard of employing any domestic staff – was:

- bringing in her husband's dirty clothes; and using our washing-machine and iron in our time to clean and press them.

Some friends in Brazil had a similar but worse experience that led to her dismissal, so perhaps this is an international custom?

Miscellaneous

Household security

When it comes to your personal security, I make no apology for summarising here advice given in Chapter 3.

1   The management of many foreigners' housing com-
    plexes will want the maid to register with them, as a
    safety and security precaution.

2   By the same token, therefore, on **her dismissal** or **your
    departure**, please remember to:
    (a) De-register the maid.
    (b) Recover her **identity pass** and **house key**.
    (c) Change the **burglar alarm code**, if appropriate.

Otherwise, you may be ripe for a burglary.

Forms of address

We and our Chinese maids always used **first names** to
address each other – a practice frowned upon by some of
our older and traditional Chinese friends, who preferred
the more formal forms of *ayi*, *taitai* (wife) and *xiansheng*
(mister).

All our maids already had **anglicised names**, so we were
spared the embarrassment of having to name them, like
slaves-owners of old.

Big brother

There is a remote risk that maids might be tempted to
report their employers to the authorities for what they
consider illegal or immoral activities. For this reason, I
recommend the Victorian code of behaviour: '**not in front
of the servants**'.

Bells

During our time in Franquist Spain, it was not unusual
for up-market apartments to be fitted with maids'

electric-bells, which we found particularly useful discretely to summon the *chacha* when entertaining (rather than having overtly to call out or pop into the kitchen).

In China, however, I am not aware of expatriate accommodation being so equipped; for which reason I suggest, for those special occasions, you consider using a small **hand-bell** (as we did in Colombia).

Post script
One last word of caution: all good things come to an end! Thus, on return to the home country, **husbands should not expect their wives to be surrogate maids!**

DRIVERS
Much of the foregoing in relation to maids applies 'as is' – but in context – to drivers, namely (in alphabetical order):

◆ bonuses and gifts;
◆ honesty before ability;
◆ love me, love my pets – especially when your dog is car-sick, as ours was!
◆ probation;
◆ social security;
◆ state employment agencies;
◆ supervision.

What follows, therefore, is additional or different.

Caveat
Although there are some excellent female drivers in China, I have assumed throughout the traditional practice

of employing a male driver.

Recruiting and managing drivers

Choosing a driver

Avoid drivers who have previously worked for Chinese bosses in general, and government officials in particular, because (as mentioned in Chapter 2) of the **status** and **authority** that some may have enjoyed through spending more time with *laoban* than anyone else – whether perceived (by themselves), ascribed (by colleagues) or real. They will try to continue behaving in similar fashion when working for you, and exercising the worst liberties.

EXAMPLE
With one such driver, I learnt the hard way, thinking naively that he would not behave in such a manner if I told him not to!

Discipline and dismissal

Ensure that, before leaving your service, the driver

♦ hands over **car**, **garage** and **office** – as well as house – **keys** and **ID cards**;

♦ leaves any **car documents** (such as log book, insurance, user manual).

♦ has settled all **outstanding traffic infractions** (mentioned below).

Traffic infractions

You need to decide who is going to pay your driver's traffic fines, and under what circumstances.

EXAMPLE

In our case: if in order to get me to my destination on time my driver exceeded the speed limit, or drove on the wrong side of the road or in the wrong direction to avoid traffic jams and, in the process, neither endangered me nor the car, then I was happy to pay any fines.

Drivers' duties

There are three types of driver:

Dedicated personal driver

This is the best arrangement, enjoyed by most top-ranking expatriates, whereby the driver – as well as the car – is solely at your and your family's disposal 24 hours a day, seven days a week. In other words, when you are not using the car and/or driver, your wife and/or family and/or even friends have prior claim over company staff or work, who have none at all.

Dedicated company driver

The next best arrangement, enjoyed by many middle-ranking expatriates, whereby the driver – as well as the car – is at your disposal whenever you want, and otherwise available for other company staff and duties. Only if there is no other call on the car and driver can your family use them without you, if at all.

Shared or pool company driver

By far the worst arrangement, endured by some expatriates of any rank, whereby you, your colleagues, and possibly wives either share a car and driver or have access to a pool of cars and drivers on a first-come, first-served basis.

From personal observation: such an arrangement does not work even where a car and driver is shared between just two neighbouring expatriate wives, whose husbands are away (by air) all week.

Car maintenance

Whichever type of driver, you should expect him to look after the car, including regular **cleaning**, **re-fuelling**, routine **maintenance checks** and arranging for **periodic servicing**.

Drivers as helpers

Besides normal driving and car-maintenance duties, we found that drivers were both able and willing to undertake such additional tasks as:

- minor **do-it-yourself** (DIY) in the office and at home; and **gardening**;
- solo **shopping** (such as for dog food, mentioned in Chapter 8);
- **running errands** (such as making deliveries/collections, as mentioned in Chapter 10);
- practising your **conversational Chinese** (alluded to in Chapter 2);
- repairing **bicycle punctures**;
- collecting **take-away-meals** (when I was working late at the office);
- transporting **visitors** to/from our home from/to their hotel, and taking them on **sight-seeing tours**, accompanied by my Chinese PA;
- taking/collecting children to/from **school**;
- taking the **dog** – in our case a very car-sick one – for walks and to the vets and kennels;

and, in general:

- anything that would allow them to **build face** by showing off about, and so basking in the reflected glory of, '*laoban*' (for the reasons explained in Chapter 2; and alluded to in Chapter 6).

Terms of employment

Wages

Additionally, since drivers are more akin to a company employee than a maid, you may consider rationalising their pay structure as I did by means of:

1 *In general:*
   - (a) **Job evaluation** and **performance appraisal**.
   - (b) Rolling up any **allowances** into base pay, especially those that are intrinsic to a role (such as **meal allowance**, mentioned below).
   - (c) Maintaining as separate genuine allowances those that are a function of **performance** or **cost-of-living**, expressed as a percentage of base pay.

2 *In particular:*
   - (a) Basing his **daily working hours** on yours plus travel time between your home and the office.
   - (b) Including **regular overtime** and **weekend working** in his base pay.

Meal allowance

Since many of your business and social engagements – for which you will require the car – may involve a meal, you need to make arrangements for your driver to eat and agree who pays.

EXAMPLE

In our experience common practice, depending on the occasion, includes:

1 Inviting him to **eat with you** – such as when shopping.
2 Paying for a **simple meal in a separate room** – such as while waiting for you at a banquet in an hotel (where a special drivers' canteen is sometimes available).
3 Providing cash to **buy his own food somewhere else** – such as while waiting for you at a friend's house.

Personally, I never felt comfortable eating with my driver, in case it gave him ever greater illusions of grandeur spending even more time with *laoban* than anyone else.

Working expenses

Drivers will inevitably incur such working expenses as road **tolls**, **parking** fees, **fuel** costs, traffic **fines** and **meals** (mentioned above) – for which I recommend you provide a small **cash float** to be replenished on presentation of the corresponding **vouchers**.

Dress code

Whilst not advocating the provision of working clothes let alone a uniform for your driver, I do recommend that you agree a 'smart casual' **dress code** that is mutually acceptable (to your taste and his pocket) in order to avoid any embarrassingly gaudy or shabby appearance that might prejudice your company image.

Days-off and holidays

Whereas you can do without a maid for a day or week or two, not having a driver available – whether through illness, holiday or similar – can severely impede your mobility, other than resorting to using public transport (i.e. taxis).

Taxi drivers, however, are unlikely to want to hump shopping home on a Saturday, run you to church on a Sunday, rush you into hospital at midnight, take dogs for a walk, collect you at unsocial hours, collect your friends... and wait to take them home; know where you live/work; or speak rudimentary English, etc.

In short: not having a driver on call 24/7 can be more of a problem than mere inconvenience, for which reason it is not uncommon for senior expatriates to employ or be provided with a **relief driver**.

However, such an arrangement can cause jealousy of the main driver – who considers the car to be 'his' – towards the relief. In our case, this contributed to our eventually sacking the former and retaining only the latter, who preferred working 24/7 to having a relief. We had to make a conscious effort, therefore, to ensure he took time off when we knew that we did not need him.

EXAMPLE

Each time we went away together by air, as long as our driver took us to the airport and collected us on our return, I was happy for him to take leave in-between times.

Taking liberties
The greatest liberty that drivers may take is to use your car for **private use** or worse still **hire and reward** as a **taxi**.

The best counter-measure – which we employed – is to insist that, when you are not using it, they leave the car in the garage (at work or home) and never allow them to take it home. Until you can fully trust your driver, the only exception, in our experience, is when to do so may genuinely cause your driver real hardship – such as when you arrive home at midnight, after a prolonged business or social commitment, and need to leave at crack of dawn for the office or airport. Otherwise, to travel between his and your home, you may consider providing your driver with a cheap pedal- or motor-cycle, depending on the distance.

The main liberty that one driver took – for which we eventually dismissed him – was **abusing the car-phone**. As elsewhere in the world, many employees consider private calls using company phones a perk of the job, to which some employers are prepared to turn a blind eye within reason. On this occasion, however, he had blatantly exceeded 'reasonable' use.

Other **in-car liberties**, which are more **annoying** or **bad habits** than anything, with which you may have to deal include:

1   **Sleeping** in the car whilst waiting for you – preferably on his own, and not with your friend's driver (as mentioned below).

2   **Smoking**, **eating** and **drinking tea** (from an old jam-jar) – which we banned as giving a poor impression to guest-passengers.

3   Playing the **Chinese-language radio** which we accepted but also counter-balanced with Western tapes and

compact disks, ranging from classical music to modern Christian worship songs.

4 **Driving far too fast** for your comfort.

Miscellaneous

Forms of address
Most expatriates whom we know, like ourselves, and their Chinese drivers always used **first names** to address each other. Only a handful preferred the term *laoban* (boss).

None of our drivers had an **anglicised name**, which one asked me to give him, like a slave-owner of old, whilst the other preferred being addressed by his Chinese name.

Big brother
Additionally, take appropriate measures to ensure that:

1 You do not say to anyone in the car (including over your mobile phone) **anything sensitive** that you would later regret if understood and repeated by your driver to the authorities or your business competitors.

2 And conversely **anything sensitive** that you do say to anyone in the car (including over your mobile phone) cannot be understood and repeated by your driver to the authorities or your business competitors.

Relationship with other drivers and their bosses
Your driver will:

◆ Inevitably, rub shoulders with **other drivers** as a natural consequence of your interaction with their bosses.

◆ Probably build strong relationships (*guanxi*) with the drivers of those people with whom you have most frequent and regular contact.

EXAMPLE

One of our drivers became so friendly with my best friend's driver that the two of them would sleep in the same car whilst waiting for both of us!

Thus besides the impression that he may cause by his behaviour and dress, mentioned above, you need to:

1   Ensure that your driver does not pass on any **intelligence** to other drivers about your **business** or **social activities**.

2   Coax **intelligence** out of him about their bosses.

Relationship with your maid

Your **maid** and **driver** are also likely to develop a bond – some may even be married to each other – of which the two main dangers are:

1   Their wasting time **gossiping**, whilst the driver is waiting for you.

2   The driver consequently becoming privy to and passing on **intelligence** about your **domestic life**.

The way that we tackled this situation was to keep the two of them apart as much as possible, in particular not allowing the driver into the house except to use the **toilet** – which one never did nor wanted to!

Time management

Managing your driver's time is, therefore, critical to his effectiveness – especially minimising **unproductive waiting time** by helping you in other ways, as suggested above. There is only so much time he need spend cleaning the car!

EXAMPLE

We eventually devised a **scheduling system** for the maid and driver combined, as follows.

First thing most mornings, I would review my diary for the next few days, including travel plans and social engagements, with my PA who would then phone my wife to review her personal and household needs.

Subsequently, my PA would draw up two written **work-sheets** (in Chinese):

1 One for the **maid**, which she faxed home.
2 Another for the **driver**, detailing: dates, times, passengers (normally my wife and/or self), destinations, waiting-time tasks, odd-jobs, shopping-lists, etc.

She would also agree where and when to accompany my wife and/or self (such as shopping or interpreting).

Relationship with foreign wives

If you are a husband, then your driver should accord the same rank and respect to your **wife**.

However, be aware that:

1 Vestiges of the **patriarchal society** do still linger in the way that your driver will probably open the car door for you before your wife.

EXAMPLES

1 When it rained, my driver was in a real quandary as to whom he should shelter under the umbrella, despite instructions to give priority to my wife.
2 At other times, he was embarrassed opening the car door for Western females wearing revealing dresses.

---

2   Although as mentioned elsewhere Chinese men are not attracted to **Western women**, they do believe them to be promiscuous and thus fair game – in line with their schizophrenic view of the West as technologically highly advanced, but morally corrupt – so that drivers may 'try it on' while the boss is away.

One way of redressing the situation is to include your wife in the driver's **performance review**, thus making it clear that his continued employment depends as much on her as you.

Company flag

Until you and/or your visitors are able to pick your driver out from a whole crowd of Chinese, I suggest you give him a **company flag** to hold aloft – akin to tourist guides in China – so that he can be easily distinguished from all the others waiting for their passengers.

Convenience or curse?

It is very convenient to know that, at whatever time of day or night you need to arrive at or leave a crowded business or social engagement, you do not have to worry about parking or finding the car, respectively.

EXAMPLE

On leaving the Great Hall of the People one night, after attending a sold-out ballet, we found our driver waiting for us right outside the main exit, having parked the car only a few yards away in Tiananmen Square. I never did find out how he had managed it! Thereafter, we became quite accustomed to similar experiences.

Such convenience can, however, also be a curse if you enjoy a drink or too. No longer having to observe the **drink and drive** laws, we know of many expatriates who have, reputedly, regularly indulged in **alcohol abuse**, relying on a sober driver (sometimes ours) to take them home.

Thankfully, I was forewarned and, so, now are you.

My favourite experiences

In early 1998, I was fortunate to be the first owner in Beijing of a white Mercedes 'E' Class which, because of its then rarity, drew quite a lot attention, not least from the traffic police who, on account of its luxury status, thought I must be a VIP (although I could still be seen, as we had chosen not to have smoked-glass windows).

My driver was not slow to take advantage, especially on two occasions:

◆ At Chinese New Year, when the traffic in Beijing was more crowded and chaotic than usual, a traffic policeman removed a 'no entry' crash-barrier to allow us safe passage along a road closed to the general public!

- ◆ Just as we were leaving the Summer Palace car park after dinner with the chairman of British Telecom, at which the British Ambassador was also present, my driver spotted their cars leaving with Chinese police outriders. Quick as a flash, he snuck in behind them and joined the convoy, crossing Beijing non-stop in record time!

Post script

When we left China, to take enforced early retirement, it was our devoted driver, Xue, who accompanied us on our last journey to the airport and bade us farewell, amidst many hugs and tears; and then took our dog to live with him.

If you only make one friend in China, make it your driver.

Poor in worldly possessions, but rich in generosity, friendship and loyalty, you may experience more Chinese hospitality during one visit to your driver's home than at all the banquets to which you are invited.

Keeping Dogs

This chapter is dedicated to **Bismark** (or **Bai si**), our Chinese-bred basset hound out of Hong Kong parents and Anglo-French grandparents, who features so prominently below and at the time of writing is alive and well in Shunyi County, Beijing District.

GOVERNMENT REGULATIONS

During the rule of **Mao Zedong**, the Chinese government tried to eliminate domestic dogs from their cities. (The cynics' immediate reaction may be 'by eating them', but they would be wrong as explained below.)

In the face of whatever permitted resistance there was to such a **ban**, the government introduced stringent **regulations** to keep urban dogs under strict control – which, in our time, were that dogs must be:

1   Of a **size** not exceeding 35 centimetres at the shoulder,

2   **Kept indoors** (i.e. at home or in your housing complex) and **off the streets** between 7 a.m. and 8 p.m.

3   **Inoculated** (see Figure 10).

4   **Registered** annually with the PSB, which issues:
(a) An **identity tag** (to be attached to the dog's collar)
(b) A **photocard** (to be held by the owner)

at the prohibitive cost of **RMB 5,000** (c. £380 or US$ 600) the first year, and half thereafter – not to mention the challenge of persuading your dog to sit still in a passport photograph booth!

5 **Insured** for third party liability.

Otherwise, the dog may face summary execution (by revolver) in front of the owner.

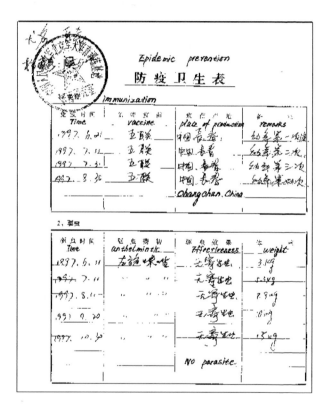

Fig. 10. Bismark's vaccination certificate issued by the PLA Dog Breeding Unit.

Penalties for breaching regulations

If other foreign dog-owners pooh-pooh these regulations to you, my advice would be: they have been lucky so far, but you may not be in the future, according to our experience.

Whilst Chinese nationals may be able to flout the regulations, foreigners are soft targets for the PSB, living as they may in prescribed housing. Hence, when we moved to **within the Beijing city boundary** (in 1998), we found that the property management company arranged for the PSB to visit our housing complex to register residents' dogs.

Some of our friends living **in the countryside outside Beijing**, where the regulations were more flexible, had been allowed (prior to 1997) to import their alsatians, labradors, dalmatians and similar dogs into China, only to be told later that their dogs were too tall and would have to be repatriated or destroyed unless they complied with the **height regulation**. Short of chopping their legs in half, how could the owners comply?

Thankfully, after much wrangling, a blind eye was turned – *but the dogs still remained illegal and, hence, always susceptible to the regulation being enforced.*

Height restriction

I am often asked: 'why such a restriction on height?', to which I usually reply, tongue in cheek:

- ◆ *either:* to protect the monopoly of pekinese
- ◆ *or:* to fit into an oven!

in order immediately to allay the fear that many foreigners have that the Chinese might eat their dog – which they will not (as explained below).

Revision of regulations
In April 2003, the media reported that, in Beijing, the competent authority is to:

♦ revise its regulations;
♦ reduce the registration fee from RMB 5,000 to RMB 2,000 (c. £150 or US$ 240);
♦ relax the rules for elderly and **handicapped** dog-owners.

However, in view of the concern over SARS and erroneous links to dogs (mentioned below), no such changes had yet been made at the time of writing.

ACQUIRING A DOG
For foreigners, there are basically two options for acquiring a dog in China:

1 **Adopting** an existing one from a departing expatriate.
2 **Purchasing** a new one.

The following guidelines apply to the second option only, as being peculiar to China.

What dog to buy?
Buying a dog in China is an adventure in itself. Whilst I am used to dogs, my wife is not, which gave us our first problem: what sort of dog to buy?

The solution, thankfully, was close at hand, in the shape of the Chinese government's list of some two dozen **officially approved breeds** of domestic dogs (i.e. those not exceeding 35 centimetres at the shoulder).

Since the restriction on height is also one of choice, we – as people looking for a real he-dog or hound, not a toy – were in a real quandary. Luckily, the copy of the approved list which my Chinese PA had from her days at *China Daily* had been annotated by hand with 'basset hound' – at c. 25 kilos, a 'big dog with short legs'.

However, just because a particular breed of dog is approved does not necessarily mean it is available in China.

Hence the second problem: where to find the breed of dog you want – in our case, a basset hound – without importing one?

Where to buy a dog?
There are basically three options for anyone buying a dog in China.

1 Pet shops
An obvious starting point is a **pet shop** such as the one in Beijing (contact details below) which had featured in the *China Daily* article written by my Chinese PA; and where, therefore, I was:

◆ offered a warm welcome, hefty discount, and, of course, a wide choice of **pekinese** and **shitzus** ('lion dogs');

- politely told that bassets were difficult to come by, but could be found if we gave them time, which we did.

Meanwhile, we showed interest in a shitzu and – in sheer desperation of not finding a basset – were on the verge of buying one when we discovered that it was:

- two years old;
- incontinent;
- shaking not from excitement but distemper or rickets.

2 Street sellers

If we had wanted a diseased dog, we could have bought any one of the many pekineses on sale in the **streets**. Some of our friends did so, and lived to regret it, although the dogs did not: they died quite quickly.

You have been warned: however adorable, beware of puppies sold in the street.

3 Dog brokers

You may find, as we did, by asking other dog-owners, that there is a **dog broker** in your locality.

EXAMPLE

Thus it was that, when all seemed lost, suddenly the phone rang: 'I hear you are looking for a basset hound. I know where there is one', the caller said and proceeded to give me details of a seven-month old basset puppy at the **People's Liberation Army** (PLA) **Dog Breeding Unit** (described immediately below). In the home of Chinese whispers, word had gone round the expatriate doggy community and reached the local dog broker.

Thankfully, following on from the previous point, if you live in or near Beijing there is a fourth option.

4 PLA Dog Breeding Centre

At Chang Ping, north of Beijing en-route to the Great Wall, the **PLA** has a large centre breeding three types of dog:

- large guard dogs for army use (e.g. Alsatians, Dobermanns and Rottweilers);
- basset hounds presumably for similar use as **sniffer dogs**;
- toy dogs for sale (e.g. pekinese and shitzus).

This is the option that we chose, of which I cannot speak highly enough, as will become clearer below (contact details below).

Purchase price

Forewarned by the dog broker that the asking price for a seven-month old basset puppy was the local equivalent of £1,000 (c. RMB 13,000), but might be negotiable, I went armed with US$1,000 in cash and thus entered into a bizarre negotiation, through an interpreter, with a PLA soldier taking instructions over the phone from his commandant.

It was at this moment that I realised what the much-vaunted 'socialism with Chinese characteristics' really means: capitalism! Thus, the PLA negotiator was not lured by the offer of a lower price in foreign currency; and only after much wrangling accepted to split the difference at US$1,100, but still insisting I pay in Renminbi.

Perhaps the high prices asked by reputable breeders such as the PLA, in addition to the stringent regulations (described above), explain the:

◆ paucity and unpopularity of thoroughbred healthy dogs;

◆ abundance of half-starved flea-ridden mongrels.

Value for money

At the risk of stating the obvious: if you are paying a lot for an allegedly pure-bred dog, ensure that you obtain **proof of purchase** and a copy of its **pedigree** (see Figure 11). While yours may not necessarily be a perfect specimen, it could still be carrying the genes of a past and/or future champion.

Fig. 11. Bismark's proof of purchase (left) and pedigree (right) issued by the PLA Dog Breeding Centre.

At the very least, on leaving China a **pedigree** may be a useful negotiating tool in finding an appreciative new owner prepared to pay a reasonable price.

EXAMPLE

In Colombia: after paying £100 in early 1974 – a lot of money in those days – for a German pointer puppy bred by a Crufts judge, imagine our delight, on receipt of her pedigree, at discovering that she had been sired by the supreme champion of all the Americas (North and South)! On relocating to Spain at the end of the same year, her new owner offered us £80.

Indeed, the PLA offered to take Bismark off our hands for breeding purposes when we left China...but, true to socialist principles, for free! Thankfully, as mentioned below, our driver was so fond of Bismark that he offered him a home.

KEEPING A DOG

Veterinary services
Veterinary services are available for small animals. However, in our experience, they are:

♦ **few and far between** – since, in a country where animals either work or are eaten, but not kept as pets, most Chinese veterinary surgeons are horse rather than doggy doctors;
♦ **expensive** – as many are foreign.

If you live in Beijing, we thoroughly recommend the **PLA Dog Breeding Centre** where – in our time at least – the lady commandant was the leading and perhaps only Chinese canine veterinary surgeon in China. Besides excellent and expert care, the fees (in 1998) per consultation, often including any prescription, were only RMB 50 (equivalent to £4 or US$6). At regular intervals, we would arrange for Bismark to have a check-up and his claws clipped, when he was always genuinely pleased and happy to co-operate – what better recommendation could you want!?

Kennelling and dog-sitting

Many expatriates rely on **maids** and/or neighbours to look after their dog while they are away, which we did for short absences from home (such as over a weekend, or brief mid-week business trip).

However, at RMB 50 per day (in 1998), including food – and sometimes a free medical check-up – again the **PLA Dog Breeding Centre** was hard to beat; and certainly met with Bismark's approval, judging by the insouciance he always displayed on arrival and departure.

Having paid what we considered a small fortune to buy and license Bismark, we were pleasantly surprised at how little the PLA charged us for veterinary services and kennelling. Looking back, I now realise that the PLA had Bismark's best interests at heart, in that the:

- **purchase price** ensured that the dog went to owners who were so keen and foolish enough to pay that amount of money that they could give him a good home where he would be really wanted;
- **veterinary bills** ensured that he remained healthy.

As with everything else in China, charity begins at home. Hence, foreigners are fair game. In this instance exploit them, but look after the dog.

Obedience classes

The **PLA Dog Breeding Centre** also offered obedience classes: one for English speakers, another for Chinese speakers. In Bismark's case, he speaking Chinese and we speaking English, it was a lost cause – insofar as training any basset is concerned, which the Centre warned us was quite impossible and Bismark was eager to prove by coming bottom in the IQ test! After all, with a nose second only to a bloodhound and the devotion of a saint (remember the basset who played the part of the nanny in Walt Disney's cartoon version of *Peter Pan*?), he had nothing to prove – unlike the pekinese, shitzus and similar!

Off the lead, however, and away from the scrutiny of other dog owners, Bismark was the star pupil; and even taught me the Chinese art of taking him for a walk on a bicycle.

Dogs and maids

Dogs are also a valuable judge of character when it comes to choosing a **maid**, as follows.

Maids quickly realise that for some foreigners – including us – it is a question of 'love us, love our dog', so that one way to impress is to cherish the family pooch, however obnoxious and naughty around the house. Thus, it was very obvious at interview how the older maids would make a fuss of Bismark quite overtly: they did not bother to be subtle, probably thinking all foreigners were stupid, as mentioned elsewhere.

However, it was Bismark's behaviour when we returned home after he had been alone all day with the maid that told us how she really treated him. For one maid, that was her redeeming feature, such that we could go away and happily leave Bismark with her overnight; and at all times rely on her to help feed and exercise him.

Dogs and drivers

The same is true of **drivers**, especially as in our case where the dog suffers from travel sickness.

Thankfully, our driver Xue was a genuine dog-lover, having one to guard his family smallholding. Indeed, on our leaving China, he offered to give Bismark a home, rather than see him go to a stranger or back to the PLA (as mentioned above).

Thus, he had no hesitation in not only transporting Bismark to/from the PLA Dog Breeding Centre on numerous occasions, often alone; and driving Bismark and us to the nearby countryside, and waiting, whilst we went for walks; but also, cleaning out the car afterwards and shopping for dog food.

To restrain Bismark whilst **in transit**, we managed locally to purchase a large metal cage.

Dog walks

During the **week**, we had to contend with walking Bismark in the **city**:

- on the **lead**;
- along **pavements**;
- **outside our housing complex** only before 7 a.m. and after 8 p.m.;

- **inside our housing complex** at any time;
- carrying a **poop-scoop** to collect and dispose of his droppings.

In this last context: although one housing complex where we lived boasted a **dog's toilet**, we never managed to find it. Instead, Bismark was easily satisfied with the lamp-posts, and managed to strip his favourite one (outside our house) of most of its paint at the base – which says more of the quality of the paint than anything else!

At the **weekends**, however, thanks to our dog-friendly driver there were many **country walks** (e.g. in Shunyi County) over fields, through woods and across ditches – free of lead and poop-scoop – for a hound to enjoy.

Sometimes we reversed roles, and Bismark took me for a cycle-ride on the lead – a very Chinese pastime.

Dogs with Chinese people and tradesmen

On our **walks** outside the housing complex, the people were a problem. Brought up mainly without dogs, the Chinese we met – adults and children – all seemed to have an inherent fear of them. Some even either burst into fits of hysteria or shouted at me, presumably to go away.

The same was true of **tradesmen**, who would not enter the house until Bismark had been closeted away. However, once they were the other side of a fence or door from him, and/or realised how friendly and relatively harmless he was, the less scared they gradually became.

Finally (as mentioned elsewhere): your landlord and/or housing management company will normally have an army of **gardeners** of indifferent ability at their disposal, whom they may deploy to cut your lawn using hand-shears. In such an event, it is only courteous to clear the garden of droppings beforehand.

Feeding dogs

Food for Bismark was never a problem:

- proprietary western **tinned meat** and **dry biscuits** were readily available – the latter in large bulk bags at some super-stores (such as *Wanfujing*);
- in restaurants (and even the China Club in Beijing), we often asked for **doggy bags** to take the leftovers home, and never met opposition. I do suspect, however, that some waiters thought that *we* were going to eat the food, rather than waste it on Bismark;
- at the kennels, I do not know what the **PLA Dog Breeding Centre** fed him, but Bismark always looked fit and well afterwards.

Eating dogs

I am constantly called upon to allay the fears about which many foreigners are quite adamant without ever having visited China: *that the Chinese might eat their family dog –* which they will not.

True, Chinese do eat dogs. However, according to those of my Chinese friends whom I trust, **edible dogs** (like frogs in France) are specially bred at such great expense that they would certainly not be wasted on foreigners!

Indeed, whilst I enjoyed eating food in China that most Westerners would find abhorrent – thanks to five years at an English boarding school – dog was never on the menu. Nor can I recall meeting anyone who readily owned up to eating dog, especially a family pooch!

Nevertheless, in the global tradition of restaurants offering speciality dishes, there are eating houses with dog on the menu, such as Korean restaurants (try opposite the Lido Hotel in Beijing).

Dogs and SARS

On a similar note: while it is well known that the Chinese eat civet cats, it has only recently come to public light that they may carry the virus responsible for **SARS** – so you have been warned!

By analogy, however, contact with dogs has been unfortunately and apparently erroneously blamed by some local governments for passing **SARS** onto humans, sadly resulting in dogs being killed in the streets of some cities (such as Nanjing, the capital of Jiangsu Province) out of sheer ignorance.

Fireworks

Unfortunately, any dog – or adult for that matter – afraid of **fireworks** will suffer many miserable days on end in China, particularly in the country areas where some people like to toss and swirl fireworks around their heads like demented Dervishes.

Thankfully, due to his army upbringing, Bismark was happily abroad in the fields, totally nonplussed by the many and regular whiz-bangs going on around him, whilst his fierce friends were cowering at home.

CONTACT DETAILS
Beijing KPK World Pet Zoo Co Ltd
34 Gongti North Road
Dongcheng District,
BEIJING 100027, China
Tel: +86 (010) 6552 6177

Highly recommended
People's Liberation Army Dog Breeding Centre
Chang Ping
BEIJING
China
Tel: +86 (010) 6073 2877

Climate and Clothing

CLIMATE

It is difficult to summarise the **Chinese climate** because, as described below, it:

♦ is so **variable**;
♦ embraces such an **extensive territory** and **complex topography**.

1 **Climatic variations.**
China is dominated by **dry** and **wet monsoons**, causing **stark differences** of **temperature**.
(a) **Winter**:
 – cold and dry northern **winds** from high latitude areas bring bitter cold;
 – temperatures between the north and south can differ by some 40°C;
 – the warmest areas are in the south and southwest (such as Hainan Island, which has a summer climate all year round; and Sichuan);
 – temperatures can be 5°C to 18°C lower than other countries in the same latitude.
(b) **Summer**:
 – warm and moist (rain-bearing) southern **winds** from sea areas at lower latitude bring unbearable heat and produce **rainfall** in the form of **cyclonic storms**;

- temperatures throughout most of the country are remarkably uniform;
- the coolest spots are in the far northeast (such as Heilongjiang, which has a winter climate all year round).

2   **Geographical extension**.
China stretches:

♦ *from the* **frigid zone** in the north;
♦ *to the* **tropical** and **subtropical zones** in the south; with most of the country lying in the northern **temperate zone**.

The Yangtze River, with **Shanghai** at its mouth, is the official North-South dividing line below which public buildings are not entitled to **central-heating**.

Thus, there is no one season when the Chinese weather is ideal: even **spring** is **unpredictable**. However, the majority of places are normally quite pleasant in **autumn**, when the weather is most **temperate**.

Overview
China can be divided into the following seven climatic zones.

1   **North East China** – including **Beijing** – where:
♦ **summer** is short, warm and humid, with much **sunshine** and unpredictable **rainfall**;
♦ **winter** is long; and very cold and dry due to strong continental **winds** from the northern deserts of Siberia and the Mongolian Plateau.

2   **Central China** – including **Shanghai** – which has four distinctive seasons; and where:

- **summer** is hot and humid, with occasional **cyclones** and **typhoons** in its coastal regions;
- **winter** can be bitterly cold;
- **rainfall** is plentiful all year round.

3 **South China** – including **Guangzhou** – in the **subtropics**, where:
- **summer** is hot, wet and humid, with heavy **rain** between April and September (including occasional coastal **cyclones** and **typhoons** between July and September);
- **winter** is humid and mild, although January to March can be chilly.

4 **South West China** – a mountainous area, which characteristically has vertically seasonal zones, where:
- **summer** temperatures vary according to the altitude;
- **winter** is mild and wet, with some **rain**.

5 The **Tibetan Region** – a high plateau, with an **Arctic climate** – where:
- **summer** is warm during the day, but very cold at night;
- **winter** is severe, with frequent light **snow** and **frost**;
- **rainfall** is heaviest in Summer.

6 The **Western Interior** – an **arid desert** – where:
- **winter** is cold;
- **rainfall** is even throughout the year.

7 **Inner Mongolia** – comprising mountain ranges and semi-desert lowlands, with an extreme **continental climate** – where:
- **summer** is warm, with heavy **rain**;
- **winter** is cold;
- **winds** make the temperatures even colder in winter and spring.

North East China

1 **Summer** (May to August) can be **very hot**, with temperatures reaching 38°C in **Beijing**, coinciding with the city's **rainy season**.

2 **Winter** (December to March) can be:
   (a) **Very cold**, with temperatures ranging from −20°C in **Beijing** to −40°C further north, where you may find the strange sight of sand dunes covered in **snow**.
   (b) **Dry**.
   (c) **Dark**, bereft of sunshine.

3 The best weather is in **spring** and **autumn**, when temperatures:
   (a) Range from 20°C to 30°C during the day.
   (b) Drop a lot at night.

4 Annual **rainfall**:
   (a) Varies from 63 cms to 70 cms.
   (b) Occurs mainly in Summer.

5 **Fog** can occur:
   (a) Inland: more than 40 days per year.
   (b) Along the coast: more than 80 days per year.

Beijing

In Beijing, the **temperate continental climate** produces four clearly contrasted seasons as follows.

1 **Summer** (June to August) is **rainy** and **humid** (i.e. **hot** and **sticky**) with:
   (a) A mean **temperature** of 26°C, which can easily exceed 30°C and sometimes 40°C.
   (b) High **humidity**.
   (c) Heavy afternoon **thunder-showers**.

(d) High levels of **air pollution**.

(e) **Mosquitoes** in July.

2   **Autumn** (September to early November) is the best and most pleasant season, **neither dry nor humid**, with:

(a) Little **rain**.

(b) Clear skies.

(c) **Breezy** days.

3   **Winter** is **long** (mid-November to March) and **cold**, with:

(a) Temperatures generally below **freezing**, and sometimes falling as low as −20°C.

(b) Northern **winds** cutting like a knife through butter.

(c) High levels of air **pollution**.

EXAMPLES

1   Natural and artificial lakes remain **frozen** for several weeks, if not months, providing instant public rinks for ice-skating, a popular sport such as at the Summer Palace over the Chinese New Year (see Figure 12).

Fig. 12. At Dragon Villas where we first lived the outdoors roller-skating rink was filled with water at Christmas and converted into an instant ice-rink, where our son (pictured above) used to play ice-hockey.

2 In Shunyi County, the area surrounding Dragon Villas: it was not unusual to see anglers drive across a **frozen lake**, cut a hole in the ice through which to fish, and set up a primitive brazier and/or barbecue!

3 The morning that a large UK delegation arrived at Beijing airport in January 1998 to launch the Britain in China campaign: **snow** fell so suddenly and violently that – like many others – I had to abandon my car (with driver), walk the last kilometre or so to the arrivals terminal, welcome my CEO and wait for the car to arrive. If memory serves me right, my PA was following in a second car, in case mine did not make it!

4 In January: even our hardy PLA-bred basset hound, desperate for exercise and to relieve himself, could not survive outside longer than ten minutes at midday, despite wearing a dog-coat!

4 **Spring** is **short** (April to May), **dry** and **dusty** and characterised by a phenomenon known as '**yellow wind**' or '**dirty rain**' plaguing the capital – that is: fine **dust** blown from the Gobi Desert in the Northwest.

EXAMPLE

When I was once caught in a short April shower, my dark suit became so speckled with dirt that it resembled a camouflage jacket and had to be dry-cleaned!

Central China

1 **Summer** (April to October) in the **Yangtze River Valley** – where the cities of **Wuhan, Chongqing** and **Nanjing** are China's three famous '**furnaces**' – is
   (a) **long**;
   (b) **humid**;
   (c) **hot** with high temperatures.

2 **Winter** temperatures can:
   (a) fall well **below freezing**;

(b) be as cold as in Beijing – particularly south of the Yangtze, where public buildings are **not heated** (as mentioned above).

3   **Spring** and **autumn** probably offer the **best** weather.

4   It can be **wet** and miserable at any time except Summer; and annual **rainfall** is about 76 cms.

Shanghai

Shanghai has four distinctive seasons.

1   **Summer** (May to September) is **long**, **hot** and **humid**, with:
(a) Stifling **humidity**, unless there is a **breeze** blowing off the river. Thankfully, many public buildings and private homes are now **air-conditioned**.
(b) **High temperatures** (mid-to-upper 30°C) – the hottest months being July and August, when temperatures can reach 40°C.
(c) Very tiresome **damp** during the **rainy season** (mid-June to early-August), when it can **rain** for days on end – accounting for some 60% of the annual **rainfall** of about 120 cms.
(d) Occasional mild **typhoons** ('big winds').

2   **Autumn** (October and November) is the **best season**, with average temperatures of:
(a) During the day: 24°C.
(b) At night: 14°C.

3   **Winter** is **short** (December to February) and **cold**, with:
(a) Very **low temperatures** dropping well below **freezing** – January being the coldest month.

(b) A blanket of chilling **drizzle**.

(c) Occasional **snow**.

4   **Spring** (March and April) is very **pleasant**, but with:

(a) **Unheated** public buildings (since the city is officially designated south of the Yangtze).

(b) Intermittent **showers**.

(c) Occasional **cold** spells.

South China

1   **Summer** (July to September):

(a) Is a season of **typhoons** – on average eight per year – bringing high **winds** and heavy **rains** to South-Eastern coastal areas.

(b) **Experiences temperatures** averaging 26°C, but reaching 38°C.

2   **Winter** is:

(a) **Short** (January to March).

(b) Not as cold as in the north.

3   **Autumn** and **spring** are the best seasons, when:

(a) Daytime temperatures range from 20°C to 25°C.

(b) Sometimes, however, it can be miserably **wet** and **cold**, with **rain** or **drizzle**.

4   **Rainfall** is:

(a) About 76 cms annually.

(b) Especially abundant in summer.

Guangzhou

Guangzhou is a **temperate**, **sub-tropical** city, lying only a few miles south of the Tropic of Cancer, where:

1   **Summer** is:

(a) Very **hot**.

(b) Characterised by daily afternoon **showers.**

2 **Winter** is:

(a) **Dreary** (chilly, damp and overcast).

(b) Not as cold as the rest of China.

CLOTHING

When it comes to the **dress code** in China, there are **few formalities** and the Chinese tend to be **conservative but pragmatic**. Thus, foreigners can wear what they like, within reason, as long as they do not offend the **Chinese sense of propriety** (see Figure 13).

Fig. 13. My trademark bow-ties drew less attention in China than in the UK. (Hosting a press conference at the China World Hotel, Beijing, January 1998.)

Non-business dress code

In general terms, except as noted later, you should **dress for comfort and the climate, rather than style** according to the following guidelines:.

Season	Temperature	Clothing
Summer	22°C and above	T-shirts, short-sleeve shirts or blouses; slacks, shorts or skirts; cap or hat; rainwear, sandals
		Note: Shorts are not appropriate for visiting religious shrines
Autumn	10°C to 22°C	Western suits, trouser-suits or sports jackets and slacks; dresses; light woollen sweaters or cardigans; rainwear, travel shoes
Winter	10°C and below	Coat, padded jacket, woollen sweaters, cotton clothes, hat, gloves, lined shoes
Spring	10°C to 22°C	Western suits, trouser-suits or sports jackets and slacks; dresses; woollen sweaters or cardigans; long-sleeve shirts or blouses; travel shoes

Business dress code

In general terms, except as noted later:

1   Be comfortable, but not too relaxed.

2   It is not done, for example, for men to wear **shorts** to official business meetings although it may be accep- table to do so when visiting a farm or factory.

3   Avoid dressing in **all-white clothes** (such as some safari suits), which are more appropriate to funerals – not to mention trying to keep them clean!

4   **Shirt-sleeves** are the norm; and the most formal you will normally ever need is a **suit** (see Figure 14).

5 **For women**: a simple dress (with a high neckline, back and sleeves), blouse and skirt, slacks and jacket or a trouser-suit are adequate for anything short of an official state banquet in the Great Hall of the People.

Fig. 14. With my wife and the Principal of Shanghai Finance College (in **blouse and skirt**) and members of faculty (in **shirt-sleeves**), following my installation as a guest professor (hence the suit and tie), September 1998.

6 **In winter**: wrap up well against the bitter cold, with several layers of warm clothing under a good coat, plus hat, scarf and gloves. **Thermal underwear** is a matter of personal choice.

EXAMPLE

We found **normal underwear** quite adequate, when supplemented with thick shirts, blouses and pullovers.

7 **In summer**: wear light and loose-fitting **cotton** or **linen clothes** to combat the stifling heat; and also carry a pacamac and/or folding umbrella (in your briefcase) to fend off the **rain**.

EXAMPLE

In practice, however, many expatriate families, such as ours, will be cocooned in heated and air-conditioned houses, offices and cars, especially during the working-week; and only venture outside at weekends, when sight-seeing, dog-walking, playing sport, shopping, etc.

Older publications recommend taking with you to China as many clothes as possible, especially business suits, shoes and evening wear; and stocking up in Hong Kong. However, good-quality Western-style clothing is now readily available in most large **department stores** (see photographs in Figure 15), in response to the growing demand of the **young fashion-conscious Chinese**.

Fig. 15. Number One Department Store, Shanghai, February 2003: fashionable ladies' shoes and men's fashions (Levis, Adidas and Jack Jones).

Nevertheless (according to my wife), locally-made **female underwear** designed for the waif-like Chinese ladies tends to be too small for the fuller Western figure.

Sexually provocative clothing

True to their distaste for public immodesty, the Chinese also object to **provocative clothing**.

Thus **women** should not wear clothes that are excessively

revealing – such as plunging neck-lines, see-through blouses, tank tops, hemlines above the knee and shorts.

EXAMPLES

1 My driver was embarrassed by Western females climbing in and out of the car wearing Chinese **slit-dresses**.
2 My son was annoyed at how Chinese males stared at his wife's **skimpy tops**.
3 At the time of writing permission for the US pop-singer Britney Spears to appear live in China may depend on her agreeing to wear more subdued **stage costumes** than those she proposes wearing in other countries during the same tour. (However, having attended the hugely-successful concert of the pop-violinist Vanessa Mae in Beijing in 1998: might this be a retrograde ploy on the part of the Chinese authorities to quell the insurgence of Western music and artistes? I hope not; but we shall see.)

Modesty applies equally to **men's clothing**.

EXAMPLES

1 Beijing workmen walk the streets in summer wearing only a vest (above the waist) rolled up to their armpits, like a bikini-top, in an attempt to maintain decorum whilst sunbathing.
2 I was stared at when wearing **cycling-shorts**.

When in doubt: use your common sense.

Business meetings

Westerners should wear **Western business attire** not least because it has now been largely adopted by senior Chinese officials (as in the photograph in Figure 16, with my most senior female and male Chinese colleagues in Beijing in 1997, wearing typical modern **Chinese business dress**) according to the following guidelines.

Fig. 16. Typical modern Chinese business dress.

1 *In winter:*
   (a) Bundle up to keep warm.
   (b) If the meeting room is not heated, you can always keep your coat on!

2 *In summer:*
   (a) No one will expect you to wear a jacket and tie.
   (b) Nevertheless, make no assumptions: it is better to arrive in jacket and tie and be invited to remove them, than to dress down only to find that the Chinese have dressed up for the occasion!

3 Should you wear **jewellery**, be aware that:
   (a) On the one hand, modest gold jewellery and a quality watch may gain you face.

(b) On the other hand, the Chinese propensity for public modesty could be offended by overly 'flash' jewellery.

Banquets

As a general rule, standard **banquet attire** is a dark lounge suit and tie for gentlemen; and a demure dress or trouser suit for ladies.

There is no need to dress in **formal evening wear**, unless the invitation specifically so requests.

Jewellery should be tasteful and unostentatious.

Balls and dinner-dances

Black-ties and **evening gowns** may be expected at embassy balls or, for example, the China Club (Beijing) dinner-dances, when local tailors can make quite acceptable **dinner jackets** (tuxedos) at fairly short notice.

EXAMPLE

In 1997 in Beijing: for the British Embassy Ball – which my employer was co-sponsoring – a local tailor made one three-piece and two two-piece **dinner-jackets**, based on my existing one, between Monday and Friday, visiting our office three times (to measure, alter and fit), for no more than £100 each.

Northern China – Beijing

In **Northern China** in general, and **Beijing** in particular, typically:

1 In **summer**:
   (a) Wear tropical or light-weight clothing.

(b) *During the day:* a pair of sunglasses and a light-weight hat will keep the sun at bay.

(c) *In the evening:* take a light-weight pullover or jacket if going outside.

2 In **winter**:

(a) Until the end of November: a good coat should be sufficient.

(b) From December to March: you will need very thick, **wind-proof** clothing and possibly **thermal underwear**. Since the weather is dry, the locally-made padded jackets made of cotton or silk are very suitable and can be bought from large department stores. Fur hats with fold-down ear-flaps are readily available at reasonable prices (but ensure the red star has been removed!). (See Figures 17–20.)

Fig. 17. Celebrating Easter in Tiananmen Square, Beijing, **spring**, 31 March 1997 – in anoraks and coats.

Fig. 18. Celebrating the return of Hong Kong in Tiananmen Square, **summer**, 30 June 1997 – in lightweight clothing.

Fig. 19. Visiting the Summer Palace, Beijing, **autumn**, September 1997 in open-neck shirts and blouses.

Fig. 20. Dog-walking in Shunyi, Beijing, **winter**, January 1998 – in pullover, padded jacket, deerstalker, scarf, gloves and stout boots.

Fig. 21. With the Principal (far left) and faculty members at Shanghai Finance College, **spring** (late March) 1998 – in buttoned-up jackets.

Fig 22. Celebrating Lantern Festival in Yuyuan Bazaar, Shanghai, **winter** (mid-February) 2003 – all in anoraks and coats, and some with hoods, umbrellas and face mask.

Fig. 23. With the Principal (front row, far right), faculty members and students at Shanghai Finance College (after being installed as a guest professor), **autumn** (September) 1998 – mostly in open-neck short-sleeved shirts and blouses.

Central China – Shanghai

In **Central China** in general, and **Shanghai** in particular – according to one guide-book – you will typically need:

1 In **summer**:
   (a) An ice-block for each armpit.
   (b) An **umbrella**.

2 In **winter**:
   (a) Silk **long-johns**.
   (b) Down **jackets**.
   (c) An **umbrella**.
   (see Figures 21 to 23).

Southern China – Guangzhou

Although not as cold in **Winter** as the North, it is still advisable to carry some warm clothing with you. (See Figures 24 and 25.)

Going native

Very occasionally, you may be fortunate to receive an invitation that requests 'black tie or equivalent Chinese evening wear' (such as we did once from the China Club, Beijing) in which case I recommend that you:

1 **Consult** a Chinese friend or colleague as to what is and, more importantly, is not appropriate.

2 **Remember** that Chinese clothing is designed for the oriental, not Western, mien and figure.

3 **Ask** a Chinese friend or colleague for their honest opinion as to how you look in Chinese clothing.

Fig. 24. With a group of Western and Chinese colleagues in a Guangzhou restaurant, **spring** (early April) 1997 – mostly in jackets and ties.

Fig. 25. My wife sight-seeing with a group of Chinese friends in Guangdong Province, **autumn** (October) 1997 – in shirts, slacks and cardigans.

4   Wear Chinese clothing only if they say that it suits you *and* you are not self-conscious but can ignore being teased – everyone else may be less brave than you and in Western attire.

Fig. 26. With my wife at the China Club, Beijing, September 1998. The plain imperial-yellow silk (what appear to be) 'pyjamas' that I am wearing were chosen with the help of my Chinese PA in preference to the rather gaudy mandarin jacket favoured by many foreigners.

(10)

Communications

POST

From personal experience of living and working in Beijing in the late 1990s, I offer the following advice and guidelines (which, whilst possibly outdated in detail, should be still relevant in general).

1   The **international public postal system** is **slow** and **unreliable** by Western standards. At best, air-mailed letters and postcards will take a week or more to reach their destination.

EXAMPLES

1   Many **Christmas cards** exchanged between friends outside China and ourselves never reached them nor us.

2   Post reputedly forwarded from our first house in China to our second, and subsequently from the latter to our UK home, never arrived.

3   **Postcards** that we sent air-mail at the beginning of our week-long visit to Shanghai in February 2003 did not reach the UK until several days after our return home.

---

2   The **public postal system** should, therefore, be your method of written communication of last resort: **fax**, **e-mail** or **private carriers** are infinitely preferable, even for local communications.

EXAMPLES

In the late 1990s, whilst living and working in Beijing:

1 Whenever possible and practicable, I always used **e-mail** to communicate in writing with anybody and everyone in and outside China.

2 (a) Where e-mail was either impossible or unsuitable, I always communicated in writing via **fax** with Chinese and foreign government, business and personal contacts in and outside China.

 (b) We installed a **fax** machine in our UK home, where N° 2 son was living; whilst N° 3 son's school did the same in his boarding house so that we could maintain fast and efficient bilateral contact.

 (c) Happily, we found that other key home contacts already had **fax** machines, such as our bank, solicitor, dentist and N° 1 son's workplace.

3 Where e-mail and fax were either impossible or unsuitable, and for parcels and similar, especially if destined outside Beijing and overseas, I normally used **private carriers** (such as DHL or UPS). Within Beijing, I used my driver, as recommended below.

4 As a general rule, I used the **public postal system** only *in extremis*, even for non-urgent or unimportant communications.

3 Using your **driver** or other **member of staff** to deliver or collect letters, invitations, packages, travel documents and similar is the only sure way of guaranteeing their safety and security.

EXAMPLES

1 Where e-mail and fax were either impossible or unsuitable, and for parcels and similar, all destined within Beijing, I normally used my **driver** for deliveries and collections, especially when urgent and/or confidential.

2 After moving from one house in Beijing to another, our **driver** used to collect the post from the former rather than rely on any forwarding system.

4   If you do have to use the post inside China:

(a) Remember that most **Chinese postal workers** cannot read pinyin (i.e. the romanised spelling system for transliterating Chinese characters), let alone English or other foreign language.

(b) Ask a Chinese colleague or friend to **write the address in Chinese characters** – even if it is only the name of the destination country for overseas mail.

(c) Provide your family and friends (including Chinese) with a **Chinese-language version of your address in China** which they can photocopy and use as an **address label**.

(d) Similarly, provide your Chinese friends with a **local-language version of your address outside China**.

EXAMPLE

As mentioned in Chapter 6: we designed our personal **moving notices** and **name cards** to be used in these two ways.

(e) The most convenient place to **buy stamps** and **post letters** is probably your local large hotel, leisure club or community centre – perhaps in your own housing complex.

(f) **Stamps** and **envelopes** are not always pre-gummed, and may, therefore, need to be **glued** on and shut, respectively.

5   One question we are sometimes asked at Farnham Castle is whether you can buy Western **Christmas**, **New Year**, **Easter** and **birthday cards** to which the answer is: yes but they are expensive and garish by our standards, reflecting Chinese taste.

6   In this connection may I commend the growing expatriate practice of sending a standard **Christmas letter** ('round robin') recounting the highlights of your life in China as an efficient means of keeping others up-to-date with what you are doing – in **hard-copy** (by **post** or **fax**) or **electronic format** (via **e-mail** or, as we now do, on your **website** if you have one). From comments we receive, our 'end of term report' (as one friend describes it) seems to be not only much appreciated but even looked forward to; and has the added advantage of generating a reply in similar vein.

TELECOMMUNICATIONS

According to Interfax China's *Snapshot of China Mobile Phone Market Report 2003*, China now boasts the largest telecom network capacity in the world, where mobile is poised to overtake fixed-line telephony, as follows.

1   The number of **telephone users** (fixed-line and mobile) in China became the world's largest in 2002, accounting for over 15% of the world's total.

2   By mid-2003, that number had increased by approximately one-eighth to some 472 million, split roughly 50:50 between fixed-line and mobile users.

3   **Mobile phones** have spread like wildfire, achieving an overall **penetration rate** of c.18% compared with only c.1% in 1997, when we first arrived in China; and their increased use for **local calls** (c.48% year-on-year at mid-2003) is rapidly catching up with **fixed-line**. **Global System** (or Standard) **for Mobile** (GSM) networks cover all cities and virtually all counties.

4 This **penetration rate** is only 1% behind **fixed-line phones** at c.19% – an almost threefold increase since 1997 – which are gradually losing **domestic long-distance** market share to an increased use of **mobile** and **internet service provider** (ISP) phone services (c. 26% and c.43%, respectively, year-on-year at mid-2003).

5 To recover market share, fixed-line operators are offering **voice forwarding** (mobile to fixed-line) services.

6 By 2007 – based on a forecasted compound average growth rate (CAGR) of just over 13% – some 785 million Chinese or about 60% of China's current population will be telephone users, accounting for more than one-fifth of the world's fixed-line and mobile total (split approximately 47:53, respectively).

Fixed-line/wired telecommunications

Telephone and facsimile
Maintaining contact with family, friends and business associates via **phone**, **e-mail** or **fax** should not be a problem, for the following reasons:

1 **Fixed/wired telephone lines** are increasingly reliable, both within and between major cities, and internationally.

2 Thankfully, most major hotels and multi-national companies employ English-speaking **switchboard operators**. However, the widespread use of **Domestic Direct Dialing** (DDD), **Subscriber Trunk Dialing**

(STD) and **International Direct Dialing** (IDD) obviates their need when making phone calls.

3   Local department stores offer a wide range of good-quality and well-priced **handsets, extensions, answerphones** – including the cordless variety – and **fax machines**. Before purchasing, however, ensure that the instructions are in a language you understand, unless you have a Chinese-speaking friend or colleague who is prepared to translate them for you!

4   Accommodation in most foreign housing complexes, and rooms in most Western style hotels, are equipped with two telephone lines:
   ◆ *either* one for voice, the other for fax/data;
   ◆ *or* one for personal, the other for business use.

EXAMPLES

1   As mentioned above, we frequently communicated between our China and UK homes via **fax**.
2   When travelling on business outside Beijing, I was able to maintain **fax** and **e-mail** contact by connecting my laptop or personal organiser (PDA) to the corresponding phone socket in my hotel room.

Public pay phones
When calling from a **public pay phone** (which I never had occasion to do) it is better to use a **pre-paid phone-card** than coins since the light weight and small size of the latter can make them unreliable and cumbersome to use, especially for long-distance and international calls.

However be aware that some **phone-cards** can be used only for local (i.e. regional) calls so make sure that you buy ones valid throughout China.

International phone credit cards

Apart from public pay phones, there may be occasions when you need to make expensive, long-distance calls chargeable to your employer using a phone not normally billed to them directly – such as from an office that you are visiting or hotel where you are staying on holiday.

For such occasions, to avoid the hassle of paying cash and/or embarrassment of not having enough of the right change, I recommend an **international phone credit card**, domiciled on your own bank and reimbursable by your employer.

EXAMPLE

My employer provided me with, and paid for, an **international phone credit card**, primarily so that I could keep in contact with our China office (by voice, fax and e-mail) whilst on home leave.

Phone etiquette

As explained in Chapter 12: because of the language barrier and issues of face, discussions between foreigners and the Chinese tend to be conducted face-to-face rather than over the phone and via interpreters; and meetings arranged between intermediaries.

Thus, you will probably not need to speak Chinese very often on the phone.

However, on such rare occasions (for example ringing home and asking the maid if your spouse is there), the phrases listed in Appendix 8 may prove useful (as they did for me).

Big brother

Some foreign business(wo)men have reported that they suspect their Chinese hosts of listening in on phone conversations with the home office during a recess in negotiations as a means of pre-empting the next stage. 'Forewarned is forearmed' for the Chinese...so beware.

Telegrams and telex

In today's world of high-tech communications, we tend to overlook the 'humble' **telegram** and out-dated **telex.**

Nevertheless, these services may and should be still available – for example, at hotel reception and business centres, respectively.

Mobile/wireless telecommunications

Mobile phones

China is now the biggest **mobile phone** market in the world, as per the foregoing statistics. Visit any major city, and it seems that nearly everybody is using one, and not necessarily the apparently more affluent.

Mobile phones can be expensive to buy, but cheap to run (as explained below). Options include:

1   Purchasing a **local SIM card** for your existing handset.

2   Buying **pre-paid re-chargeable local SIM cards** (but note that reception may be weak outside major cities).

3   Renting a **local mobile phone** such as from an international hotel, but only for a short stay.

When buying a **non pre-paid SIM card** – with or without a handset – you will need to provide a permanent local address and/or referee (such as your employer) for billing and payment purposes.

International roaming
Alternatively, if your home network provider has a **roaming agreement** with **China Mobile** or **China Unicom**, in theory you should be able to use your own GSM phone quite seamlessly.

In practice, however, this option can be very expensive.

EXAMPLE
In February 2003, during our visit to Shanghai, the bill for using my UK Nokia Communicator, including e-mail, was some £100 for just one week!

Details of such agreements are available at the websites of:

♦ **China Mobile**: www.chinamobile.com
♦ **China Unicom**: www.netchina.com.cn

Charging your existing handset
Should you use your **existing handset**, in whatever way, ensure that you have a **mains adaptor** for your **charger**!

Expatriate lifeline
For expatriates who find themselves in a difficult situation that defies their command of Chinese, **mobile phones** are a **lifeline** to:

1 **Interpreters**: thankfully, my Chinese PA was prepared to take our mobile phone calls at almost any time of

day or night in order – for example – to explain to:

- a **shop assistant** or our **maid** what we wanted
- our **driver** when/where to take/collect us.

2 **Drivers**: when daytime meetings over/under ran, or evening events had no set duration, we and our driver relied on our and his mobile phone to ensure a prompt rendezvous.

3 **Emergency assistance**: some employers (including mine) provide mobile phones – vulgarly known as 'rape phones' – for the personal safety of spouses.

Value-added services

Both of China's mobile phone operators (mentioned above) have for some time offered:

- **text short messaging service** (SMS) (*xiaolingtong*) which is so popular that the number doubled between 2002 and 2003 to reach c.180 billion (including over 7 billion at Chinese New Year 2003 alone!), no doubt due to its being cheap, convenient, portable and fashionable...but not, necessarily, secure (see below);
- downloads of **ring-tones**;
- transmission of **pictures**.

and are now adding:

- mobile **internet**;
- enhanced or **multi-media messaging service** (MMS).

Security

Given the reported filtering of internet and e-mail traffic, mentioned below, SMS texting is probably equally monitored – especially after the role it reputedly played in disseminating such a volume of rumours, true and false, about SARS sufficient to contribute to mass hysteria and panic.

Costs

It pays to shop around for the best deal, since:

1 Officially, China operates a **two-way billing** system for **mobile voice** services – that is: both parties to the call share the cost.

2 In practice, however, it seems that – despite the government's best efforts to enforce its tariffs – operators are competing on price, including a **quasi one-way billing service**.

3 At the time of writing, **hand-set prices** average some RMB 1,500 or US$ 180; and range from RMB 5,000 to RMB 600 approximately (some US$ 600 to US$ 70).

Pagers

A relatively cheap, but less versatile, alternative means of keeping in touch on the move is to buy a **pager** with one year's **pre-paid service** (which automatically lapses unless you renew it).

TELE- AND VIDEO-CONFERENCING

During my time there (the late 1990s), the only viable method of **tele-conferencing** within and outside China was by means of **telephone conference calls** or – as we often did – participants at each end sitting around a **hands-free speaker-phone**.

Video-conferencing and **in-house television** (apart from closed circuit over short distances) which I had trialed and researched, respectively, in the UK in my previous role were then of neither a quality nor cost nor reliability to be a realistic alternative.

Today, however, with the advances in telecommunications technology, **video-conferencing** is now feasible in China either privately, or by hiring the public facilities provided by a number of business-to-business service companies in major Chinese cities (such as Regus, whose offices I visited in Beijing).

On a less grand scale I am aware of several friends who maintain face-to-face contact with family and friends overseas by converting their personal computer (PC) into a **video-phone** by attaching a **web-camera** and **voice-compatible modem** and dialling via their standard internet connection.

E-COMMUNICATIONS – E-MAIL AND INTERNET

The advent of **e-mail** and the **internet** has posed two problem for 'fortress China' – how to build a new 'Great Wall' to prevent its citizens from:

1   Being exposed to outside – for which read 'corrupting' – influences.

2   Exposing to outside agencies the truth – whatever that is – about China.

Consequently, we are aware of individuals and organisations (see below) whose e-mail and internet access has been:

- monitored by the PSB
- limited to national networks.

Nevertheless, we enjoyed and continue to enjoy unlimited e-mail and internet access with Chinese subscribers.

> **EXAMPLE**
>
> In the late 1990s, when my employer merged with another, I was puzzled to find that the latter's staff had little or no **e-mail** and **internet** access, whereas all mine had been making fulsome use of both for some time, especially for on-line market research (e.g. Reuters). The answer may lie in the fact that we were one of the first foreign companies to participate by invitation in a Chinese national internet system for our business sector.

Today, 'Chinese internet use in general is exploding, with annual growth rates of almost 100%' (*China Business Handbook 2003*, p.33).

Indeed, several years ago, the Yankee Group estimated that by 2005 internet users in China 'will surpass the number in the United States' (*China-Britain Trade Review*, Aug 2000) which, if the accuracy of their 2001 forecast is anything to go by, will be achieved.

The great firewall of China
Despite our experiences of freedom of **internet access**, mentioned above, according to *China Perspectives, N° 47*, Mar Apr 2003, pp. 10 ff:

1 Access is blocked to the websites of:
   (a) 'The big English-language press organs...
   (b) Foreign organisations interested in subjects deemed to be politically sensitive...

(c) Several content providers linked to education, and more precisely to the field of health.'

2 Research by Harvard Law School during the second half of 2002 concluded that, whilst simultaneously accessible from the USA, 25% of the foreign websites to which they simulated access from China were inexplicably inaccessible at least once and nearly 10% on several occasions.

3 'The **filtering of the data** available on the Chinese internet, both on the web and in news groups, is also standard practice in China...

4 Internet cafés are supposed to install programs which memorise the activity of users, who must first give proof of identity to the manager of the establishment...

5 The existence of "**data packet sniffers**" which make it possible to identify "subversive" foreign sites, of **e-mail filters** and of **Big Mamas** on news groups is now largely recognised...

6 The **control architecture** of the internet in China only allows at best interstitial and temporary freedom of expression. Only the most experienced manage to circumvent censorship, at the risk of serious consequences.'

Did we really escape notice? You have been warned!

Digital imaging

When we first travelled overseas (in the 1960s and 1970s), the only cost-effective ways to capture those special moments (e.g. the death of Franco and coronation of Juan-Carlos of Spain) for those back home were photographs and audio-cassettes. Later, in China, in the 1990s, we upgraded to a video-camera; but the tapes still had to be posted home.

Today, **digital** (video) **cameras** and some **mobile phones** allow your grandchildren to send you, over the internet, copies of pictures that they have just done at school or short footages of their birthday party or school nativity play.

Internet cafés
After some initial security problems – resolved by reportedly wholesale closure followed by tough licensing laws – **internet cafés** are now not only popular but also freely accessible in major cities, subject to the scrutiny mentioned above.

Local ISP
Should you require a local ISP, I suggest you contact: **Eastnet China Ltd**: www.eastnet.com.cn

Useful websites
The Bibliography includes a number of websites – that I have scrutinised from many hundreds listed on various search engines – which contain useful references to living and working in China.

Additionally, 'all of China's ministries are now accessible on the internet, though not all their websites have English language versions' (*China-Britain Trade Review*, Jan 2000).

E-COMMERCE

One consequence of China's accession to the WTO has been the lifting of restrictions on the use of the internet domain '**.cn**' (in December 2002), including making it available to qualifying non-Chinese.

EXAMPLE

Even I have acquired a Chinese domain name (minim.org.cn) and, hence, e-mail address (china.consulting@minim.org.cn).

As a result, 'the country is poised to become one of the most dominant e-commerce players in the Asia/Pacific region – and the world' (*The Next Frontier of Global E-Business*, NeuStar).

However, the following obstacles currently hamper transacting business and buying goods on-line.

1   **Unsophisticated banking systems** (despite initial incursions into on-line payment and internet banking systems).

2   Predominantly **cash culture**, encouraged by a vicious circle of a:
    ◆ preference for paying cash;
    ◆ limited use of credit-cards.

3   **Distrust of protection under the law** – actual or perceived – as regards the:
    ◆ replacement of defective goods;
    ◆ security of payment;
    except in person and for cash, respectively.

4   *Guanxi* – the way that business in China has been traditionally conducted between 'connected' people

(as described in Chapter 2) means that some:

- **Chinese customers** may dislike dealing with anonymous traders;
- **foreign dot.coms** without *guanxi* may have difficulties in securing the necessary licences;

apart from any technological considerations, such as: availability of terminals, quality of web services, access cost and speed of access, costs and reliability of networks; or government regulation.

Nevertheless in the wake of SARS, when some Chinese consumers were tempted to switch to **on-line shopping** in order to reduce their exposure to infection in public shops, China's e-commerce has experienced an epiphany – which just goes to prove that every cloud has a silver lining!

Small office/home office (SOHO)

If further proof were needed of China's capacity for **e-commerce**: when, in mid-2003, the Chinese authorities placed all 700 employees of Alibaba.com under house quarantine – after one of them was hospitalised with suspected SARS – the company was soon up and running from their homes via broadband (*China-Britain Trade Review*, Sep 2003).

PRACTICAL CONSIDERATIONS

Time difference

You will need to consider how (to resolve any problems that) the **time difference** between China and your home country may impact on telecommunications as follows.

1   Greenwich Mean Time (GMT) is eight hours behind China, with the result that, for example, when you have almost completed a full day's work and are thinking of clocking off, your **European colleagues** are just arriving at their office.

2   Consequently, for example, most:
   - **faxes** and **e-mails** from the West will normally arrive **outside working hours**;
   - **phone conversations** with the West will often be **during unsociable hours** for one party.

3   With **faxes** and **e-mails**, the time difference can work for or against you, respectively, as follows:
   (a) **Non-urgent** ones can be answered the next day, during your working hours and before the originator arrives at their office.
   (b) **Urgent** ones, requiring immediate attention – or at least before the close of the originator's working day – may have to be:
      - *not only* **dealt with in the evening** when, for example, co-respondents (especially Chinese) may not be readily available;
      - *but also* **sent to your home**.

4   Consequently, do not be surprised if your employer (like mine):
   - *not only* insists on your having a business fax-cum-e-mail facility at home (at their expense);
   - *but also* uses it to send you urgent and confidential communications, especially overnight and at weekends!

5   However, from personal experience, every cloud has a
    silver lining – if not two – since you can always:

    ◆ take your mind off the appalling traffic conditions
      whilst being driven at break-neck speed between
      home and the office by drafting replies;

    ◆ return the favour by swamping your home office
      with similar communications to arrive at an equally
      unsociable time!

EXAMPLE

I would frequently wake up in the morning – including at the weekends –
to find various **faxes** and **e-mails** waiting for me in my study, which I
dealt with in these ways.

---

6   Expect to receive and have to make **phone calls during
    unsociable hours** for you, both for business and private
    purposes – again especially confidential ones.

EXAMPLES

1 One evening, just as we were leaving a bar where we had been
  celebrating a successful negotiation, I received a call on my **mobile
  phone** from my boss in London about a most urgent and confidential
  matter. To play for time – i.e. sober up – I explained that I was away
  from the office, but would ask my driver immediately to take me there
  (rather than home) from where I would ring him back.
2 Whilst my employer was going through an international merger,
  confidential **phone calls at mid-night** were *de rigueur*.

---

7   To avoid **confidential faxes** being sent to a general
    office and seen by all-and-sundry, you should install a
    separate line in your personal office.

8   Phone conversations with friends and family in the
    West will also probably occur at awkward times for

one party, especially during the week when your sleeping hours may coincide with their working day; and may need to be scheduled in advance.

EXAMPLES

1 One the one hand:
   a We tended to ring our children and parents late on a Sunday evening, when it was early afternoon in the UK.
   b When I was trying to arrange the music for our second son's wedding in the UK, I sometimes had to get up in the early hours of the morning to ring the people involved in their evening time, when they had got home from work.
2 On the other hand: when our first grandchild was born in the UK in the middle of the night, we received the phone call at breakfast time.

Who pays the bills?

Unless you have no family or friends with whom you need or wish to maintain contact, your bill for **personal long-distance phone calls** (including **fax** and **e-mail**) is likely to be fairly high, even by the standards of expatriate salaries – a fact that most caring employers readily recognise (in our experience) by subsidising such calls to a greater or lesser extent.

I recommend, therefore, that, before moving to China, you agree with your employer who pays what.

EXAMPLES

My employer paid:
1 **All mobile phone calls** (including my wife's), on the basis that they were normally connected with and/or occasioned by business issues, language difficulties or considerations of personal safety and security peculiar to China.

2 **50% of all private phone calls**, whether local or international. Accounting was made easy by our having two phone lines at home, as intimated above: one for personal, the other for business use.

3 My **international phone credit card**, which it provided for me, as mentioned above.

Special tariffs

There are a whole host of telecommunications service providers offering **special tariffs for expatriates to phone home** – too numerous and varied to mention here.

Alternatively, your ISP may allow you to '**piggy-back**' and use their connection for voice as well as data transmission.

For details, I suggest you:

◆ contact your fixed and mobile phone and internet service providers;
◆ consult the plethora of magazines specifically aimed at expatriates;

both in China and your home country.

Dialling codes

As elsewhere in the world, to phone another country from China: dial the international access code **00**, followed by the country code, area code (without leading 0) and number.

For China, the:

◆ **country code** is **86**;
◆ most important **area codes** are listed as Appendix 9.

Useful phone numbers

Useful phone numbers are listed as Appendix 10.

Hotels

As well as their in-room facilities, most **hotels** frequented by business(wo)men have well-equipped **business centres**, offering **phone, fax, e-mail** and **internet** services.

However, as elsewhere in the world, they tend to charge high rates, especially for international use; and may impose a minimum charge, regardless of the length of your call or transmission.

Thus, if you are living in one for any length of time, I suggest that for use that is personal and/or not chargeable to your business you should consider:

1 **Installing a private line**, subject to your having a residence permit or Chinese person prepared to vouch for you.

2 Arranging with a friend, colleague or your employer **to borrow** their home or office facilities.

3 **Reversing the charge**, by dialing 108 followed by the country code, etc. ...provided you can persuade the person whom you are calling to collect!

Other tips for hotel-based expatriates:

4 Give prospective callers your room number, which the hotel switchboard is more likely to recognise than your foreign name.

5   Before connecting your laptop or similar to the phone socket in your hotel room, check that so doing will not 'fry' your modem!

MEDIA

Press

For those who cannot read Chinese: **English-language** and **foreign newspapers** and **magazines** are available in international bookshops and hotels (such as *China Daily*, *International Herald Tribune* and *Time*, respectively) or, if not, on a subscription basis from home or via the internet.

Whilst it would be invidious of me to comment on or recommend any one in particular, suffice it to say:

◆   do not believe everything you read in the newspapers, especially those from Chinese publishing houses and targeted at foreigners
◆   if you cannot decide, choose the one with the best crossword!

EXAMPLE

Presumptuous as it may seem: during one posting when I used little written English even outside work on a regular basis apart from tackling crosswords, I asked my employer to send me *The Times* rather than *The Daily Telegraph*, because I no longer found the latter's puzzles sufficiently challenging!

Another source of information specifically aimed at the expatriate market are the **foreign community**:

- **magazines**, which are readily available in international hotel lobbies and clubs or, again, some on-line;
- **notice-boards**, such as in the foreign supermarkets, full of advertisements for events, items wanted and for sale, personal services (such as maids, drivers, language teachers) and similar.

Finally my wife occasionally paid well over the odds and treated herself to a **woman's magazine** from the bookshop of our nearest international hotel in Beijing (Lido).

Radio and television

There are English-language news bulletins by the Chinese state **radio** and Beijing **television** (to which I sometimes listened whilst getting up and going to bed).

For **reliable** and **impartial news broadcasts**, however, I would recommend the:

- World Service of the **BBC radio** (via a short-wave radio);
- **CNN** and **BBC television** rolling news programmes which are invariably available in foreigners' accommodation and international hotels.

$$\left(11\right)$$

Transport

AIR

Given the size of the country, the most common and quickest form of transport that foreign business people use to travel any significant distance within China – although some major cities are within driving distance of each other, such as Beijing-Tianjin or Guangzhou-Shenzhen – is **air**, as follows.

1   Thankfully, China now has many **domestic airline companies** operating **modern aircraft** on **internal routes**, for whom **safety** has become a priority, resulting in a marked reduction in the number of **accidents** (as mentioned in Chapter 3 and detailed in Appendix 3).

2   Nevertheless, it is probably preferable to fly with **the better-known airlines** such as **Air China, China Eastern Airlines** or **China Southern Airlines** as they are more likely to provide an acceptable **level of service**, even if not wholly up to Western standards for those used to the creature comforts and pampering of international business or first class.

EXAMPLE

We frequently travelled business class with **Air China** both domestically and internationally and always felt very safe and reasonably comfortable. With **other domestic carriers**, however, we normally flew First Class, but still felt less safe and comfortable. Nevertheless, we did appreciate the separate check-in desks and departure lounges...and some of the gifts were very acceptable!

3   Your office (and/or hotel, as appropriate) should be able to **book flights** for you through CITS, local travel agents or airline offices – but possibly not until only a few days in advance of the flight.

4   It is advisable to **re-confirm your return flight**.

EXAMPLES

1   My Chinese PA used to visit CITS with wads of cash to purchase my airline tickets.
2   On arrival at my destination, I would invariably ask the hotels' reception or business centre staff to re-confirm my return flight – a service that many Western-style five-star hotels automatically offer to guests staying in their executive rooms.

5   There is a **departure tax**, payable at the airport in cash in Chinese currency, of RMB 50 or RMB 90 for all domestic or international flights, respectively – so do remember to have your money ready.

6   Airlines often ask you to **check in** two hours before departure. However – if this seems 'over the top' – from our experience, for:
   (a) *International flights*: this is very necessary in view of all the **departure formalities** and **security checks**.
   (b) *Domestic flights*: one hour may be quite sufficient especially if travelling first or business class, for which there is usually a **fast-track check-in**.

7   Most importantly give yourself ample time to get to the airport through the thronging urban traffic, especially if travelling during the rush hour. It is better to arrive early at the airport, and savour the first/business class lounge, than late, and miss the plane.

8   Nevertheless, I still have vivid memories of often having to hang around airports, waiting for **delayed arrivals** and **departures**.

9   The free **baggage allowance** is:
    ◆ *economy class*: 20 kilos;
    ◆ *business class*: 30 kilos;
    ◆ *first class*: 40 kilos.

10 Additionally, first-class passengers are allowed two 5-kilo pieces and others one of **hand** ('carry-on') **luggage**, although this is rarely weighed which may explain why few people bother to check in luggage on a domestic flight: it is quicker just to lug it on and off the plane.

EXAMPLE

It is not an uncommon sight – especially between mainland China and Hong Kong – to see Chinese passengers struggling onto planes with trolley-type **carry-on luggage** that they can hardly lift and which barely fits into the overhead lockers.

11 **Cabin staff** can speak, and **flight announcements** are made in, **English** as well as Chinese.

12 All flights are **non-smoking**.

13 Chinese **airports** can be quite daunting for the first-

time visitor, but you will soon get used to their idiosyncrasies as follows:

(a) Be prepared for **long queues** and/or interminable **scrutiny of travel document**s and/or repeated **security checks**.

(b) Have all your **travel documents** easily to hand at all times, and be ready to offer them open at the right page.

(c) Stand behind the lines painted on the floor in front of the various **check-in** and **security desks**; and do not move forward until signalled by an official (who may shout at you if you do!).

(d) Smile at, be polite to, but do not try to make small or clever talk with the **check-in** and **security officials**.

(e) **Departure lounges** tend not to be as comfortable, and **luggage trolleys** – unless your driver can grab one for you – as plentiful, as in the West.

(f) As with all things in China, **patience** is a virtue.

14 At all times – when booking, re-confirming and travelling – have your **passport** available.

Travelling with children

According to TravelChinaGuide.com: 'Since the Chinese are fond of children, **traveling with children** in China is not difficult, but it can be a challenge. In order to keep your child healthy, safe and comfortable during travel, some tips are offered' in general (see: www.travelchina-guide.com/essential/children.htm) and in particular for **air travel**, as follows:

1 '*For an infant (up to 2 years of age):* the **fare** for international and domestic flights is 10% of the full fare; the infant cannot occupy a seat. Limit one lap child per accompanying adult.

2 *For a child (2–12 years of age):* the **fare** for a seat on a domestic flight is 50% of the full fare.

3 *Child up to 12 years old:* is free from the **airport construction fee** but **departure tax** is required.

4 If you purchase a ticket for your child, **reserve adjoining seats**.'

RAIL

The following comments are based on research, rather than personal experience, since few senior expatriates have cause and/or inclination to use the Chinese railway system for business travel.

National railways

1 **Train seats** come in the following four **options** or **categories** (more politically correct terms than 'classes' in socialist China!).

   (a) **Hard seat:** upholstered, but invariably crowded, dirty, noisy and smoky.

   (b) **Soft seat:** more comfortable, non-smoking, less crowded and with plenty of leg room.

   (c) **Hard sleeper:** comprising open six-berth (in three tiers) compartments, similar to some European youth hostels, with the best berths in the **middle tier** (as they are unlikely to be commandeered by other passengers as day-time seats, and have good headroom).

(d) **Soft sleeper:** comprising closed four-berth (in two tiers) luxury – quiet, clean, even air-conditioned – compartments with Western-style toilet and washing facilities; and costing almost as much as flying.

2   Should you be adventurous enough to take the train:
   (a) Other than for short journeys, you are not only advised for reasons of comfort and security but also expected as a foreigner to travel in **soft sleeper**, for which specific **personal safety** recommendations are listed in Chapter 3.
   (b) On **long-distance trains** the **restaurant cars** are better than they used to be; but still have set opening hours, between which you are advised to rely on providing your own refreshments, including tea, coffee powder and dried milk (for which **hot water** is readily available).
   (c) The **safety record** of the railway system is good (as mentioned in Chapter 3, together with basic general **personal safety** recommendations).
   (d) The **toilets**, irrespective of class, are not usually very hygienic; and you are advised to take your own toilet paper, soap and towel.
   (e) Few routes have **air-conditioned carriages**.
   (f) Trains are invariably **punctual**.

3   When **buying tickets**:
   (a) **At the station**, the easiest place to buy tickets is the counter in the soft seat waiting room for current and next-day tickets.
   (b) **Sleepers** can be booked up to four days in advance.
   (c) **Long distance tickets** should be bought 24 hours, if not several days, in advance.

Local/urban railways

1 The cities of Beijing, Guangzhou, Shanghai and Tianjin (and soon Nanjing) are served by an **underground railway** (aka metro, subway or 'underground dragon') of which the key features are briefly as follows:

(a) The **underground** is:

- **fast:** up to 70 kilometres per hour (kph). Indeed, given the high volume of urban traffic, this may be the quickest means of public transport if you are in a hurry, although crowded in the rush hour;
- **clean:** smoking, graffiti and garbage are banned;
- **cheap:** less than US$1 per journey, with free transfers between inter-connecting lines;
- **safe:** being well-lit and well-policed;
- **bilingual:** with **station announcements** in English, and **signs** and **schedules** in *pinyin*, as well as Chinese.

(b) Currently, there are no **bulk-buy savings** or **travel cards**; but, to save queuing, you can buy **pre-paid tickets**.

(c) The **sign** outside a station is:

- *either*: a blue 'D' for *ditie* (the Chinese for 'subway');
- *or*: a red 'M' for metro.

(d) Stations do not usually have **toilets**.

(e) Some **drivers** may skip stations to make up lost time!

2 Apart from traditional urban trains, some major cities are introducing **elevated light-rail** and **magnetic levitation** (aka *maglev*) systems, the latter capable of speeds of up to 500 kph.

Future developments

1 With the prospect of the **2008 Olympics** in Beijing and **World Expo 2010** in Shanghai, more 'bullet' style trains are expected, possibly including a *maglev* connecting Beijing with Tianjin, Shanghai and Guangzhou.

2 'Between metropolitan cities and on major corridors, dedicated passenger lines and **high speed railways** shall be built so as to construct a fast dedicated passenger traffic network with the high speed railways as the backbones and with Beijing and Shanghai and Guangzhou as the centers' according to the then Vice-Minister of Railways (Cai Qinghua), speaking at the National Railway Working Conference in 2003.

ROAD

Road safety is a major problem in China, as detailed in Chapter 3 – but gradually improving with the introduction of good quality **express highways** in, around and in some cases (e.g. Beijing-Tianjin; Guangzhou-Shenzhen) between major cities.

Cars

1 Most expatriates are provided with a **company car** and **driver**, for good reasons, as explained and detailed in Chapters 1 and 7, respectively.

2 It is becoming easier to hire a car (with driver) in the bigger cities, where **car hire companies** (such as Avis) are springing up as the number of affluent Chinese with driving licences increases. Indeed, **renting cars** has become something of a vogue, with many Chinese

using them in preference to taxis for business purposes.

EXAMPLES

1 During the late 1990s we **hired** a car (with driver) each time a group of senior executives visited China for several days to attend multiple meetings when my own car (with driver) was insufficient on its own. On such occasions, when punctuality and safety were paramount, this was preferable to using **taxis**.

2 In 2002, during our visit to Shanghai, we hired an executive car with driver and English-speaking tour guide for an afternoon at a cost of approximately US$90 or £60.

Taxis

1   If you do not have your own transport, the best way to get around any city is by **taxi**, which should be reasonably cheap (starting at about the equivalent of US$1.50 or £1), hassle-free and – outside rush-hour – easy to flag down.

EXAMPLE

One Chinese friend of ours, who lives in Shanghai, got rid of his private car on retirement, and now relies on **taxis** as an equally efficient but cheaper means of reduced transport.

2   Nevertheless, be prepared for crowded and chaotic streets that may take a long time to negotiate, and leave plenty of time for your journeys.

3   Bearing in mind that **taxi drivers** (who are of both sexes):
   ◆ are surprisingly bad at finding their way around;
   ◆ rarely speak anything other than Chinese;

- cannot generally read *pinyin*.

do ensure that you have a Chinese character map and/ or your destination, home and office addresses written down in characters. It also helps if you have your own directions, and sit in the front with a map: if you look helpless, you may literally be 'taken for a ride'! When in doubt ensure that the driver knows where you want to go *before* getting into the taxi.

EXAMPLES

1 My Chinese bilingual PA provided me with home-made **'flash-cards'** in Chinese characters (for the taxi driver to read), *pinyin* (for me to read out) and English (for me to understand) of the main destinations to which I used to catch a taxi when my car and driver were otherwise occupied (usually by my wife!).

2 Many hotels provide guests with a similar card, listing their address and the main tourist attractions for you to point at or tick whichever you require.

3 We found that greeting the taxi driver in Chinese and subsequently commenting on the heavy traffic (*che tai duo* – literally 'cars too many') gave the impression that we were Chinese-speaking!

4   When hailing a taxi from an **hotel** – whether you are staying there, or attending a meeting or banquet, or just passing by – you will often find that there is a **bell-hop** on duty who can help you by:

(a) Telling the taxi-driver your destination.

(b) Writing down your destination (in Chinese) and the taxi registration on a card for you to keep.

5   Taxis usually **charge** by distance and time taken, so check that the driver turns on the **meter** at the beginning of each trip (although most drivers are surprisingly honest).

6 When it comes to **paying**:
   (a) Beware of and protect against the **financial scams** mentioned in Chapter 3 by carrying **small change**.
   (b) Always ask for a **receipt** (*ka-fa-piao*), showing the fare, taxi and driver details, as well as a phone number to call in case of problems (e.g. mislaid or forgotten luggage), which – judging by our experience in Shanghai in 2002 – may well be a machine-issued ticket rather than a hand-scrawled note.
   (c) You may find that some taxi-drivers in the main cities (such as Shanghai) are now able to accept payment by **credit card**.

7 If you find a taxi driver whom you particularly like, ask for a card: most have phones, and can be hired for the day (probably more cheaply than an executive service, such as mentioned above).

8 In the event of a problem: make a note of the driver's details as shown on the **identity card** or **driver's licence** displayed in the taxi.

Buses

1 Some **foreign housing complexes** provide **shuttle buses**, especially at the weekends, to local shopping centres. In all honesty, we can say that their drivers are the worst we have come across anywhere in the world (as mentioned in Chapters 3 and 6).

2 Many **hotels** have **courtesy buses** – downtown or airport – of which we have had good experience.

3 For transporting large numbers of people, it is

possible to hire a small **private coach** with driver rather than a fleet of cars.

EXAMPLES

We hired a **private coach** with driver on two occasions:

1 When accompanying a group of senior executives and their entourage to the Ming Tombs and Great Wall.
2 For a company outing to and picnic in the countryside.

4 Some **long-distance buses** are equipped with television, air-conditioning and toilets (as in the West) and fall into two categories (akin to trains): **soft seat** and **soft sleeper**.

Bicycles

1 China is *the* country to **buy** a good (export-standard) quality locally-built **bicycle** at a very reasonable price.

EXAMPLES

We bought the following top-of-the range **bicycles** in Beijing in 1997:

1 Two adult road-bicycles for about RMB 900 (approximately US$ 110 or £70) each.
2 A genuine **BMX** for some RMB 1300 (approximately US$ 155 or £100).
3 A light-weight (carbon-fibre and aluminium) **high-performance semi-professional mountain bicycle** for RMB 8,500 (approximately US$1,025 or £655) – which would have cost half as much again in the UK.

2 Looking back, I wish I had bought – and brought back to the UK – a **bicycle with integral trailer**, which many foreigners find very useful for carrying shopping and small children around the larger expatriate housing complexes.

3 **Riding a bicycle**, however, other than off-road, is another question! (As mentioned in Chapter 3.)

4 Always remember:
   (a) Where you have left your bicycle – especially in the huge **cycle parks** outside some large stores – as you might not recognise it amidst the myriad of similar machines!
   (b) To leave your bicycle **protected** and **locked** against malefactors.

5 If your bicycle suffers a **puncture** or **accident**, you will normally find that there is a **road-side repairer** nearby (although not always as up-market as the Shanghainese one illustrated in Figure 27).

Fig. 27. Roadside bicycle repairer.

6   Do not be surprised to see the Chinese using a bicycle as a:

(a) **People carrier** with father, mother and child on the saddle, rear pannier and cross-bar, respectively.

(b) **Goods vehicle** with drums of tar balanced either side of the rear wheel, or furniture piled high on the rear pannier, or towing a trailer full of people or goods.

EXAMPLE

When we bought various white electrical goods for the office, the vendor wanted to deliver them by bicycle before we insisted on more conventional transport.

Motorbikes

1   Some city authorities are trying to clamp down on the burgeoning **motorbikes**, which we found more numerous the further south we went, especially in Guangzhou.

2   For the 'Peter Pans': second world war-style **motorbikes with sidecar** are available at very reasonable prices (approximately US$1,500 or £1,000 in the late 1990s).

EXAMPLE

In 1998, a small group of British expatriate businessmen rode all the way from Beijing to London on such motorbikes!

Pedicabs (aka rickshaws)

Last but not least: apart from the **rickshaw** tours (pictured in Figure 28) which are well worth trying once, you may find **pedicabs** plying their trade as an alternative to motorised taxis, for those who have time and money to waste.

Fig. 28. A pedicab.

WATER

1 I have already referred to **ferries** in Chapter 3, in the context of their potential risks.

2 As practising boating enthusiasts, we have:
   - ♦ enjoyed public **river cruises** out of Guangzhou and Shanghai;
   - ♦ been disappointed not to find any **private boating facilities**.

(12)

Work Practices

EXCHANGING GIFTS AND FAVOURS

Appropriate gifts

1   Although it's the thought that counts, as mentioned in Chapter 1, it is nevertheless important to select appropriate and avoid inappropriate gifts – particularly as giving the wrong gift to somebody you have not met before could cause offence.

2   To be on the safe side, therefore: consult your Chinese advisors, for whom – infuriatingly – choosing the right gifts may be the most important task in planning a business event.

3   Goods imported from the home country have prestige value and help win points in the face game.

EXAMPLES

I have found that the following are much appreciated:
1 Crystal (e.g. Waterford) fruit bowls.
2 Porcelain (e.g. Wedgwood) wall-plates.

---

4   In theory, it is customary for foreigners to present a **large collective gift** to their Chinese hosts, rather than several small gifts to individual members. This practice not only satisfies Chinese **egalitarianism** and **collectivism** but also avoids accusations of offering/ receiving **bribes**.

5   In practice, however it is now customary (instead of or in addition to a collective gift) to give **small individual gifts** to the Chinese, who may keep them if they are of nominal value (say: no more than **RMB** 200, equivalent to about US$25 or £15).

6   In either case, gifts should correlate with the recipients' status.

7   Giving a very valuable gift to a powerful individual, especially in private, could risk you and the recipient being accused of **bribery** – a crime under Chinese law – and should, therefore, be avoided.

Reciprocity

In the spirit of the Chinese proverb, quoted in Chapter 1, that 'courtesy demands reciprocity':

1   Gifts and favours given in return for those received should roughly **correlate** in magnitude with each other, so as not to cause a loss of face; and over time should **balance** each other out. Note: It helps to keep a **record** of gifts and favours exchanged and refused, and also avoids repetitions.

2   Be wary of the expensive gift that precedes a request for a favour; and do not be afraid politely to decline a gift from someone for whom you have never done, nor intend to do, a favour. With apologies to Virgil: '**Beware of Chinese bearing gifts**'.

Etiquette

In China, exchanging gifts is an intrinsic element of courteous behaviour with its own etiquette – which normally includes:

1 **Wrapping gifts** in (preferably) red paper, material or similar.

2 **Presenting gifts** with a slight bow and both hands – as a sign of respect and courtesy.

3 **Ritually refusing gifts** up to three times, before finally **accepting** – in keeping with the Chinese tradition of public displays of modesty, and to avoid accusations of personal material gain. Note: Never **retract a gift**, unless you sense genuine reluctance; nor **reject unwanted gifts**, unless unwelcome.

4 **Not opening gifts publicly** in the presence of the giver, but privately at home – which would otherwise contradict the Chinese view that the thought counts more than the gift.

Tipping

1 In theory, **tipping** is officially forbidden in socialist, egalitarian China as the patronising and exploitative act of a capitalist regime – since serving the motherland, not cash, should be sufficient motivation and reward for doing a good job.

2 In practice, however, service personnel in many high-class venues frequented by foreigners now explicitly seek **tips**, with an implicit alternative of poor service since cash, not patriotism, buys goods.

3 As with all gifts, **refusal** is part of the **acceptance ritual** to avoid which you could always slip the tip into the recipient's pocket in private. However, given government policy, do not persist if the refusal seems genuine, but trust the recipient's instinct for the risk involved.

NEGOTIATING TECHNIQUES

Chinese negotiating tactics

1   When negotiating with the Chinese, you may find that they try to:
    ◆ control the arrangements;
    ◆ exploit your and their weaknesses;
    ◆ exploit your remorse;
    ◆ trip you up;
    ◆ embarrass you;
    ◆ play you off against your competitors;
    ◆ approach you via a third party;
    ◆ pretend to be annoyed with you;
    ◆ go over old ground with you;
    ◆ quote their law at you;
    ◆ manage your expectations.

Dos and don'ts for negotiating with the Chinese

Since most of their tactics involve **face**, your best counter is to **play the Chinese at their own game** and **not rise to the bait** as follows.

1   **Always**:
    ◆ prepare beforehand;
    ◆ remember that the final decision(s) may be made by persons not at the meeting(s);
    ◆ inflate your price;
    ◆ play to the Chinese strengths;
    ◆ look for opportunities to empathise with the Chinese;
    ◆ display long-term commitment to China;
    ◆ go over every detail of the contract;

♦ be prepared for much back-tracking, repetition, ambiguity and inevitable misunderstandings;
♦ take detailed notes;
♦ be able to walk away from the table;
♦ know where the exits are;
♦ check your ego at the door;
♦ be careful what you say to the media.

2 **Never**:
♦ try to resolve problems individually;
♦ concede too easily;
♦ hesitate to cut your losses;
♦ reject a Chinese position out of hand;
♦ assume that the Chinese may make decisions for economic reasons alone;
♦ assume there is such a thing as 'China plc';
♦ speak off the record;
♦ lose your temper;
♦ lose your patience;
♦ embarrass the Chinese;
♦ gloat at a successful agreement.

Overcoming objections

1 Where not already included above, Scott D. Seligman (*op. cit.,* pp. 146–148) suggests that, to overcome objections, you should:
♦ appeal to a higher-level decision-maker;
♦ ask the right question; push the right button;
♦ be 'Mr nice guy';
♦ show respect; be modest;
♦ take risks;
♦ use your *guanxi* to go through the back door (*zou houmen*);

2   When all else fails, try the three 'Fs' – be: **f**irm, **f**air and **f**riendly.

BUSINESS MEETINGS

Making arrangements
Arranging meetings is a nightmare, and flexibility the solution.

1   **How**
   (a) To maintain the protagonists' **face**, meetings are usually arranged by **intermediaries** who have the right *guanxi*.
   (b) Thus '**cold calling**' is not normally appropriate in China.

2   **When**
   The Chinese tend to:
   (a) Dislike committing to future appointments (in case they cannot keep them) but prefer to **make arrangements** as late as possible, when they have a clearer idea of other obligations – say: not more than two weeks ahead.
   (b) **Finalise arrangements** with visiting foreigners only after they have arrived in China, contending that anything could happen in the meantime to abort the visit.
   (c) **Rearrange** and even **cancel meetings** at the last minute – usually on the face-saving grounds that they have been unexpectedly summoned by the powers that be.

In such ways do the Chinese put foreigners (even Prime

Ministers) in their place, and remind them who is in charge!

3 **With whom**
   (a) Consistent with the rules of **face**, meetings should take place between principals of **equal rank**.
   (b) Thus, until the **foreign principal's identity** is confirmed, that of the Chinese principal may not be revealed.
   (c) Additionally, the Chinese may treat foreign visitors in proportion to their **country of origin**, gauging their commitment to and respect for China by the distance travelled: the greater, the better.

Preparation

Besides being good standard business practice, carefully **preparing meetings** should prevent your falling prey to Chinese tactics (mentioned above) for negotiating new concessions or information.

1 **Agenda setting**
   (a) The Chinese expect meetings to have (for them) a **beneficial purpose** – otherwise, why give up their precious time? They may only agree to meet you if you have something new to say or benefit to offer.
   (b) Moreover, the Chinese **dislike surprises**, preferring to:
       ◆ **collectively agree** their position in advance of a meeting in order to **present a united front**;
       ◆ **react** to others' ideas, rather than bear the onus of setting the agenda themselves;
       ◆ select the **proper participants** for a meeting.

(c) Thus you should exchange beforehand (in Chinese) a:

+ **detailed agenda** of the topics for discussion;
+ **brief curriculum vitae** of each participant;

(d) Otherwise, you may be fobbed off with Chinese participants who are not the decision makers whom you require.

2 **Briefing**

(a) Ensure that every member of your group is fully briefed about what they may (not) say in general – and in particular as to the:

+ **aims** and **objectives** of the meeting; individual **contributions** and **roles**; and meeting **etiquette**;
+ recent and planned developments in **China**; details of the **Chinese organisation**; and personal and career details of the **Chinese participants**;
+ **questions** that they may (not) ask of the Chinese; **questions** that the Chinese may ask of them; and **answers** that they may (not) give;
+ plans and achievements of **your organisation**, and its **main competitors**, in relation to China; and the history of its previous relationship and meetings with the Chinese organisation.

EXAMPLE

I used to prepare a full **briefing-pack** for each programme of meetings between my international board members and senior Chinese government officials (at about six-weekly intervals), including a literal transcript of an opening speech, follow-up remarks and questions, and answers to **frequently asked questions** (FAQs).

(b) Otherwise, meetings can quickly resemble Daniel going into the lion's den.

Logistics

1 **When**

As a general rule, meetings should:

(a) **Last** no more than 30 minutes to one hour, following the Maoist principle that 'meetings should not go on too long'.

(b) **Start/finish** no earlier/later than half-an-hour after/before the beginning/end of the working morning or afternoon.

(c) Allow for the process of **interpretation** – which can reduce the effective discussion time to a half or a third.

2 **Where**

(a) Meetings are normally held in **purpose-built conference rooms** – not offices – with chairs **formally arranged** around the perimeter of the room or a central oblong table.

3 **Note taking**

(a) Ensure you have a **bilingual note-taker**, in order to counter the **Chinese** who tend to:

♦ bring a **note-taker** with them, whose **minutes** could later (be used to) embarrass you or your organisation when quoted by someone (not) present at the meeting;

♦ when **negotiating**, try to trip you up, embarrass you or go over old ground with you, against which comprehensive notes are the most effective **defence**;

- ask interminable multiple **questions** in one long sentence which are easier to answer if written and broken down into their component parts by your note-taker.

(b) Moreover, you need someone in your party who can:

- monitor the **interpreter**(s) – otherwise you will not know if what you said/heard was what the Chinese heard/said;
- ensure your **interpreter** does not converse directly with your interlocutor – which I have known some try to do!

4 Interpreters

In addition to the normal rules for using interpreters in China you should observe the following guidelines:

(a) Even the Chinese who speak foreign languages commonly conduct meetings with foreigners via interpreters as a:

- ploy to gain **face-saving** thinking time;
- status symbol to enhance their importance or **face**.

(b) Consequently, **never**:

- assume that your Chinese interlocutors do not understand your language;
- make **asides** in your own language, in case you are overheard and understood.

(c) Similarly, even if you speak Chinese, you should consider providing your own interpreter, in order to avoid giving the impression that you are not senior enough to warrant one and thus not their equal – which would cause them and you a loss of **face**.

(d) In China, interpreters often enjoy **intimate relationships** with their principals and/or wield **influence** in their own right. Thus, a Chinese man's female interpreter may also be his mistress. Ensure, therefore, that your relationship with your interpreter is (seen to be) above reproach.

5 **Caution**

(a) From the foregoing, it follows that there is no such thing in China as **speaking off the record** – since anything you say may be taken down and later used in evidence against you by the Chinese when and however it benefits them.

Preliminaries

1 **Arrival**

(a) **Punctuality** is a virtue and tardiness an insult in China where:

- ◆ **visitors**: are expected to arrive exactly on time – neither late nor early;
- ◆ **hosts**: should pre-assemble in the meeting room ready to greet their visitors – to keep whom waiting is even ruder;
- ◆ **latecomers**: should apologise profusely to show they mean no insult.

(b) A representative of the host (such as the interpreter) should **meet** the **visitors** – say at reception – and **accompany** them to the meeting room.

(c) **Visitors** should enter the meeting room in **rank order** to allow the hosts to identify the principal and main secondary visitors; otherwise, they may mistake whomever does enter first as the principal visitor.

(d) If the Chinese greet the foreigners with **applause**, the correct response is to applaud (not wave) back.

2 **Welcome and introductions**

(a) The principal host and visitor should introduce their colleagues in **rank order** and, where appropriate:

   ♦ participants of **equal rank** in **age order**;
   ♦ **women** to men.

(b) The Chinese seldom hold **one-to-one meetings**, but are invariably accompanied by colleagues (including observers, apprentices and even covert Party members). You may, therefore, be out-numbered and/or not introduced to everyone, which is just one method that they use to try to put foreigners in their place.

(c) During **introductions** greet appropriately (as described in Chapter 2), smile, nod your head and exchange **name cards**.

3 **Name cards**

The Chinese lay great store by **name cards** (aka visiting or business cards).

(a) **Having** name cards means you are '**somebody**'; hence, **not having** any may be construed as your being a '**nobody**'.

(b) The more name cards you collect, the more important people you have met – thus increasing your **face** and *guanxi*.

4 **Seating**

(a) Important visitors should be **escorted** to their seats, and the **principal visitor** placed in the seat of honour to the right of the principal host (or facing, if at a table).

(b) Others may sit where they like though it is customary to sit in **rank order**.

Structure

Meetings between foreigners and Chinese officials are **structured dialogues** between both principals. Other participants act as observers and speak only on their principal's explicit invitation, since **to interrupt a speaker is rude**.

1 **Beginning**
   (a) The Chinese code of courteous behaviour **favours circumlocution** and frowns on blunt speech (for which they often criticise foreigners). You should, therefore:
   - begin with small talk and ice-breakers such as general observations or questions before easing into the focus of meeting;
   - avoid laying all your cards on the table at the outset.
   (b) The **Chinese principal** will not interrupt; and may reply in similar vein, including a lecture on China for the 'illiterate' foreigners, for which you should show appreciation by smiling and later asking clarifying questions.

2 **Middle**
   (a) The Chinese will normally ask **you to speak first** which is not only good manners, but also a ploy to gain the upper-hand by lobbing the ball back into your court and back-footing you;
   (b) The exchange may take two forms of which you should declare at the outset which one you propose to use namely a:

- **comprehensive discourse** by the first speaker, followed by a **similar reply** (like a **debate**);
- series of **mini-exchanges** (like a **ping-pong match**);

of which, when in doubt, I favour the latter as kinder on the attention span of both parties!

(c) Because of their rote-based education, the Chinese possess and value a **good memory**. Thus, when you:

- **speak**: the less you use notes, the greater the impression you will cause;
- **reply**: the Chinese will expect you to remember and deal with all the points in the order raised.

(d) One word of caution: if the Chinese nod or grunt whilst you are talking, they are indicating under-standing *not* agreement.

3 **End**

(a) Meetings **end** naturally or when the principal host decides – when, to avoid any misunderstandings, you should:

- **summarise** what was achieved or agreed (including action points) at the meeting;
- agree a **contact name** on both sides for future dealings;
- remember to hand over your **gifts**!

(b) Before taking leave, the Chinese may request a **group photograph** (for their collection of *guanxi* memorabilia, in the same way as name cards).

(c) To **take your leave**, shake hands, smile, nod your head and say *zài jiàn!* ('goodbye').

(d) Thereafter, it is normal for:

- the **principal host** to exit the meeting room immediately, as a sign that formalities are over and it is time to relax;

♦ a **member of the host party** (such as the interpreter) to accompany the visitors back to reception.

(e) Contrary to Western practice, having brought the meeting to an abrupt ending, the Chinese tend to **protract the farewells**.

(f) After a meeting – to avoid any misunderstandings – you should write to the Chinese, in their own language, **thanking** them for the meeting, and **summarising** what was achieved or agreed (including action points).

Techniques

In addition to the normal guidelines for negotiating with the Chinese:

1 **Sell, not tell**.

Make **your solution** out to be **their idea** – as follows.

(a) **Always**:

♦ **ask** what do **they need** and how could **you help**;

♦ **suggest your offering** as **their solution**.

(b) **Never:**

♦ **remind** them what **you have done** for them;

♦ **tell** them what **you will do** for or **want** from them – which, besides revealing your hand, demonstrates a total disregard for their needs and face;

♦ **tell** them what **they need** and that **you have the solution**.

2 **Asking and handling questions**

(a) **Always**:

- allow the speaker to finish before asking questions;
- ask **clarifying questions** only;
- defer with a face-saving reason – such as: 'I will get back to you' – if asked a **difficult** or **awkward question** that you cannot immediately answer.

(b) **Never**:

- **interrupt** a speaker;
- ask the Chinese or your colleagues **unrelated questions**, that could cause a loss of face if they cannot answer;
- introduce **new requests**, since the Chinese do not make 'off the cuff' decisions, as mentioned above;
- say '**no**' or '**I don't know**' – a sure-fire face-losing way of shutting the door to further discussion.

3 **Asking favours and making promises**

Consistent with the rules for '**face**' and **reciprocity**:

(a) **Always**:

- accompany any request with the offer of a **face-saving way out**;
- be prepared to (ask the Chinese to) **return a favour**.

(b) **Never**:

- **ask for a promise** or favour that the Chinese cannot keep or deliver – which would cause a loss of 'face';
- **make a promise** that you cannot or do not intend to keep.

BUSINESS ENTERTAINING

Making arrangements
In addition to *how*, *when* and *with whom* as for Business Meetings, described above:

Invitations
    (a) For very formal banquets, **printed invitations** may be issued in English and Chinese (one or two weeks in advance), which recipients should answer – in writing or by telephone – and may need to produce to gain entry.

    (b) To ensure that they reach the right people on time, banquet invitations should be **delivered personally** (e.g. using your driver) or **electronically** (e.g. by **fax** and/or **e-mail**).

Preparation
In addition to agenda setting and briefing as for business meetings, described above:

Menu
    (a) I strongly advise you to delegate deciding on the **number** and **choice of dishes** for Chinese guests to someone who understands the peculiarities of their palate and stomach, within an agreed budget.

    (b) Except on very informal occasions, it is a good idea to provide a printed bilingual menu for the:
  - **Chinese**: to add to their collection of *guanxi* memorabilia, in the same way as name cards and photographs at business meetings;
  - **foreigners**: to know what they are eating (if they cannot read the other's language)!

(c) Do not forget to check your own language version to ensure it makes sense and that the food is acceptable to foreigners!

Logistics

In addition to note taking, interpreters and caution as for business meetings, described above:

1 **When**
   (a) As a general rule, banquets should:
   - **last** no more than two hours;
   - **start** immediately at the end of the working morning or afternoon – not least because smaller, private ones may follow on from a meeting.
   (b) With **evening banquets** in particular, the Chinese:
   - prefer to go straight from/after work and finish at a reasonable hour, when they can still find public transport;
   - may, therefore, not be able to attend and/or get transport home if an evening banquet starts later than 6 p.m.

2 **Where**.
   - Banquets are normally held in a **reserved private room** in a **restaurant** (of an hotel or club) – furnished with **large round tables**, so as to seat more (up to a dozen) guests at each one and allow them to face one other.

3 **Guests' spouses and drivers**
   (a) Despite sexual equality at work – mentioned in Chapter 2 – **Chinese spouses** do not usually attend business banquets, even if the foreigners' are

invited.

(b) When present spouses usually sit at the same table as their partners, with the **principal guest's spouse** seated on the left-hand of the principal host.

(c) It is customary for the host to provide a meal for the **guests' drivers** (ranging from supplying a simple meal in a separate room to giving them cash to buy their own food elsewhere).

4   **Interpreters**

(a) Interpreters usually **sit** to the right of their principal guests.

(b) Agree beforehand how and when the interpreter(s) will **eat**.

Preliminaries

In addition to arrival, welcome and introductions, and name cards as for business meetings, described above:

1   **Arrival**

(a) The (principal) hosts may invite the (principal) guests briefly to relax in easy-chairs, drink tea (*not* alcohol), smoke and indulge in small-talk, until the banqueting staff indicate all is ready.

(b) If you are asked to sign a **guest book** or scroll, I suggest contenting yourself with writing an over-size signature with a felt-tip pen – unless you are adept at drawing Chinese characters with a brush without losing face or incurring mock praise.

2   **Seating**.

The organiser should work out beforehand where the principal host(s) and guest(s) will sit, as follows:

(a) Seating is **hierarchical**, by rank – when, as in the

West, the **right-hand side** is of higher status than the left.

(b) Consequently:

- ◆ **hosts** should receive a **guest-list** beforehand in rank-order (which may not be finalised until the last minute, just like business meetings);
- ◆ **guests** should wait to be shown to their seats, normally indicated by bilingual **place cards**.

(c) The **principal host** always faces the door.

(d) At **large banquets**, with **several tables**, attended by **mixed guests** from various organisations:

- ◆ the most senior from each should sit at the top table (the furthest away from the door);
- ◆ **subsidiary hosts** (at other tables) should be in their principal's sight-line.

3 **Cautions**

(a) Guests unable to attend may send a **substitute guest**, possibly of different rank, which will upset the seating protocol.

(b) **New faces** at a banquet that accompanies negotiations could be the real decision-makers who are too senior to attend the routine meetings. This is your opportunity to impress them.

Etiquette

In China, banqueting is an intrinsic element of courteous behaviour with its own etiquette which normally includes:

1 **Toasting**.

Alcohol aplenty is essential and **toasting** mandatory, as follows.

(a) Drinking alcohol should not start until the

principal host proposes the **first toast**; and, a few courses later, the **principal guest** replies – both with the words: *gan bei* (bottoms up).

(b) At banquets with **several tables**, the **principal host** and **guest** should visit each to propose a toast.

(c) Thereafter, anyone may propose a toast: indeed, you should **never drink alcohol alone** but always find someone to toast (extending your glass towards them with both hands).

2 **Drinking**.

To observe the face of **sobriety**, you should:

(a) **Always**:

 ♦ **sip beer, soft drinks** or **tea** between toasts;

 ♦ **fill your neighbours' glasses** and **as fully as possible** as a sign of respect and friendship; and wait for them to reciprocate;

 ♦ **refuse alcohol politely** by turning your glass upside down or placing your hand over it or citing health reasons;

 ♦ continue to **toast with a soft drink**, to save face!

(b) **Never**:

 ♦ **fill your own glass** but wait for your neighbour to fill it: it is impolite to put your needs above others';

 ♦ **stop drinking alcohol** in the middle of a banquet: your hosts may incorrectly conclude they have offended you;

 ♦ **become drunk** or **behave drunkenly**: you will lose face;

 ♦ **serve alcohol beforehand**, when you are the host.

3 **Serving food**.

Chinese practice for serving food differs from Western, as follows:

(a) Dishes are placed in the centre of the table for everyone to **serve each other** rather than themselves.

(b) **Guests** should **ritually praise** the food's presentation and taste during and at the end of the banquet. (Beware, however, of **ritually praising** food that you do not like: your host may remember, and serve the same again next time!)

(c) Consistent with the Chinese practice of **ritual humility**, hosts should respond by **ritually apologising** for serving a meagre meal – which cynics might consider fishing for compliments.

(d) In the **absence of waiters**, hosts should monitor their guests' plates and serve them throughout the meal.

(e) When serving **fish** the head should point towards and be offered to the principal guest.

4 **Serving others and yourself**.

The Chinese practice of serving others rather than yourself is changing through foreign influence. You should, therefore **observe how the Chinese behave** and **follow suit**, but meanwhile:

(a) **Always**:

   ◆ wait until the principal guests have been served with **their first course** before serving others or yourself;

   ◆ serve **your neighbours** with the **choicest morsels** – as a sign of respect and friendship – using **public** (*never* personal) **chopsticks** or **cutlery**;

and wait for them to reciprocate;

◆ **help yourself** to the **nearest dishes** and **portions** using **your chopsticks** or the **public chopsticks** or **utensils**.

(b) **Never**:

◆ **start the first course** until the principal host has served the principal guest(s) – by selecting the best morsels and placing them on their plates – and/or raised his chopsticks as a signal to 'tuck in';

◆ **reach** across the table, or **help yourself** to the **best portions**.

5 **Rice**

(a) Since a banquet is a demonstration of the host's prosperity, it may not be appropriate to serve **rice**, being a staple food.

(b) Consequently, to demonstrate your satisfaction: **never ask** for it; and, if served, you need **only pick** at it.

(c) In contrast: at a **private meal** – in deference to the importance of rice in Chinese history and culture – to leave rice is impolite.

(d) The **correct way to eat rice** is to raise the bowl to your mouth with one hand, and 'shovel in' the rice with the chopsticks.

6 **Eating**.

Whilst you must accept any food offered, it is normally acceptable, if ungracious, to **refrain from eating** it – except when your host serves you personally, when not to eat it would be an insult. Sometimes, like me, you just have to grin and swallow! Otherwise, you can eat as much as you like, provided that you:

(a) **Always:**
- ◆ **pace** yourself, eating slowly and steadily;
- ◆ **sample** every dish – even if you only lick the food; or pop it into your mouth, take it out and put it back on your plate;
- ◆ when faced with **something you dislike** or **distrust**: accept but do not eat it, push it around on your plate a bit, or pretend to sample it;
- ◆ use your chopsticks or spit discreetly into a cloth **to remove something from your mouth**;
- ◆ **praise** the food during and at the end of the banquet.

(b) **Never:**
- ◆ **rush** or fill up too early;
- ◆ **stop eating** in the middle of a banquet: your hosts may incorrectly conclude that they have offended you;
- ◆ **refuse** food: as well as impolite, the Chinese may interpret your behaviour as a ritual refusal, and take no notice;
- ◆ **use your fingers** to remove something from your mouth: touching food is impolite;
- ◆ **over-praise** food you do not like, as explained above.

7 **Touching food**.
Touching food is generally impolite, with a few exceptions.

8 **Chopsticks**.
If you have difficulty using **chopsticks** (*kwaizi*) at least have a go, and then use the **porcelain spoon** provided at your place setting. The Chinese will not take offence: they cannot all use a knife and fork!

Otherwise, you can use **chopsticks** any way you like even to spear food, as I have seen one Chinese government minister do, provided that you:

(a) **Always**:
- ◆ use your **right hand** and keep your **left hand** on the table;
- ◆ **hold the chopsticks** as far away from the tip as possible, which is considered a sign of good breeding;
- ◆ **when not in use** lay them on the rest provided or the rim of your plate.

(b) **Never**:
- ◆ **play** with your chopsticks, **point** them at anyone, or **lay them** directly on the table;
- ◆ leave them **stuck in your rice-bowl**: they would resemble incense sticks in a bowl of ashes offered to the dead;
- ◆ pick up food dropped on the floor: touching food is impolite.

9 **Conversation**.

In addition to the rules of conversational etiquette mentioned above under negotiating techniques and business meetings:

(a) If you do not speak Chinese, and your neighbours your language: you should still try to communicate with them somehow (e.g. in a third language). Not to do so is a social blunder.

(b) Some say: wait for the fish to arrive before talking business.

(c) To repeat previous advice: *never* **speak off-the-record**.

10 **Gifts**.

In addition to the protocol for exchanging gifts and favours mentioned above:

(a) Each side should let the other know of its gift, to avoid the embarrassment of one party coming empty-handed and being unable to reciprocate.

(b) **Individual gifts** may be left at the place settings.

(c) **Collective gifts** should be presented publicly and formally at an appropriate moment (such as when making or responding to the main toast).

11 **General table manners**.

(a) Leave any **bones** and **shells** on your plate.

(b) Where **finger bowls** are provided, dry your hands on the **towels** provided (mentioned below).

(c) It is rude to **blow your nose** in public, and especially at table. Rather: excuse yourself, and 'perform' in private.

(d) **Eating noisily** is no longer as acceptable as it used to be other than to show appreciation and enjoyment of **noodles**.

(e) **Smoking** between courses is not unusual.

(f) You may eat **soup** with a porcelain spoon or sip it from the bowl – in either case holding the bowl in one hand.

(g) Use one hand to wield a **toothpick**; the other to shield your mouth.

(h) **Towels** are provided before and after a banquet for the diners to wipe their hands and face: hot in winter, cold in summer.

(i) Although Chinese **women** do not, foreign **female guests** may drink and smoke in public in moderation without incurring any shame as the Chinese expect foreigners to behave oddly!

12 **Helpful hint**.

When in doubt: **do what the Chinese diners do**.

Coda

1 **Closure**.

(a) The **host** will **close** the banquet after the last course by thanking the guests for coming, asking if they have eaten enough – to which the correct reply is 'yes' – and rising from the table.

(b) Thereafter **guests** should take their leave as after business meetings – including posing for **photographs** – but quickly, without any *Tischgespräch* or 'over-coffee table-talk': to linger is impolite.

(c) Finally the **host** should **pay the bill**, alone, once everyone has left.

2 **Karaoke**.

(a) You may be invited to a post-prandial '**karaoke**' session, for which ability is thankfully not a prerequisite!

(b) Do not worry, therefore, if you dislike karaoke: one song only, and your individual and corporate face is saved.

3 **Showing appreciation**.

It is polite and *de rigueur* for **hosts** to over-order, and **guests** to leave something on their plates to show their hunger has been satisfied – for which reason you should:

(a) **Never** finish all the food or empty all the bowls: your **host** would be embarrassed, thinking he had left you hungry.

(b) **Always** tell your **host**, at the end, that you have eaten enough and the food was delicious – even if untrue!

4 **Return invitation**.
   (a) Following the respective codes of **generosity** and **reciprocity**, mentioned above, the:
   - **host** settles the bill;
   - **guests** reciprocate with a return banquet, otherwise the hosts may feel insulted and withdraw their goodwill.
   (b) Only very close friends 'go Dutch' (split the bill) in China.

5 **Follow up**.
   Follow up a banquet with a **letter**, as after business meetings.

Tips for coping with Chinese food

1 Food in China bears no relation to that served in Western Chinese restaurants.

2 **Abstaining**, as stated above, is a loss of face for host and guest alike and, hence, not an option. For which reason, I suggest you:
   - refrain from **live food**;
   - ask what an **unknown dish** is only after trying it: sometimes it is better not to know beforehand!
   - familiarise yourself with such **euphemisms** as: 'field chicken' for 'bull frogs'; and 'sea cucumber' for 'sea slugs';
   - ask in Western-style restaurants for **food without MSG** if you are allergic to it as suggested in Chapter 4;
   - line your stomach with a hearty **Western breakfast**; and stock up **snacks** to stave off hunger.

3 Otherwise: **if you do not have a strong stomach, ask for an alternative assignment!**

(13)

Expat Life

NON-WORKING ACTIVITIES

Being an expatriate can be a full-time job

When briefing expatriates on life in China, I have always taken the approach that it is in their best interests for me to tell it as it is, warts and all, so that they have no illusions about the few real pains as well as many genuine pleasures that await them – as the following case study demonstrates.

CASE STUDY

A few years ago, my wife and I were asked to brief an American couple of about our then age who were due to move to China, where the husband was to take charge of negotiating and, hopefully, implementing a large joint-venture industrial project.

When we first met them, they did not seem particularly concerned at the prospect of such a move since in their profile they described themselves as experienced expatriates. However, although this is normally a welcome bonus for anyone in their middle-age contemplating a China posting – as intimated in the Introduction – we were slightly concerned that their insouciance might be ill-founded, since such experience was limited to the UK and Holland, two 'civilised' Western countries, not too dissimilar to their own, and where their native English language is widely spoken!

Our concern was justified when the wife starting waxing lyrical about how – since no dependents were accompanying them – she was looking forward to her husband sticking to a strictly Monday to Friday, 9 a.m. to 5 p.m. regime, so that they could both spend plenty of time together enjoying evening socials and weekend excursions. Like many well-paid family-free senior expatriate couples, they were rightly anticipating the prospect, whilst naively overlooking the realities, of living and working in China.

As she talked, the thought was going through our mind: 'But there is the little matter of your husband being there to do a job, and a difficult one at that, in which you have a role to play, which is why his employer has given you both this fantastic expatriate package' – a thought that was shared by a fellow colleague and Sinophile, who overheard the conversation and agreed that we should tactfully disabuse her of what, in our opinion and experience, was an unrealistic expectation.

Over the course of the next few hours, as the discussion ranged over the many issues described in previous chapters, the truth began to dawn on the wife that possibly her husband might not always be able to keep to fixed working hours, or let her have the car for shopping, or get away and go sight-seeing every weekend.

She had overlooked such fundamentals – mentioned earlier in this book – as:

1 Western head offices may work different hours from their Chinese representations but they still expect senior expatriates, such as her husband, to be available at all times, including **weekends** and **public holidays**, which may mean, for example: telephone conference calls at **unsocial hours**, or overnight faxes to be dealt with immediately, including at weekends.

2 Business in China may often be done over the dinner table at interminable banquets, which – whether a wife is involved or not – could well occupy a husband several **evenings** a week or month, and sometimes at the **weekends**.

3 **Weekends** are favourite times for a husband's visiting colleagues to fly into and/or out of China so as not to impinge on the working week – when they will expect to be entertained, with or without wives.

4 China is a big place, with long distances between major commercial centres (even by air) where business trips invariably involve the husband spending several **nights** away from wife and home – including **Fridays** and **Sundays**, so as not to lose any weekday working time.

5 Expatriate business(wo)men in general, and the very senior ones in particular, are ambassadors for their employer, with all the **time-consuming public relations** and **profile raising** that that entails, in which the spouse has a part to play.

In other words: **being an expatriate can be a full-time job**, 24 hours a day, seven days a week, 52 weeks a year. Certainly, I had to cancel my home-leave coinciding with the birth of our first grandchild, and stay in China whilst my wife travelled to the UK, when a seven-strong international investment team, headed by the Deputy CEO, decided to spend a week researching the Chinese investment market during a critical stage of a world-wide merger between our and another company.

Living 'over the shop'

Estate agents always says that the three most important factors in choosing where to live are 'location, location, location' – and this is equally true in China for expatriate business(wo)men wanting to be at the centre of its business community.

From personal experience of observing those who have tried, it is no good attempting to run a mainland-China operation from the relative comfort and semi-Western milieu of Hong Kong, or – failing that – commuting from there across the water to Guangzhou, just because you do not fancy the prospect of being far away from a safe haven in, say, Chengdu or Harbin.

You should, therefore, **live 'over the shop'** – not literally, but at least close to where your business is.

Trailing spouse: working wife, bungalow bunny or consort?

In general terms, **wives of senior expatriate businessmen** have to choose (if indeed they have a choice) between the following two options as to how they spend their weekdays.

1   Some wives – especially those without accompanying dependants and/or who do not have to work because of their husband's generous expatriate remuneration package and/or who have no particular career or skill – relish the idea of becoming a '**bungalow bunny**', joining the **ladies who lunch** at their interminable coffee-mornings, sports activities, *mah-jong* parties, shopping expeditions, etc. If you are one such, then you will not be disappointed! However, you can do all that in the West, so why not give it a miss for a change, and discover what China has to offer? If you have the opportunity, go out and learn Chinese so that you can make Chinese friends, shop at local supermarkets, experiment with local recipes, persuade your husband to lend you his car and driver, and savour China, not '**expat land**'. Children and/or dogs are not a tie, if you have a good *ayi* (as explained in Chapter 7).

2   Other wives – even those who do not have to work because of their husband's generous expatriate remuneration package and/or have no particular career or skill – harbour ideas of being a **working wife** in China as a way of killing time while hubby is at the office,

rather than becoming a 'bungalow bunny'. Perhaps teaching English? The fact that they are not qualified and/or not particularly well-educated does not seem to deter them. After all: should not the Chinese be grateful for the opportunity of conversing with the pukka English-speaking wife of a foreign *laoban*, rather than making do with a China-educated Chinese teacher of English? What arrogance! **If you do not already have a successful career at home, you are unlikely to in China** – although we know some who are the exception to the rule.

EXAMPLE

My wife was fortunate in that, with a first degree in modern languages, post-graduate teaching qualification and Diploma in Teaching English as a Foreign Language – all from UK 'ivy-league' institutions – as well as previous relevant overseas experience, she was virtually able to walk into the **British Council in Beijing** and almost immediately secure a number of prestigious teaching contracts (such as PricewaterhouseCoopers, Nokia, US Embassy). Not only that: in the process, she had to turn down an offer from one of Beijing's several higher education Institutes. Very few wives, however, are that fortunate.

Whichever of these two options she chooses, remember: **a wife is expected to support her husband as his consort** and employer's unpaid (?) ambassadress.

When the cat is away

As mentioned elsewhere, we have seen **expatriate marriages** (not only in China) break up for a number of reasons such as **leaving a trailing spouse in the home country**.

However, we are also aware of overseas postings that have failed because **the spouse could not settle abroad**...and through no fault of her own. All too often, such postings are geared towards the business and employee (usually husband), both in their pre-arrival preparation and post-arrival arrangements and welcome. Rarely does an employer really think about how the wife is going to cope when hubby has to go the office at 8.30 a.m. the morning after the welcome party...and the morning after that...and every morning thereafter. Whilst he has a job to do and may make a smooth transition from one working environment to another, within the same business and employer, and with all the support services that these can offer, she is left at home in totally alien surroundings with, initially, what to do and to whom to turn?

Do not be fooled into thinking that **regular home leave** for the husband is necessarily the solution. From personal experience and observation: working in (say) Mongolia during the week and returning to (say) Beijing to re-join your wife for the weekend might still expose her to loneliness and/or temptation for 70% of the time, for which no amount of money or 'all expenses paid' arrangement may compensate and/or avoid. Whilst a quarterly cycle of (for example) 11 weeks in China followed by two back in the home country could be even worse: and the effect on any young children quite devastating (as we discovered when I was commuting between Spain and the UK in the late 1970s).

In our experience the most successful postings are those where the husband and his employer consider the wellbeing of the wife (and family) to be at least as, if not more, important than his own.

Far away from life-long friends and family, a wife loses her entire natural support network at one fell swoop; and, the older she is – just like moving to a new neighbourhood in the home country – the more difficult she may find it, and longer she may take, to make new friends, for a whole variety of reasons (such as: difference in age, values, education), not least 'cliquism'. No matter what the books say, or others tell you: expats can be as cliquish as they come, especially the long-term ones who tend to vote conservative with a capital C and may resent sharing their circle of friends with the new-comers barging in on 'their' scene.

CASE STUDY

A few years ago, my wife was asked specifically to take part in briefing – for two days in France, no expenses spared – a French couple in their early 60s who were due to move to China, where the husband was to take charge of a number of long-established joint-venture manufacturing plants.

When we first met them, the husband made it abundantly clear that they had both already visited China on very many occasions; and consequently did not need to 'waste time' learning about how to do business there with the Chinese, which he claimed to know (erroneously, as it turned out, which we were later able to rectify on day two). Rather, he wanted us to concentrate on briefing his wife, who was most concerned about the practical aspects of living in Shanghai (about which we had previously managed to buy her a book in French).

When we narrowed down her concerns, it turned out that all the material needs that befitted a senior expatriate couple (such as personal accommodation, transport, staff, etc.) had already been agreed and arranged. So what was it that really bothered her? **How to make friends of her own nationality and tongue**.

In other words: **behind every successful posting is a happy and supportive wife** – which explains why this book is dedicated to mine!

Further details
For further details, see:

◆ *Living & Working Abroad – A Wife's Guide*
◆ *Living & Working Abroad – A Parent's Guide*.

TERMS AND CONDITIONS OF SERVICE
Your terms and conditions of service should take account, as appropriate, of:

1 **Cost of living** – as discussed below.
2 **Hardship** – such as the: quality of healthcare and educational facilities, political tensions, personal security risks, and pollution levels.

EXAMPLES

Two common features of expatriate contracts in China are:
1 **Hardship allowance** in the form of a percentage increase of base salary.
2 **Hardship leave** in the form of an increased annual leave entitlement and/or all-expenses paid short-break(s) outside China (often to Hong Kong).

---

3 **Increased risks** – such as the standard of medical care, stability and convertibility of local currency, and tax regime.

EXAMPLES

Three common features of expatriate contracts in China are the:
1 Provision of **medical evacuation** as mentioned in Chapter 1.
2 Payment of **salary in foreign currency** and partly, if not wholly, **outside China** (either in their home country or offshore).
3 Payment of tax liability in China by the employer.

4 **Additional expenses** – that is those that you may incur primarily or solely as a direct or indirect result of being required to live away from your home country.

EXAMPLES

As a guide, the benefits that we enjoyed included the full reimbursement or partial subsidy (to an extent that confidentiality precludes me from disclosing) of the following:
1 **Accommodation**, including personal linen, towelling and television.
2 **Business flights** in business-class outside, and equivalent standard inside, China – including for my wife, when required to accompany me.
3 **Car** and **driver** for business and private use as mentioned in Chapters 1, 7 and 11; and **taxi fares** for my wife and self when the car was not available.
4 **Club membership**: one social for the family (e.g. Dragon Club, Beijing), and one business for me (e.g. China Club, Beijing).
5 **Disturbance allowance** – that is: minor moving expenses other than relocation expenses and removal costs.
6 **Entertainment allowance** (including business entertaining at home) – including for my wife, when required to accompany me.
7 **Furniture** and **furnishing** allowance.
8 **Home-leave flights** twice a year: business-class for my wife and self, and economy-class for our teenage son.
9 **Hotel accommodation** in executive-class rooms in China – including for my wife, when required to accompany me.
10 **Kit allowance** for my wife and self.

11 **Language classes** for my wife and self.

12 **Maid** as mentioned in Chapter 7.

13 **Medical care** for the family in China, and **medical examination** pre- and post-China for my wife and self – as mentioned in Chapter 5.

14 **Mobile phones** for my wife and self – as mentioned in Chapter 10.

15 **Orientation visit** for my wife and self before being allowed to accept the appointment!

16 **Relocation expenses** and **removal costs** to/from China – in our case, a 20-foot container on repatriation.

17 **School fees** for our son in the UK at the boarding school he was already attending.

18 **Utility costs** (electricity, gas, water, telephone).

19 **Visa renewal** for my wife, son and self including associated travel to/from and accommodation in Hong Kong (in lieu of hardship leave).

5   **Foreign service premium** – that is, compensation (which some cynics might term a 'bribe') for leaving behind one's home country, family and friends.

EXAMPLE

Depending on the generosity of the overall package, such a premium may not be appropriate (as in our case!).

Further details

For further details, see:

◆ *Employment Conditions Abroad*, www.eca-international com

◆ *Watson Wyatt*, www.watsonwyatt.com

Cost of living

How much money you need to live in China depends on your individual lifestyle. As mentioned in Chapter 6, in connection with accommodation, buying – including eating and drinking – 'made in China' is far cheaper than sticking to imported goods and more exciting!

Opinions vary as to the differential between major Chinese and Western cities, depending on the shopping basket used in general and comparative income levels, tax regimes, schools fees, accommodation and transport costs in particular. For example I have come across one estimate of Beijing as 25% cheaper, and another 25% more expensive, than New York!

Schools

For those who do not favour their children remaining in the **home country** – boarding (the option we chose) and/or living with guardians – there are three options for educating expatriate children in China:

1   **Home tuition**.

2   **International schools**, such as in Beijing, Dalian, Guangdong, Nanjing, Qingdao, Shanghai, Tianjin, Wuhan and Xiamen. For a complete list, see *The China Business Handbook*, Alain Charles Publishing, London, 6th edition, 2003, pp. 40–41.

3   **Local schools**, of which there is a growing number authorised to enroll foreign students such as: Jingshan Primary, Fangcaodi Primary and 55 Middle School in Beijing (the subject of an article in *China Economic Review*, Aug 2001).

The issues surrounding these options are not necessarily peculiar to China.

Company credit card

As mentioned in Chapter 10, in connection with e-commerce, China has traditionally been a cash culture and only recently seen a significant growth in the use of credit cards. To avoid being caught short, I recommend carrying safely a reasonable amount of cash, as well as plastic; and, before making a major purchase (such as items of furniture), find out beforehand what payment method is expected and/or acceptable.

Unfortunately, Chinese bank notes are of relatively low denomination – as you will find out when trying to cram sufficient into your wallet, not to mention standing behind someone in a queue paying RMB 20,000 or RMB 30,000 in multiples of RMB 100!

Personal finance

Whatever your terms and conditions of service, before arriving in China ensure that:

♦ Your **personal finances** (e.g. tax, state pension contributions, etc) are in order in your home country. This may require registering yourself as non-resident for tax purposes in your home country.
♦ You consider:
  – moving your funds and/or being paid **offshore**, to take maximum advantage of non-resident tax status, where applicable;
  – continuing to pay voluntary contributions to your home country **state pension scheme**.
♦ You find a quick, easy, legal – and preferably 24-hour telephone, fax or on-line – method of **transferring funds** between your home country and China. This will

undoubtedly involve your opening a local bank account with a multi-national (such as Citibank, Standard Chartered or – as we did – HSBC).

Entry visas, residence cards and work permits

Normal practice is for employers to take care of obtaining all the necessary permissions for their (senior) expatriate staff to live and work in China.

Repatriation

Last, but by no means least, is the **repatriation** process to the home country at the end of your time in China. Sadly, many employers still fail to see this as an issue, erroneously assuming that you will be readily familiar with living and working conditions in the country of your birth and their national operation, respectively.

In some cases, such repatriation may be simply and easily satisfied by the (equivalent of) **induction training** for new employees in a similar role

EXAMPLES

On returning after ten years abroad to the computer centre of my employer in the UK, where I had previously worked only in the overseas department of their London Head Office for less than a year:

◆ It took me six months to work out how to obtain office stationery;

◆ I could not understand why colleagues did not shake hands on arrival in the morning – and was even criticised in a performance review for wanting to do so!

In other cases, however, a **country briefing** and **cultural orientation** may be necessary, depending on how long you have been away and what changes have occurred –

especially if your children have been born and only ever lived abroad.

EXAMPLES

On returning to the UK after 10 years abroad, where two of our sons were born and grew up speaking Spanish as their first language:

1 Our children saw English as a foreign language; school changing rooms as an arena to demonstrate their bull-fighting skills with a towel; and the British royal family as usurping Don Juan-Carlos and Doña Sofia of Spain.
2 My wife and I found that the **monetary system** had been decimalised several years earlier, replacing familiar coins with ones we simply did not recognise.
3 The whole family had to (re-)learn an alien: **highway code** (for traffic driving on the left, not right); system of **weights** and **measures** (pounds and feet, not kilos and metres); and commercial opening hours, including **licensing laws**.

Finally, if – like me – you are **retiring** on your return from China, it is important that you take advantage of whatever **pre-retirement** activities your employer offers, in order to achieve **closure to your career**. Although we attended a retirement seminar, our peculiar circumstances were such that we had no opportunity for a UK retirement party and hence no opportunity to exchange plaudits and gifts with colleagues of many years standing – which still rankles.

POST SCRIPT

Everyone needs a Vivian
Throughout the book, I have often made reference to my Chinese bilingual PA...Vivian.

It will not come as surprise, therefore, to learn that, as a result of, and in response to, the many practical questions during my briefings at Farnham Castle, my clients and I have come to the conclusion that 'everybody needs a Vivian' – with the brief to:

◆ Help the expatriate boss operate at a personal and professional level as efficiently and effectively as possible as if he were bilingual Chinese-English and fully conversant with living and working in China.
◆ Translate idiomatically and interpret idiomatically for the boss.
◆ Act as confidential PA and confidante to the boss – including: arranging travel, appointments, permits and other work-related personal and personnel issues.
◆ Supervise the boss' domestic staff (e.g. driver and maid).
◆ Support and coach the boss and family members, insofar as required by their unfamiliarity with the Chinese language, culture and mores.

Expatriates to avoid

In our experience, I recommend that you avoid those expatriates:

◆ Whose favourite pastime – especially on a Friday evening in their expats only club, staffed by Chinese – is '**China bashing**', deprecating their Chinese colleagues in no uncertain manner. Bigoted, uninformed, arrogant and wholly out-of-touch with reality – that is why they cannot get on with the Chinese (rather than vice-versa, as they would claim). As intimated in previous chapters, lording it over the Chinese leads nowhere, except eventually back home. Indeed, one wonders why foreigners choose to interact with the Chinese if all they do is complain about them to other foreigners?

♦ Who have '**gone native**' and spend their Friday evenings running down the home country – do they have a hidden agenda for working abroad?

♦ Who say they are going to learn Chinese and about China when they return home: far from being Sinophiles, they display rank ignorance.

Keeping it real

One day you will have to say goodbye to China and the expatriate lifestyle, and return to normality. Gone your chauffeur-driven Mercedes, large house with servants, banquets with politicians and diplomats, first-class travel, seemingly unlimited expense account, private school and medical fees, tax-free salary...the list goes on! Gone too your face and *guanxi*.

Back home, you may find colleagues and neighbours are wary, even jealous, of ex-expats:

At work

You may have to re-establish your street-credibility and take a drop in job level – as I did in my mid-30s after ten years overseas – until you can prove you can do a proper job, rather than 'swanning around' as many mistakenly imagine expatriates to have done.

In the community

You may feel frustrated and rejected as you try to muscle in on the social scene without waiting your turn to be invited – the main way that many expatriate communities encourage you to behave for their own survival, on the premise that: 'if your house is on fire and you see a fireman, you do not ask him how long he has been one before allowing him to put the fire out', to quote one expat friend in Spain.

How to cope

How you cope depends on your peculiar mindset. On the one hand, some expatriates go native and try to re-create a mini 'China in Britain' haven into which they can retreat from the real world. On the other hand, we have a very English home, tastefully decorated with choice Chinese antiques and other carefully selected memorabilia alongside similar artifacts from other countries where we have lived and worked, that serve as a happy reminder of a privileged experience.

As my mother used to say: 'better to be a has been, than a never was'. After all, how many people have a photograph at home of their informal private meeting with a former British Prime Minister?

This is how we have coped: constantly reminding ourselves that expatriate life is artificial and savouring our memories, which we now share with you.

Appendices

APPENDIX 1 – CONDITIONS IN CHINESE PRISONS

Prison conditions vary hugely. It is most likely that a foreign national would be held in one of the better prisons. Foreign national prisoners are generally held separately from Chinese prisoners.

However, there is often **no hot water** in the men's facilities and the available **cold water** is often **insufficient** to launder clothes. **Cells** are said to be freezing in winter and stiflingly hot in summer, as there is **no heating** or **air conditioning**. In some prisons, prisoners are held two to a cell and each cell has its own balcony. In others, cell-mates sleep communally on a raised platform or on the floor. Some cells do not have enough room for all the prisoners to lie down at once, and many are so **crowded** that there is less than one square metre per prisoner. There is **no furniture** in the cells and the **lights** are on 24 hours a day. **Lice** and **mosquitoes** are a problem in Chinese prisons and many prisoners suffer from **scabies**. In some institutions, prisoners must **remain silent** most of the day.

What is provided and can be obtained

Prison guards run **stores** in the prisons selling essential items, cigarettes, foods such as dry noodles, fried fish/

meat and candy. The prices are usually expensive. Prisoners are provided with three **meals** a day.

Health
Prisoners can obtain medical treatment in prison or in community hospitals. **Medical care** is free and prisoners receive a **health check** once a year. A **clinic** is provided in the prison and experts are brought in if required.

Hygiene
Prisoners are required to provide their own bedding, towels, toothpaste, soap, sanitary towels and other **daily necessities**. Although it is possible after sentencing to secure **prison uniforms**, generally prisoners supply their **own clothing** to which prison stripes are affixed. After sentencing, all male prisoners routinely have their **heads shaved**.

Work opportunities
Under Chinese law, all **able-bodied** prisoners **must work**, but prisoners who are unable to work because they are old, ill or otherwise unfit to work do not participate in work. It is unlikely that this 'opportunity' to work is given to foreign nationals. In 1990, about 10% of the prison population did not participate in work activities. Some of the prisons offer opportunities to work in the laundry, the print shop and work making clothing, road signs and shoes; the **wages** are meagre.

Access to money
The safest way to send **money** to an inmate is through the consular division of your home-country's ministry of foreign affairs. The consul in China will be notified of the

money deposit and will arrange for the inmate to receive the money in local currency. It is difficult to judge how long this process will take. It is usually no longer than three weeks but in some cases may only be taken in quarterly by the Consular staff on a visit and held in the prisoner's account at the prison to be used as required.

Visits

Pre-trial detainees are not allowed to receive visitors; packages can be sent but their contents will be scrutinised. Once sentenced, prisoners can receive **monthly family visits** lasting from 20 minutes to one hour, depending on the facility. The **Law on Criminal Reform** stipulates **two visits a month** lasting 30 minutes.

Visits should be arranged initially through your nearest Consular representation, who will contact the relevant authorities. Generally prisoners can **get two 20-minute visits per month** but sometimes the authorities, if requested by the Consulate, will grant additional visits.

Communications

Local newspapers are available in detention centres. Once sentenced, prisoners may subscribe to **approved papers** and receive **approved books** and **magazines**. **Telephones** are never available to prisoners. Prisoners are entitled to receive **letters** and **parcels** from friends/relatives but individual prisons have differing regulations about receipts of parcels. In most places, **food** cannot be sent in. Letters and papers from organisations (such as Prisoners Abroad, universities, etc) are not allowed.

Education and training

Prisons have sufficient **educational facilities** for only a fraction of the prison population. Since 1981, the Chinese government has included education of criminals in its national education programme. Where conditions permit, special educational institutions are set up for formal and institutionalised **legal**, **moral**, **cultural** and **technical education** of prisoners. By the end of 1991, nearly three-quarters of all prison and reform-through-labour branches had established such special schools. Each school has a dean, teachers' office, and a teaching programme and curriculum prepared each term, each year. Prisoners study about **two hours a day**. The **teaching staff** is specially selected for the school; some are chosen from among the prisoners with a higher education level.

Source

Fact sheet: China – General Prison Information

Prisoners Abroad

89–93 Fonthill Road Finsbury Park, London N4 3JH, UK

Telephone: + 44 (0)20 7561 6820
Facsimile: + 44 (0)20 7561 6821
E-mail: info@prisonersabroad.org.uk
Website: www.prisonersabroad.org.uk
Charity No: 280030
Issued: February 2001
Used: With kind permission

The information in this fact sheet is constantly changing and is subject to variation. Although every effort has been made to ensure that it is correct and up-to-date, Prisoners

Abroad cannot be held responsible for any errors or inaccuracies. They would welcome notification of any changes you are aware of.

Prisoners Abroad

Prisoners Abroad is a UK charity providing information, advice and support for prisoners and their families. They can provide information, limited financial assistance in certain situations, vitamins, a regular newsletter and support for families. Prisoners Abroad collaborate with the FCO on a variety of projects aimed at delivering services to British nationals held in prison overseas. They can keep in touch with prisoners and their families throughout the term of the prison sentence and help them on release.

APPENDIX 2 – LOCAL CONSULAR SERVICES IN CHINA

What your local Consul *can do* for you in China

Emergency services

- Issue emergency (and sometimes) full **passports**.
- Contact relatives/friends to ask them to help you with **money** or **tickets**.
- Tell you how to transfer **money**.
- In emergencies only **cash a personal cheque** for a very limited amount in local currency, if supported by a valid banker's card or similar.
- Help you find local **lawyers**, **interpreters**, **doctors**, **dentists** and **hospitals** who speak English and/or your language.

- Inform next of kin of an **accident**, **serious illness** or **death**; and advise on procedures.
- Put you in touch with organisations who help trace **missing persons**.
- Speak to the **local authorities** on your behalf.
- Only as a last resort, in exceptional circumstances, and as long as you meet certain strict rules, give you a **loan** to return to your home country, but only if there is no one else who can help you.
- Help your family back home contact you in an emergency.

If you are arrested or in prison
Immediately:

- **Contact** you after being notified by the local authorities of your arrest.
- **Visit** you as soon as possible if that is what you want.
- Give you information on suitably qualified **local lawyers** who speak your language and the **legal system** (including details of any legal aid available; and prosecution, remand, bail, and appeal procedures – so that you know what is happening and are aware of your rights).
- Tell you about the **prison system** (including visiting arrangements, mail and censorship, privileges, work possibilities, social and welfare services).
- Pass a message to your **family** if you want. To save money, your family can find out what is happening to you by contacting the China desk at the consular division of your home country's ministry of foreign affairs.

- Ensure that any **medical problem** you have is brought to the attention of the prison doctor; and, if necessary, ask for independent **medical advice**.
- Take up (at your request) any justified complaint about **ill treatment** or **discrimination** with the police or prison authorities.
- Put you in touch with any **charity** in your home country for prisoners abroad.
- Make representations to the local authorities if your **trial** is unreasonably delayed, or is not conducted according to due process.
- Help you find an **interpreter** to ensure that you understand the charges against you and can understand what is being said at court hearings (in accordance with international human rights standards).

In the long term:

- **Visit** you on a regular basis.
- Make sure that you have a **lawyer**, or know how to change the one you have if you are not satisfied with the existing arrangement.
- Send you **money, food** and **clothing** from your family.
- Provide information on how to apply for **transfer to a prison in your home country**.

If you die in China
- Keep the **next of kin** informed; and ensure your family does not feel alone.
- Advise on the options for and cost of **local burial, local cremation** and repatriation of the deceased and personal property back to the home country.

- Provide a list of local **funeral directors**; and, if no firm is available who speaks your language, help your family with the arrangements.
- Where there is evidence of **suspicious circumstances**, press for an investigation by local authorities and pass on the results.
- Safeguard your **personal possessions** (if you were unaccompanied), until they can be repatriated.

Non-emergency services
- Issue **birth-certificates** and **passports** for any children born in China.
- Assist with **absentee-voting**.
- **Notarise** documents.

(All of which services we have used, but not in China.)

Note
The Consulate may lawfully charge **fees** for some services.

What your local Consul *cannot do* for you in China
- Get you **better treatment** in hospital than is given to local nationals.
- Pay your hotel, legal, medical or any other **bills**.
- Pay your **travel costs**, except in special circumstances (mentioned above).
- Do work normally done by lawyers, investigators, law officers, travel agents, airlines, banks or motoring organisations.
- Act as interpreters, search for missing luggage, settle disputes with hotel managers or landlords, provide a *poste-restante* mail service, call your credit card

company or bank or replace stolen travellers cheques.
- Get you **accommodation**, a **job**, **work/residence permit** or **driving licence**.
- Demand you be treated as one of their subjects if you are a **dual national** in China.
- Perform **marriages**.

If you are arrested or in prison
- Get you **better treatment** than is given to locals.
- Give or pay for **legal advice**, **start court proceedings** on your behalf, or interfere in local judicial procedures to **get you out of prison**.
- **Investigate** a crime.
- Formally assist **dual nationals**, who are only recognised as Chinese under Chinese law.
- Pay for **prison comforts**. If you do not have money or are unable to earn money working in prison, your family and friends can send **money** directly to you or via the Consul.
- Forward **parcels** to you on behalf of family and friends (since the system has been abused in the past when drugs have been sent into prisons).

If you die in China
- **Investigate** the death.
- **Pay** burial or cremation expenses.
- **Pay** for repatriation to your home country.
- **Pay** any debts that may be outstanding.

Sources
- UK Foreign and Commonwealth Office www.fco.gov.uk/travel
- US Department of State, travel.state.gov/china.html

APPENDIX 3 – FATAL CHINESE AIRLINE ACCIDENT STATISTICS

Carrier		Accidents	Killed
Air China	(from 1988)	1	128
CAAC	(to 1988)	3	130
China Eastern		2	4
China General Aviation		1	108
China Northern		2	124
China Northwest		2	215
China Southern		3	222
China Southwest		1	61
Wuhan Airlines		1	51
Xiamen Airlines		1	82

Source: *AirSafe.com*, www.airsafe.com

APPENDIX 4 – SARS GUIDELINES

In early 2003, the Beijing office of **Dezan Shira and Associates** (www.dezshira.com) published the following comments and recommendations, based on advice taken from a variety of different sources including high level medical professionals both in China and overseas.

◆ 'SARS is difficult to catch. However, most cases are contracted when in close proximity to someone who **sneezes** or **coughs**. When this happens, small droplets of their saliva, which may contain the microscopic bacteria, can be spread into the air and also onto surfaces such as lift buttons and doorknobs. If **breathed in** or **transmitted via touch to the mouth** this can cause SARS to be transmitted.

- SARS, apart from when someone sneezes, is not transmitted by air, so open spaces are safe.
- Try and avoid crowded areas. If you have to go to such places, wear a **face-mask**. Remember to change your mask if possible twice a day.
- If in public areas and **touching** things such as lift buttons, doorknobs or other places where people have **touched** with their hands, try not to put your **hands** close to your mouth, nose or eyes. Wash your **hands** regularly especially after being in public areas. Always wash your **hands** thoroughly after visiting the bathroom.
- Try and avoid using other peoples mobile or other **telephones**. Try and **eat** with close family and friends only and try to avoid sharing dishes in restaurants with other people all using chopsticks in the same dish.
- Cures such as boiling vinegar or smoking cigarettes are not effective and can actually be harmful. We advise you to take vitamin C supplements, avoid public areas whenever possible and to maintain high levels of **personal hygiene** for you and your family.
- SARS spreads through a **lack of hygiene**. It is difficult to catch. However just follow basic sanitary procedures and you are unlikely to be affected. Do be vigilant however and follow medical and travel instructions whenever issued by the Government or other authorities.
- If travelling, please check beforehand that flights will take off on schedule and will arrive on time. Wear **face-masks** during all flights for the time being. If feeling unwell, stay at home.'

APPENDIX 5 – SAMPLE JET-LAG CALCULATOR

In June 2003, the MASTA on-line jet lag calculator offered me the following advice for travel between the UK and China, based on my normal sleep-time of 11 p.m. to 7 a.m., for stays of three days or more:

What to do	UK to China	China to UK
On the flight	◆ Maintain a sufficient non-alcoholic fluid intake so as to avoid dehydration ◆ Have the occasional stroll to guard against muscle cramp ◆ Sleep only at times that coincide with those at the destination	
	Exposure to light on travel	
	Adjust your activities and lifestyle to coincide with those at the destination	
Day 1 at the destination	Be active in bright light between	
	12:00 and 18:00 hours local time	
	Relax and avoid bright light between	
	04:00 and 10:00 hours China time	20:00 and 02:00 hours UK time
Day 2 at the destination	Be active in bright light between	
	10:00 and 16:00 hours China time	15:00 and 21:00 hours UK time
	Relax and avoid bright light between	
	02:00 and 08:00 hours China time	23:00 and 05:00 hours UK time
Day 3 at the destination	Be active in bright light between	Enjoy!
	08:00 and 14:00 hours China time	
	Relax and avoid bright light between	
	00:00 and 07:00 hours China time	
Thereafter	Enjoy!	

Source: www.masta.org/travel-tools/jetcalc.asp

APPENDIX 6 – OUR SHIPPING LIST

Apart from clothes and other personal items such as anyone would take on holiday, we flew the following items to China on several flights, and were only once charged for excess baggage.

The list comprises items that are:

◆ personal (e.g. photographs);
◆ difficult or **impossible to obtain locally** (e.g. picture hooks);
◆ **available locally** but of **poor quality** (e.g. potato peeler).

Lounge	Dining Room	Kitchen
Books	Candlesticks	Cafetiere
Cassettes	Coasters	Cake tins
CDs	Cutlery	Cheese board
Games	Meat carvers	Cheese knife
Hearthrug	Napkin rings	Ice-cream scoop
Ornaments (small)	Tablemats	Iron (steam)
Photographs,		Meat charger
pictures and	**Other**	Meat roasting tin
certificates (all	Barbecue utensils	Milk jug
framed)	Cable clips	Potato peeler
Picture hooks	(electrical)	Sugar bowl
Video player	Desk set	Tea strainer
and videos	Garden games	Thermos bag
Hobbies	Racquets	Tin opener
Fishing tackle	(squash and tennis)	Trays
Music stands		
and scores		
Violin		

APPENDIX 7 – CLIMATIC DATA

Average maximum and minimum temperatures and rainfall

Beijing (North China)

Average Data	Jan	Feb	Mar	Apr	May	Jun
Average High (°C)	1/3	3/5	10/12	19/21	26/28	30/32
Average Low (°C)	−10/−8	−8/−6	−2/0	6/8	12/14	17/19
Maximum (°C)	12	18	28	32	37	40
Minimum (°C)	−17	−15	−7	−1	4	9
Rain (mm)	<5	5/10	5/10	20/25	35/40	75/80
Average Data	Jul	Aug	Sep	Oct	Nov	Dec
Average High (°C)	30/32	29/31	25/27	19/21	9/11	2/4
Average Low (°C)	21/23	20/22	13/15	6/8	−2/0	−8/−6
Maximum (°C)	40	42	33	29	24	19
Minimum (°C)	17	12	2	−2	−12	−14
Rain (mm)	205/210	180/185	<5	15/20	5/10	<5

Shanghai (Central China)

Average Data	Jan	Feb	Mar	Apr	May	Jun
Average High (°C)	7/9	8/10	12/14	18/20	23/25	27/29
Average Low (°C)	−1/1	0/2	4/6	9/11	14/16	19/21
Rain (mm)	45/50	60/65	80/85	90/95	110/115	160/165
Average Data	Jul	Aug	Sep	Oct	Nov	Dec
Average High (°C)	31/33	31/33	27/29	22/24	16/18	10/12
Average Low (°C)	23/25	23/25	19/21	13/15	8/10	2/4
Rain (mm)	140/145	140/145	<5	55/60	50/55	40/45

Guangzhou (South China)

Average Data	Jan	Feb	Mar	Apr	May	Jun
Average High (°C)	17/19	17/19	20/22	24/26	28/30	30/32
Average Low (°C)	9/11	10/12	14/16	18/20	22/24	23/25
Rain (mm)	35/40	65/70	95/100	185/190	265/270	270/275
Average Data	Jul	Aug	Sep	Oct	Nov	Dec
Average High (°C)	32/34	32/34	31/33	28/30	24/26	20/22
Average Low (°C)	24/26	24/26	25/25	19/21	14/16	10/12
Rain (mm)	245/250	230/235	170/175	65/70	40/45	25/30

Source: www.travelchinaguide.com, 2002

APPENDIX 8 – USEFUL TELEPHONE PHRASES

When you...	
say ...	meaning...
answer the phone	
'wéi!'	'hello!' □
phone and ask to speak to someone	
'nǐ hǎo' and 'wǒ xiǎng hé [name] shuō huà' or '[name] zài bù zài?'	'hello' and 'I'd like to speak with (name)' or 'is [name] there?'
want to know who is speaking	
'nǐ shì shéi-ah?'	'who are you?'
cannot understand	
'duì bù qǐ' and 'wǒ bù huì dǒng' or 'wǒ bù huì shuō Zhōng-guóhuà'	'sorry' and 'I don't understand' or 'I don't speak Chinese'
need to find someone who does understand	
'qǐng děng yi děng'	'please wait'
finish the conversation	
'zài jiàn'	'goodbye'

APPENDIX 9 – MAIN TELEPHONE AREA CODES

City	Code	City	Code
Beijing	010	Shanghai	021
Chengdu	028	Shenyang	024
Chongqing	023	Tianjin	022
Guangzhou	020	Wuhan	027
Nanjing	025	Xian	029

APPENDIX 10 – USEFUL TELEPHONE NUMBERS

Subscriber		Number	Subscriber		Number
Ambulance		120	Speaking clock		117
Director enquiries	Local	114	Tourist hotlines	Beijing	(010) 6513-0828
	Long-distance	113		Guangzhou	(020) 8667-7422
	Fire	119		Shanghai	(021) 6439-0630
International operator		116	Traffic police		122
Phone repair		112	Weather forecast		121
Police		110			

Bibliography

GENERAL

The Chinese Business Puzzle, Andrew Williamson, How To Books, UK, 2003. Further details: www.amazon. co.uk/exec/obidos/ASIN/1857038827/qid%3D1 086778966/026-0795224-8645254 and www. minim.biz

Country information

General

Background Note: China, US Department of State, www.state. gov

China, Encarta Encyclopaedia, encarta.msn.co.uk

China, Encyclopedia Britannica CD, de-luxe edition, updated periodically.

China, Hutchinson Multimedia Encyclopedia, updated periodically.

China, New Star Publishers, Beijing, 1996.

China ABC, Chinese Embassy, UK, www.chinese-embassy.org.uk

China Daily, www.chinadaily.com.cn

China Mail, TWL Publishing (S) Pte Ltd, Singapore, Quarterly. Further information: www.twlcic.com/cm

China Online, www.chineseculture.about.com/mbody.htm

China Perspectives, French Centre for Research on Contemporary China (CEFC), Hong Kong, Bi-monthly. Further information: www.cefc.com.hk

China Site, www.chinasite.com

China Updates, www2.fba.nus.edu.sg/chinaupdates

China-Britain Trade Review, 50th Anniversary Edition, China-Britain Business Council, London, Jun 2004. Further information: www.cbbc.org

China's Might, in: *Premier Magazine*, HSBC, UK, Spring 2003.

Chinese Embassy USA, www.china-embassy.org/eng/index.html

Columbia Electronic Encyclopedia, www.infoplease.com/ipa/A0107411.html

Country Profile: China, Foreign Office, UK, www.fco.gov.uk

Far Eastern Economic Review, Review Publishing Co Ltd, Hong Kong, weekly. Further information: www.feer com

Global Road Warrior, www.worldcell.com/wrldrw/grw/country/china/01frameset.html

Inside China Today, EINnews.com, www.einnews.com/china

Links to China, www.linkstochina.com

Living and Working in China, Employment Conditions Abroad Limited, UK, 1996. Further information: www.eca-international.com

Muzi China, china.muzi.com/index1.shtml

Near China, www.nearchina.com

People Daily, english.peopledaily.com.cn/ywzd/home.html

Teach Yourself World Cultures: China, Kenneth Wilkinson, Hodder Arnold Teach Yourself, UK, 2004.

Things Chinese, Du Feibao and Du Bai, China Travel & Tourism Press, Beijing, 2002.

Time Magazine Asia, www.time.com/time/asia/magazine

World Factbook: China, CIA, www.odci.gov/cia

Tourism and travel

About China, China E-Travel, www.chinaetravel.com

China, Baedeker, AA Publishing, updated periodically. Further information: www.theAA.com

China, Columbus Guides, www.columbusguides.com/data/chn/chn010.asp

China, Insight Guides, Damian Harper et al, APA Publications, Singapore, updated periodically. One of the few overseas-published travel books on sale at the Foreign Languages Bookshop, Shanghai, Spring 2003.

China, Lonely Planet Online, www.lonelyplanet.com

China, Lonely Planet Publications, Australia, updated periodically. One of the few overseas-published travel books on sale at the Foreign Languages Bookshop, Shanghai, Spring 2003.

China, Rough Guides, UK, updated periodically. Further information: www.roughguides.com

China Basics, China Tour, www.chinatour.com

China Guides, Hotel Travel, www.hoteltravel.com

China in Brief, China Internet Information Centre. www.chinaguide.org/english

China Now, China Now Magazine, monthly, www.china-nowmag.com

China The Beautiful, www.chinapage.com

China Today, China Today, www.chinatoday.com

China Travel Tips, Hotel Travel, www.hoteltravel.com

City Weekend: The Essential Guide to Modern China, City Weekend, Beijing and Shanghai, fortnightly.

Cultural Essentials, China Vista, www.chinavista.com

Explorer China, Christopher Knowles, AA Publishing, UK, 3rd edition, 1999. Further information: www.theAA.com

Scenic Wonders in China, VHS Format Video, English Edition, China Record Corporation, Beijing, 1998.

Survival Facts, China E-Travel, www.chinaetravel.com

Travel China Guide, www.travelchinaguide.com

Travel Tips, China National Tourism Association, www.cnta.com

Travel Tips, China Tour, www.chinatour.com

Travel Tips, China Vista, www.chinavista.com

Welcome to China, China National Tourist Office, www.cnto.org

For small (grand)children

A Coloring Book of Ancient China, Bellerophon Books, USA, 2000.

A World of Festivals: Chinese New Year, Catherine Chambers, Evans Brothers, London, 1997.

Celebrate! Chinese New Year, Mike Hirst, Wayland, London, 1999.

City/region information

Beijing/Peking

A Guide to the Palace Museum, China Esperanto Press, Beijing, 1996.

Beijing, Columbus Guides, www.columbusguides.com

Beijing, Damian Harper, Lonely Planet Publications, Australia, updated periodically.

Beijing, Insight Guides, APA Publications, Hong Kong, updated periodically.

Beijing, Rough Guides, UK, updated periodically.

Further information: www.roughguides.com

Beijing, Time Out, www.timeout.com/beijing

Beijing City Pack, Sean Sheehan, AA Publishing, updated periodically. Further information: www.theAA.com

Beijing Official Guide, Information Office of Beijing Municipal Government, updated periodically.

Beijing Opera of China, Liyuan Theatre, Beijing.

Beijing Page, www.beijingpage.com

Beijing Review, Beijing Review, Beijing, weekly. Further information: www.bjreview.com.cn

Beijing Scene Guidebook, Beijing Scene Publishing, USA, 1997.

Beijing Scene, Beijing Scene, Beijing, weekly. Further information: www.beijingscene.com

Beijing This Month, www.cbw.com/btm

Beijing Walks, Don J. Cohn, Zhang Jingqing, Henry Holt, New York, 1992.

Life in Hutongs, Shen Yantai and Wang Changqing, Foreign Languages Press, Beijing, 1997.

Pékin – Porte de la China, Geo, N° 289, Prisma Presse, Paris, Mar 2003.

That's Beijing, That's Magazines, www.thatsmagazines.com

The Summer Palace, China Esperanto Press, Beijing, 5th edition, 1997.

The Beautiful Land of Capital – Sixteen Sceneries in Beijing, VHS Format Video, Beijing Culture & Arts Audio & Video Publishing House, Beijing, 1998.

Welcome to Beijing – An Orientation Guide, Jones Lang Wootton (now Jones Lang LaSalle), Beijing, 1997.

Canton/Guangzhou

Canton: Guangzhou and Surroundings, Insight Pocket

Guide, APA Publications, Hong Kong, 1995.

Hong Kong, Macau and Guangzhou, Damian Harper and Robert Storey, Lonely Planet Publications, Australia, updated periodically.

South China Morning Post, www.scmp.com

Southern Harmony, Humphrey Keenlyside of China-Britain Business Council, in: *China-Britain Trade Review*, London, Apr 2004.

That's Guangzhou, That's Magazines, www.thatsmagazines.com

Shanghai

Culture and Recreation, Shanghai, Jinjiang Holdings Co Ltd, Shanghai, fortnightly. Further information: wh@jinjiang.com

Old Shanghai, Betty Peh-T'i Wei, Oxford University Press, Hong Kong, 1993.

Shanghai, Bradley Mayhew, Lonely Planet Publications, Australia, updated periodically.

Shanghai, Columbus Guides, www.columbusguides.com

Shanghai, Foreign Languages Press, Beijing, China, updated periodically. Available in various languages.

Shanghai, Odyssey Guides, The Guidebook Company, Hong Kong, updated periodically.

Shanghai City Pack, Christopher Knowles, AA Publishing, updated periodically. Further information: www.theAA.com

Shanghai Compact Guide, Sharon Owyang, Insight Guides, APA Publications, Singapore, updated periodically.

Shanghai Daily, www.shanghai-daily.com

Shanghai Rediscovered, Christopher Knowles, Roger

Lascelles, UK, 1990.

Shanghai Surprises, China-Britain Trade Review, Mar 2003.

Shanghai Talk, Ismay Publications, Shanghai, monthly. Further information: editorst@ismaychina.com

That's Shanghai, China Intercontinental Press, Shanghai, monthly.

That's Shanghai, That's Magazines, www.thatsmagazines.com

Welcome to Shanghai, Ossima, updated periodically. Further information: www.ossima.com

CHAPTER 2 – LIVING AND WORKING ENVIRONMENT

Business environment

Business Beijing, www.cbw.com/busbj

CBBC China Guide, China-Britain Business Council, www.cbbc.org/china-guide/index.com

China Briefing, China Strategic Ltd and Dezan Shira and Associates Ltd, Shanghai, monthly. Further information: www.dezshira.com

China Business Desk, www.chinabusinessdesk.com

China Business Guide 2004, China Knowledge Press, Singapore, 2004. Further information: chinaknowledge.com

China Business Guide, Robin Porter and Mandi Robinson, Keele China Business Centre and China Britain Trade Group, Ryburn Publishing, Keele University Press (UK), 1994. Further information: www.cbbc.org

China Business Handbook, China Economic Review, Alain Charles Publishing Ltd, London, annually. Further information: china economicreview.com

China Cultural and Language Briefing, Andrew M. Williamson in *Export Buyers Guide*, 5th edition, UK, 2002. Further information: www.minim.biz

China Economic Review, Alain Charles Publishing Ltd, London, monthly. Further information: www.chinaeconomicreview.com

China International Business, International Business Daily, Beijing, monthly. Further information: www.cib-online.net

China-Britain Trade Review, China-Britain Business Council, London, monthly. Further information: www.cbbc.org

Chinese Business Etiquette and Culture, Kevin Bucknall, Boson Books, USA, 2002.

Chinese Business Etiquette, Scott D. Seligman, Warner Books, USA, 1999.

Chinese Business World, www.cbw.com/index.html

Country Commercial Guide: China, US Commercial Service, US Dept. of Commerce, www.usatrade.gov

Culture Shock! Success to Maximise Business in China, Larry T. L. Luah, Time Books International, Singapore, 2001.

Dealing with the Chinese, Scott D. Seligman, Management Books 2000, UK, 1997.

Doing Business in Beijing, China Knowledge Press, Singapore, 2004. Further information: chinaknowledge.com

Doing Business in China, Tim Ambler and Morgen Witzel, Routledge, London, 2000.

Doing Business in Shanghai, China Knowledge Press, Singapore, 2004. Further information: chinaknowledge.com

Doing Business in the PRC, Pricewaterhouse Coopers, USA, 1999.

Doing Business with China, Kogan Page, UK, 2000.

Economist Magazine, www.economist.com/countries/ China

Global Edge, globaledge.msu.edu/ibrd/CountryIntro.asp?CountryID=17&RegionID=3

Great Britain China Centre, www.gbcc.org.uk

Inside Chinese Business, Chen Mingjer, Harvard Business School Press, USA, 2001.

Joint Venture or Go-It-Alone: which is best?, Martin Scullion and Lorraine Watkins-Mathys of Kingston University, in *China-Britain Trade Review*, London, Apr 2004.

Library of Congress, www.loc.gov/rr/international/asian/ china/china.html

PricewaterhouseCoopers, www.pwccn.com

Setting up a WFOE, Richard Leitch of Joy Mining Machinery, in: *China-Britain Trade Review*, London, Jul/Aug 2003.

The New Silk Road: Secrets of Business Success in China Today, John B. Stuttard, John Wiley and Sons, New York, 2000.

Thinking China, Apco China, www.apcoworldwide.com, 2002.

Watch out, the Chinese are coming, Fiona Gilmore of Acanchi and author of *Brand Warriors*, in: *China-Britain Trade Review*, London, May 2004.

Xinhua PR Newswire, www.xinhuaprnewswire.com

Confucianism

Analects, Confucius, classics.mit.edu/Confucius/analects.mb.txt

Confucius, Kelley L. Ross, www.friesan.com

What Confucius Thought, Megaera Lorenz, www.heptune. com

Politics and economics

16th Party Congress, China Daily, www.chinadaily.com.cn, Nov. 2002.

China – Special Report, Batey Burn Ltd, Hong Kong, (now Apco China) April 1998.

Documents of the 16th National Congress of the Communist Party of China, Foreign Languages Press, Beijing, 2002.

Evolution, not Revolution, Mei Junjie of London School of Economics and Shanghai Academy of Social Sciences, in: *China-Britain Trade Review*, London, Jul/Aug 2003.

Quotations from Chairman Mao Tse-Tung, Foreign Languages Press, Beijing, 1966.

The Significance of the 15th Party Congress (1997), Batey Burn Ltd, Hong Kong, (now Apco China) October 1997.

Economics

Market Forces, Nicholas Lardy of Institute for International Economics, in *China-Britain Trade Review*, London, Dec 2003/Jan 2004.

Putting People First, Report on NPC Mar 2004 by Nick Bridge and Gillian Cull of British Embassy, Beijing, in: *China-Britain Trade Review*, London, May 2004.

Open Door Policy

China in the WTO, Rio Longacre, Crown Relocations, New York, in: *Mobility*, June 2002.

Law Firm DLA's Guide to Legal Developments since China joined the WTO, Jack Gardiner of DLA, in: *China-Britain Trade Review*, London, Dec 2003/Jan 2004.

NeuStar's Guide for International Business People: The Next Frontier of Global E-Business, NeuStar, www.neustar.com.cn

Living environment and underpinning behaviours

Beyond the Chinese Face: Insights from Psychology, Michael Harris Bond, Oxford University Press (China), Hong Kong, 1991.

Arts & Crafts of China, Scott Minick and Jiao Ping, Thames and Hudson, London, 1996.

Chinese Love Poetry, Jane Portal (ed) British Museum Press, London, 2004.

Chinese Myths, Te Lin, Teach Yourself Books, UK, 2001.

Chinese Proverbs, Ruthanne Lum McCunn, Chronicle Books, San Francisco, 2002.

Culture Shock! China, Kevin Sinclair with Iris Wong Po-yee, Kuperard, London, 3rd edition, 1999.

Encountering the Chinese, Hu Wenzhong and Cornelius L. Grove, Intercultural Press, USA, 1999. Further information: interculturalpress.com

Feng Shui, Stephen Skinner, Siena/Parragon, UK, 1997.

Images of the Other Side: Folk Gods of China, Keith Stevens, University of Durham Oriental Museum, UK, 1992.

Simple Guide to China – Customs and Etiquette, Caroline Mason and Geoffrey Murray, Global Books, UK, 3rd edition, 1999.

The Complete Book of Chinese Horoscopes, Lori Reid, Element Books, UK, 1997.

The Handbook of Chinese Horoscopes, Theodora Lau, HarperCollins, London, 1996.

The Next Cultural Revolution, Time Asia Magazine, Special Report, 11 Nov 2002, www.time.com/time/asia/magazine

Turning Bricks into Jade: Critical Incidents for Mutual Understanding among Chinese and Americans, Mary Margaret Wang, Richard W. Brislin, Wei-zhong Wang, David Williams, Julie Haiyan Chao, Intercultural Press, USA, 2000. Further information: interculturalpress.com

Xenophobe's Guide to the Chinese, J. C. Yang, Oval Books, 3rd edition, London, 1999.

Young China, Time Asia Magazine, Special Issue, 23 Oct 2000, Vol. 156, No. 16, www.time.com/time/asia/magazine

Geography

China, Atlapedia Online, www.atlapedia.com

History

1421: The Year China Discovered the World, Gavin Menzies, Bantam Press, London, 2002.

China: A History, Arthur Cotterrell, Pimlico, London, 1995.

Daily Mail Weekend Supplement, London, 9 Jun 2001.

Inside Stories of the Forbidden City, Er Si, Shang Hongkui et al, New World Press, Beijing, 1986.

Shanghai, Harriet Sergeant, John Murray, London, 1998.

The Gate of Heavenly Peace, Video CD, Unlimited Film Sensation, Hong Kong, 1995.

The Mighty Qin, Julian Champkin in: *Daily Mail Weekend Supplement*, London, 27 Mar 2003.

The Last Emperor, Video CD, Intercontinental Video, Hong Kong, 1997.

The Opium Wars, W. Travis Hanes IIIrd and Frank Sanello, Robson Books, London, 2003.

Traveller's History of China, Stephen Haw, Windrush Press, UK, 1995.

Twilight in the Forbidden City, Reginald F. Johnston, Oxford University Press (China), Hong Kong, 1985.

University of Durham Oriental Museum, www.dur.ac.uk/oriental. museum

Women

The Good Women of China, Xinran, Vintage/Random House, London, 2003.

The Joy Luck Club, Amy Tan, Ivy Books, New York, 1989. (Also available on video and CD.)

Wild Swans, Jung Chang, Flamingo/HarperCollins, London, 1993.

CHAPTERS 3 TO 5 – RISK MANAGEMENT

General

Government departments

UK Foreign and Commonwealth Office, www.fco.gov.uk/travel

Includes: Consular Services; Country Advice – China; Death Abroad; Drugs; In Prison Abroad; Information on Biological and Chemical Agents; Security and

General Tips; The Risk of Terrorism when Travelling Abroad; Travellers' Checklists

US Department of State, travel.state.gov/china.html
Includes: A Safe Trip Abroad; Consular Information Sheet – China; Crisis Abroad – What the State Department Does; Crisis Awareness and Preparedness; Evacuation Plan; Road Safety Overseas; The Office of Overseas Citizens Services; Tips for Americans Residing Abroad; Tips for Travelers to the People's Republic of China; Travel Tips for Older Americans; Travel Tips for Students; Travel Warnings on Drugs Abroad; US Consuls Help Americans Abroad; Your Trip Abroad

Travel Advisory Alert Services
ExpatExchange.com, www.expatexchange.com
International SOS, www.internationalsos.com

Chapter 3 Safekeeping

Airline accidents and safety
AirSafe.com, www.airsafe.com
US Federal Aviation Administration, www1.faa.gov/avr/iasa

Christian church
The Bible Network, www.thebiblenetwork.org.uk

Closed areas
China International Travel Service, www.cits.net

Earthquakes
e11th-hour.org, www.e11th-hour.org/resources/timelines/

china.quakes.html

Fire safety
Smarter buildings, smart investment, China-Britain Trade
Review, London, Oct 2003.

Flooding
Lamont-Doherty Earth Observatory (Columbia University, NY), www.ldeo.columbia.edu/edu/dees/U4735/
projections/floodsCHINA.html

Insurance
Association of British Insurers, www.abi.org.uk
Clements International, www.clements.com

Lone women
Suzy Lamplugh Trust, www.suzylamplugh.org

Natural disasters
US Federal Emergency Management Agency, www.fema.gov
ReliefWeb, www.reliefweb.int/w/rwb.nsf
Red Cross, www.icrc.com

Prison conditions
Prisoners Abroad, www.prisonersabroad.org.uk

Temporary commercial imports
ATACarnet.com, www.atacarnet.com

Chapters 4 and 5 Epidemiology and Healthcare

General
British United Provident Association International
(BUPA), www.bupa-intl.travel-guides.com

Centers for Disease Control and Prevention (CDC), www.cdc.gov/travel/eastasia.htm

Fact Sheets, WHO, www.who.int/inf-fs/en

Includes: Air Pollution, Brucellosis, Cholera, Dengue Fever, Dysentery, Filariasis, Food-borne Illness, Hepatitis B and C, Leishmaniasis, Malaria, Plague, Rabies, Schistosomiasis (Bilharziasis), Sexually Transmitted Diseases, Typhoid, Typhus, Yellow Fever.

Fact Sheets, WHO, www.who.int/mediacentre/factsheets/en

Includes: Influenza, Poliomyelitis, Tuberculosis.

Health Advice for Travellers, Department of Health, UK, 1996.

Healthy Travel – Asia and India, Isabelle Young, Lonely Planet Publications, Australia, 2000.

Holiday Essentials Catalogue, MASTA, 2003.

Immunisation Schedule for the International Traveller, IAMAT, Canada, www.iamat.org

International Association for Medical Assistance to Travellers, www.iamat.org

International Travel and Health, WHO, Geneva, 2003 (and on-line at www.who.int/ith)

London School of Hygiene and Tropical Medicine, www.lshtm.ac.uk

Medical Advisory Service for Travellers Abroad, www.masta.org

NetDoctor, www.netdoctor.co.uk

Travel Health Online, www.tripprep.com

Travel Management – Advice for business travel: the wider picture, Kate Goodwin and Daragh Brennan, in: *Occupational Health Magazine*, June 1994.

Travellers' Health, Richard Dawood, Oxford University

Press, UK, 2002.

Unhappy Returns, Hannah Beech in *Time Asia*, 8 Dec 2003, Vol. 162, N° 22), www.time.com/time/asia/magazine

UK Department of Health, www.doh.gov.uk/traveladvice

World Health Organisation, www.who.int/country/china/en

World Immunisation Chart, IAMAT, Canada, www.iamat.org

Yellow Book, CDC, 2003, www.cdc.gov/travel/yb/index.htm

Aids

Tackling the Aids Challenge, Heather Xiaoquan Zhang and Lin Gu; in *China-Britain Trade Review*, Jan 2003, pp. 21–22.

Air pollution

China Gasps, Time Asia Magazine, Cover Story, 1 Mar 1999, www.time.com/time/asia/magazine

Avian flu

Avian Flu Fact Sheet, DOS, 29 Jan 2003, dostravel@lists.state.gov

Update on SARS and Avian Influenza A (H5N1), CDC, 10 Jun 2004, www.cdc.gov/flu/avian/index.htm

Blood

Blood Care Foundation, www.bloodcare.org.uk

Cholera

Cholera: Basic Facts for Travellers, WHO, 2001, www.who.int/emc/diseases/cholera/factstravellers.html

Cholera and dysentery

Special Focus: Communicable disease surveillance and response strategy – Overview, WHO, 2003, www.wpro.who.int/themes_focuses/theme1/special/themes1_speciala.asp

Deep vein thrombosis

Advice On Travel-Related Deep Vein Thrombosis, DOH, 2003, www.doh.gov.uk/blood/dvt/index.htm

Essential Information for Air Travellers on Deep Vein Thrombosis, Activa Healthcare, UK. Further information: www. activahealthcare.com

Dengue fever

Combating Communicable Diseases: Dengue, WHO, 2002.

Dengue, WHO, 1999, www.wpro.who.int/themes_focuses/theme1/focus2/themes1_focus2dengue.asp

Notice: Dengue Fever: Tropical and Subtropical Regions, CDC, Jul 2003, www.cdc.gov/travel/other/dengue_trop_subtrop.htm

Summary of the dengue situation in the Western Pacific Region – An Update, WHO, Aug 2001, www.wpro.who.int/document/Dengue_situation_in_WPR_Aug01.doc

Diarrhoea

Water Related Diseases, WHO, 2003, www.who.int/water_sanitation_health/diseases/diarrhoea/en

Doctors (English-speaking, trained to UK and US standards, list of)

International Association for Medical Assistance to Travellers www.iamat.org

Food and water-borne illness
Risks from Food and Drink, CDC, 2003, www.cdc.gov/ travel/food-drink-risks.htm

Healthcare products
Medical Advisory Service for Travellers Abroad, www.masta.org
Farnham Castle International Briefing and Conference Centre www.farnhamcastle.com

Healthcare providers
AEA International: Beijing International (SOS) Clinic, www.internationalsos.com/world-network/dir.cfm
AXA PPP Healthcare, www.axappphealthcare.com/ blue.htm?html/members/countries/china.htm
BUPA International, www.bupa-intl.com/home/index.asp

Japanese encephalitis
Position Paper, WHO, Oct 1998, www.who.int/vaccines-documents/ PP-WER/wer7344.pdf

Jet lag
On-line jet lag calculator, MASTA, www.masta.org/ travel-tools/jetcalc.asp

Malaria
Emergency and Humanitarian Action: Baseline Statistics for China, WHO, Mar 2001, www.who.int/disasters/ stats/baseline.cfm?countryID = 10)
World Malaria Risk Chart, IAMAT, Canada, www. iamat.org
How to Protect Yourself against Malaria, IAMAT, Canada, www.iamat.org

Medical records
MedicAlert®, www.medicalert.org

Prescriptions
Prescriptions, www.prescriptions.ltd.uk

Private medical insurance
Covering the Expats in: *timestwo*, Insurance Times, London, March 2004.

Rabies
World Survey of Rabies, WHO, 1998, www.who.int/emc/diseases/zoo/wsr98/HTML_version/wsr98_ a12.html

SARS
Business Contingency Plans in Dealing with SARS in China, Chris Devonshire-Ellis, Dezan Shira and Associates, Beijing, Apr 2003, www.china-briefing.com

Communicable Disease Surveillance and Response, WHO, www.who.int/csr/sars/en

Dealing with SARS, Chris Devonshire-Ellis, Dezan Shira and Associates, Beijing, Apr 2003, www.china-briefing.com

SARS: What Sells?, Charles Chaw and Paul McCabe, China Knowledge Press, 2003, www.chinaknowledge.com

Time Asia Magazine Cover Stories, www.time.com/time/asia/magazine:

- ◆ **How Scared Should You Be?**, 7 Apr 2003;
- ◆ **SARS Nation**, 28 Apr 2003;
- ◆ **Stalking a Killer**, 30 Sep 2002;
- ◆ **The Truth about SARS,** 21 Apr 2003;
- ◆ **Unmasking a Crisis,** 14 Apr 2003.

Update on SARS and Avian Influenza A (H5N1), CDC, 10

Jun 2004, www.cdc.gov/flu/avian/index.htm

Tuberculosis
Global Tuberculosis Control, WHO, 2003, pp. 69–72, www.who.int/gtb/publications/globrep/pdf/country_profiles/chn.pdf

Water-borne illness/water pollution
World Water Day Report, WHO, www.who.int/water_sanitation_health/en/takingcharge.html
Water, Water Everywhere, Paul Horton of British Water, in: *China-Britain Trade Review*, London, Mar 2004

CHAPTER 6 – ACCOMMODATION

Asia Pacific Property Digest, Jones Lang LaSalle, quarterly, www.joneslanglasalle.com.cn
Astonishing Demand in the Property Sector, *China-Britain Trade Review*, London, Mar 2004.
Beijing and **Shanghai Economic Insight**, Jones Lang LaSalle, monthly, www.joneslanglasalle.com.cn
Beijing Office and Residential Market Overview, Colliers International, quarterly, www.colliers.com/Markets/China.
China Property Market Monitor, Jones Lang LaSalle, monthly, www.joneslanglasalle.com.cn
Greater China and **Beijing Property Indices**, Jones Lang LaSalle, quarterly, www.joneslanglasalle.com.cn
Greater China Residential Market, Colliers International, quarterly, www.colliers.com/Markets/China
Guide to Household Moving – People's Republic of China, Crown Worldwide, Beijing. Further information: www.crownworldwide.com

Residential Briefings – Beijing and **Shanghai**, FPD Savills, quarterly, www.fpdsavills.com

CHAPTER 10 – COMMUNICATIONS

E-commerce

China Dot Now, *Time Asia* magazine, Time Asia Magazine, 28 Feb 2000, www.time.com/time/asia/magazine

Is China Ready for E-Business?, John Stuttard in *China-Britain Trade Review*, London, Aug 2000.

The E-Economy Strikes Back, Harvey Thomlinson of Alibaba.com in *China-Britain Trade Review*, London, Sep 2003. Further information: www.alibaba.com

Press

Reading between the lines, Eric Van Bussche of Nanfang Daily News Group, in *China-Britain Trade Review*, London, Dec 2003/Jan 2004.

Telecommunications

Everything you always wanted to know about China's telecoms sector, Simon Barker of China-Research Corporation in: *China-Britain Trade Review*, London, Feb 2000. Further information: www.china-research.com

Talking to Dragons – Snapshot of China Mobile Phone Market Report 2003, Interfax China, Beijing. Further Information: www.interfaxchina.com

Video conferencing

Sterling International, www.c-links.com.tw/ict.html

Video Conferencing with China in: *China-Britain Trade*

Review, London, Nov 2003.

VideoCentric, www.videocentric.co.uk/conferencing/
videoconferencing.html

CHAPTER 11 – TRANSPORT

Rail

China by Rail, Douglas Streatfeild-James, Trailblazer
Publications, UK, 1997.

Riding the Iron Rooster – By Train through China, Paul
Theroux, Penguin Books, London, 1989.

CHAPTER 12 – WORK PRACTICES

Negotiating

**National Feelings on Business Negotiations: A Study in the
China Context**, Xinping Shi and Philip Wright,
Business Research Centre, School of Business, Hong
Kong Baptist University, at *The Delta Intercultural
Academy*, www.dialogin.com, 2003.

Negotiating China: Case Studies and Strategies, Carolyn
Blackman, Allan & Unwin, Australia, 1997.

Non-native Speakers as Negotiators, Anne Marie Bülow-
Møller in: *Crossing Borders: Communication between
Cultures and Companies*, Høgskolen i Østfold, Report
2001:3, pp. 145–157, Norway, 2001, at: *The Delta
Intercultural Academy*, www.dialogin.com

Meetings

**Disagreement in Authentic Chinese-British Business Meet-
ings: Unpacking the Role of Culture**, Helen Spencer-
Oatey, Centre for Intercultural Training and
Research, University of Luton, 2003, www.intercul-

tural.org.uk

Managing Rapport in Intercultural Business Interactions: A Comparison of Two Chinese-British Welcome Meetings, Helen Spencer-Oatey and Jianyu Xing, Centre for Intercultural Training and Research, University of Luton, 2003, www. intercultural.org.uk

Practical tips for speaking through an interpreter, Anthea Heffernan in *China Britain Trade Review*, Jul 2000.

Lost in Translation, Alison Hardie in *China-Britain Trade Review*, London, Mar 2001.

Relational Management in Chinese-British Meetings, Helen Spencer-Oatey and Jianyu Xing, Centre for Intercultural Training and Research, University of Luton, 2003, www.intercultural.org.uk

Silence in an Intercultural Business Meeting: Multiple Perspectives and Interpretations, Helen Spencer-Oatey and Jianyu Xing, Centre for Intercultural Training and Research, University of Luton, 2003, www.intercultural.org.uk

Entertaining

A Chinese Banquet, China Online, www.chineseculture.about.com

Food

A Taste of China, Roz Denny, Wayland, UK, 1994.

China E-Travel, www.chinaetravel.com

Guide to Fine Dining in Beijing, Hualing Publishing House, Beijing, 1997.

Step-by-Step Chinese Cooking, Murdoch Books, Australia, 1991.

The Joy of Chinese Cooking, Doreen Yen and Hung Feng,

Faber and Faber for the Cookery Book Club, UK, 1967.

CHAPTER 13 – EXPAT LIFE

asiaXPAT.com, www.asiaxpat.com

ExpatExchange, www.expatexchange.com

Expatriana, www.expatriana.net

Expats in China, ExpatsInChina.com, www.expatisinchina.com

Job Pilot – Expat Corner, www.jobpilot.com

Living and Working Abroad – A Wife's Guide, Robin Pascoe, Kuperard, London, 1997.

Living and Working Abroad – A Parent's Guide, Robin Pascoe, Kuperard, London, 1994.

Career opportunities for spouses

Net Expat, www.netexpat.com

Personal finance

HSBC Offshore, www.offshore.hsbc.com

PricewaterhouseCoopers, www.pwccn.com

Tax Facts – An Essential Guide for Anyone Going to Live Abroad, Midland (now HSBC) Offshore and KPMG, UK.

Relocation

Association of Relocation Agents, www.relocationagents.com

On the Move, BUPA International, www.bupa-intl.co.uk/companyguide

Relocation Bureau, www.reloburo.com

Sterling Corporate Relocation, www.sterlingrelocation.com

Repatriation
Re-Entry Shock, Eleonore Breukel, Intercultural Communications bv, www.intercultural.nl

Schools
Council of International Schools, www.cois.org

DMOZ, www.dmoz.org/Reference/Education/International

Edvisors Network, www.edvisors.com/International/index.html

International Schools Services, www.iss.edu

Terms and conditions of employment
Employment Conditions Abroad, www.eca-international.com

Watson Wyatt, www.watsonwyatt.com

Abbreviations

The following standard English abbreviations are used in this book. The first time that each one appears, the full meaning is also given. Thereafter, only the abbreviation is used.

Abbreviation	Meaning
ABI	Association of British Insurers
AEA	Accident and Emergency Asia
ATA	Admission Temporaire/Temporary Admission
BAT	British American Tobacco
BUPA	British United Provident Association
CAGR	compound average growth rate
CCPIT	China Council for the Promotion of International Trade
CCTV	close-circuit television
CDC	Centre for Disease Control, USA
CEO	chief executive officer
Chuppie	Chinese yuppie
CITS	China International Travel Service
CNN	Cable News Network
CPC	Communist Party of China
CPI	consumer price index
CTM	Chinese traditional medicine
DDD	domestic direct dialling
DEET	diethyitolumide

DG	director general
DHF	dengue haemorrhagic fever
dinky	double-income, no kids yet
DOS	Department of State, USA
DVT	deep vein thrombosis
EU	European Union
expat	expatriate
FAA	Federal Aviation Administration, USA
Farnham Castle	Farnham Castle International Briefing and Conference Centre
FCO	Foreign and Commonwealth Office, UK
FDI	Foreign Direct Investment
FESCO	Foreign Enterprise Service Corporation
GDP	gross domestic product
GM	general manager
GMT	Greenwich mean time
GSM	global system (or standard) for mobile
HIV	human immunodeficiency virus
HR(M)	human resource (management)
HSBC	Hong Kong and Shanghai Banking Corporation
ICAO	International Civil Aviation Organization
IDD	international direct dialling
IPR	intellectual property rights
ISP	internet service providers
JE	Japanese encephalitis
JV	joint venture
MASTA	Medical Advisory Service for Travellers Abroad

MBA	Master of Business Administration
Met Office	Meteorological Office
MMS	multi-media messaging service
MSG	monosodium glutamate
NPC	National People's Congress
ORS	oral rehydration salts
PA	personal assistant
PBOC	People's Bank of China
PDA	personal digital assistant
PICC	People's Insurance Company of China
PLA	People's Liberation Army
POE	privately owned enterprise
PRC	People's Republic of China
PSB	Public Security Bureau
R&R	rest and recreation
RMB	Renminbi (Unit of Chinese Currency)
SARS	severe acute respiratory syndrome
SEZ	special economic zone
SIETAR	Society for Intercultural Education, Training and Research
SMS	short messaging service
SOE	state owned enterprise
SOS	Security Overseas Services
STD	subscriber trunk dialling
STI	sexually transmitted infection
TB	tuberculosis
TD	travellers' diarrhoea
UK	United Kingdom
US	United States
WHO	World Health Organisation
WOFE	wholly owned foreign enterprise
WTO	World Trade Organisation

Index

The entries in this index are: based on the main questions that I am asked at China briefings; grouped by association of ideas; and, of necessity, illustrative rather than exhaustive. Thus if you cannot find the word you are looking for, please try a synonym.